Advanced Information and Knowlegde Processing

Heiner Stuckenschmidt · Frank van Harmelen

Information Sharing on the Semantic Web

With 51 Figures and 13 Tables

 Springer

Heiner Stuckenschmidt

Vrije Universiteit Amsterdam
de Boelelaan 1081a
1081HV Amsterdam
e-mail: heiner@cs.vu.nl

Frank van Harmelen

Vrije Universiteit Amsterdam
de Boelelaan 1081a
1081HV Amsterdam
e-mail: frank.van.harmelen@cs.vu.nl

ACM Subject Classification (1998): H.3.3, H.2.5, I.2.4, D.2.12

ISBN 978-3-642-05823-3   e-ISBN 978-3-540-26907-6

Springer is a part of Springer Science+Business Media

springeronline.com

© Springer-Verlag Berlin Heidelberg 2010
Printed in Germany

Cover design: KünkelLopka, Heidelberg

Printed on acid-free paper 45/3142/YL - 5 4 3 2 1 0

To absent friends.

Preface

About the book

The success of the information society

The rapid progress of the "information society" in the past decade has been made possible by the removal of many technical barriers. Producing, storing, and transporting information in large quantities are no longer significant problems.

Producing on-line, digitized information is no longer a problem. Ever more of our commercial, scientific and personal information exchanges happen on-line in digital form. In the professional domain, near 100% of all office documents are produced in digital form (even if afterwards they are distributed in paper form), large parts of the scientific discourse are now taking place in digital form (with physics, computer science and astronomy taking a leading role). In the public domain, newspapers are available on-line, an increasing number of radio and television stations offer their material on-line in streaming form and e-government is an important theme for public administration. Even in the personal area, information is rapidly moving on-line: sales of digital cameras are now higher then for analogue cameras, e-mail and on-line chat have become important channels for maintaining social relations and for personal entertainment the digital DVD is rapidly replacing the analogue video tape. Compact disk (itself already digital) is under serious pressure from on-line music in MP3 format from a variety of sources. In short: production of on-line information is now the norm in virtually all areas of our life.

Storing such information in the required volumes is also no longer a problem. The drive of my laptop has truly become an on-line archive, both professionally and personally. As my professional archive, it stores the sources of around 100 scientific papers I have written (and the full sources of three books), all the Master theses of the dozens of students I have supervised, the slides for countless presentations I have given, all the e-mail I have sent in the past 10 years plus all the e-mail I received in that period that I deemed worth keeping. But it also acts as a personal archive: my laptop holds all my favorite music, all the digital photographs I have ever taken, drawings and songs by my children, all my bank transfers of the past 10 years, and all my tax filings of the past 8 years. All of these data easily fit in a few tens of gigabytes, and occupy only a part of the storage capacity of my laptop.

Transport. Once we have created and stored our information on-line in digital form, it is also possible to move the information around in almost unlimited fashion: The Internet has solved most wide-area networking problems with its nearly universally supported TCP/IP protocol and its DNS host-addressing scheme. This global connectivity is now routinely available not only in offices, but also in households. Connectivity is also no longer a problem: a rapidly increasing percentage of households is on 1 Mbit/sec permanent connectivity, and connectivity at the workplace is typically at much higher bandwidth still.

The remaining problems

Given these nearly solved problems on production, storage and transport of information, what are the main remaining problems, if any? In an ironic way, it is exactly the above solutions that have created the most urgent remaining problems:

- *Information finding.* The large-scale and near-universal availability as a consequence of the successful technology mentioned above is as much a curse as it is a blessing. The more information is available, the harder it is to locate any particular piece of it.
- *Information integration.* Even when it is possible to find any particular piece of information, it is very hard to combine this information with any other piece of information we may already possess.

Typically, information is only meaningful in the context of other information, but most mechanisms we have available for publishing, locating and retrieving information deal with single, isolated instances of information, at the grain size of a document, a Web page or a diagram, and do not help us at all in integrating this information into what we already know.

Together, we call this problem with information finding and information integration the problem of *information sharing.* This general problem of information sharing occurs at many different levels, ranging from the overcrowded hard disk of our own PC, to knowledge-management problems in organizations, and to the sea of unstructured information on the World Wide Web.

The main thesis of this book is that the problem of information sharing (i.e. finding pieces of information and meaningfully relating them with other pieces) is only solvable by giving the computer better access to the *semantics* of the information. Thus, for a document, we do not only need to store such obvious metadata as its author, title, creation date, etc, but we must also make available in a machine-accessible way the important concepts that are discussed in the document, the relation of these concepts with those in other documents, relating these concepts to general background knowledge, etc. Similarly, for digital images, we would not only want to store format and size, but also that it is a satellite image of a specific area of land, where that area is located (e.g. by referencing a vocabulary of geographic locations), etc.

If computers had access to such *metadata* about the information items, they would be able to support us in finding relevant items, and in combining multiple items into a coherent answer to our questions. In this book we discuss active research on exactly this topic:

- how can the semantics of our information items be made available in a machine-accessible form?
- how can such metadata be exploited in retrieving and integrating information?

Of course it is crucial that the intended meaning of the metadata is shared between the different parties involved (e.g. those creating the metadata, and those using it). It is here that *ontologies* play a crucial role: shared formalized models of a particular domain, whose intended semantics is both shared between different parties and machine-interpretable (because it is "formalized").

It has been argued that ontologies are a key technology for resolving the open problem of meaningful information sharing. However, most approaches rely on the existence of well-established data structures that can be used to analyze and exchange information. This book investigates ontology-based approaches for resolving semantic heterogeneity *weakly* structured environments, and in particular the World Wide Web. In doing this, we have to provide solutions for the following problems that arise from the nature of the Web:

Missing conceptual models: On the Web, we have no access to the conceptual model of an information source or the resulting logical data model. This lack of structure makes it difficult to refer to the context of information items, which is necessary for stating context transformation rules.

Unclear system boundaries: On the Web, it is not possible to clearly determine which information has to be taken into account, because information sources are added, removed or changed frequently. Therefore, we cannot rely on a fixed set of context-transformation rules.

Heterogeneous representations: On the Web, we can also not assume that ontologies are represented in a uniform way, because different representations are being used. This means that we also have to perform an integration on the ontology level.

Addressing these problems, this book contributes to a framework for ontology-based information sharing in weakly structured environments such as the *Semantic Web.*

Intended readership

This book is describing state-of-the-art research on these questions. As such the book is of potential interest for practitioners and applied researchers in the area of information systems, database technology and the Semantic Web.

For practitioners in areas such as e-commerce (exchange of product knowledge) and knowledge management (in particular in large and distributed enterprises), the book provides decision support for the use of novel technologies, information about potential problems and guidelines for the successful application of existing technologies.

The book draws on a large number of techniques from very different areas, such as terminological reasoning, inductive logic programming and query rewriting. To researchers in these different areas, the book provides evidence for the usefulness of various techniques from these different areas.

Organization of the Book

The topic of information sharing is a rather general one that stands for many different problems and technologies. In this book we try to give an overview of some of the most relevant technologies, restricting ourselves to the ideas and the technologies of the so-called "Semantic Web". Consequently, topics like ontologies, content metadata and reasoning about conceptual knowledge re-occur at many different places. Different methods for creating, maintaining and using ontologies and metadata are presented in the different chapters. Some of these technologies build upon each other, others are rather independent, but still contribute to the overall picture of technologies for information sharing on the Semantic Web. We tried to reflect this dependency in the overall organization of the book that is presented in the following.

The book is organized into four main parts.

Part I

introduces the general problem of information sharing and the need for explicit representations of information semantics in order to share information in a meaningful way. Further, it introduces the notion of ontology as a way of representing information semantics that has proven its value in different application domains. We also introduce the Web Ontology Language OWL as a standard for representing ontologies on the Semantic Web.

Part II

covers the creation of explicit representations of the information semantics. This includes the development of ontology encoded in OWL based on a given information sharing problem and the mostly automatic annotation of information sources with metadata that uses terms from ontologies to describe the content of an information source. We describe the basic methods for creating ontologies and metadata and describe experiments with real data and integration problems.

Part III

describes the use of the representational infrastructure created using the methods described in Part II for the purpose of information sharing. We discuss the semantic integration of terminologies used by different information sources and the integrated retrieval of information from multiple sources based on the result of the integration. Special attention is paid to the use of conjunctive queries that contain terms from ontologies. After discussing basic notions, we report the use of Semantic Web technologies for retrieving statistical information that revealed the need to take spatial relevance into account. We summarize with a description of the functionality of existing systems for information sharing and explain how the different aspects discussed in this part of the book are implemented in these systems.

Part IV

takes us back to some more fundamental questions concerning the use of ontologies for information sharing in a distributed environment such as the Semantic Web. In particular, we re-consider situations where the ontology itself is distributed across the Web. We extend the import mechanism of the Web Ontology Language by introducing the notion of modular ontology. We define a non-standard semantics for modular ontologies and compare the expressiveness of the model with OWL. We study the evolution of a modular ontology, in particular the impact of changes in a modular ontology, characterize changes according to their impact on other modules and define an update strategy that guarantees consistency of the overall model.

The drawing below illustrates the dependency between the different sections of the book. It is meant to guide readers only interested in particular aspects of information sharing. The first three chapters contain the motivation for the work and the introduction of central notions and representations such as ontologies and the Web Ontology Language OWL. All other parts of the book make use of these basic notions and can therefore only be completely understood after reading Chap. 1 to 3. Readers already familiar with Semantic Web technology, in particular ontologies and OWL might want to skip this part and only use it as a reference. After having read part I, the reader can decide to continue with part II or IV depending on the preferred focus.

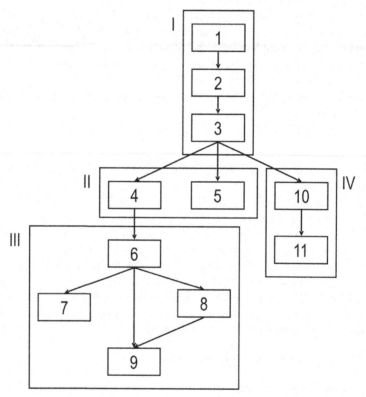

Acknowledgements

Some of the content of this book has previously been published by organizations that are not part of the Springer Group. We thank these organizations for the kind permission to use the material for this book, in particular

- AAAI Press
- Elsevier

- IDEA Group Publishing

Some of the material reported here is the result of joint work with colleagues not mentioned as authors. We would like to thank the following persons for the fruitful cooperation in the past that led to the results reported in this book, as well as their permission to use material of joint papers and tutorials:

- Grigoris Antoniou, ITC-FORTH, Greece (Chap. 1)
- Fausto Giunchiglia, DIT, University of Trento, Italy (Chap. 6)
- Jens Hartmann, AIFB, University of Karlsruhe, Germany (Chap. 5)
- Catholijn Jonker, Vrije Universiteit Amsterdam, the Netherlands (Chap. 7)
- Michel Klein, Vrije Universiteit Amsterdam, the Netherlands (Chap. 10 and 11)
- Eduardo Mena, University of Zaragoza, Spain (Chap. 9)
- Christoph Schlieder, University of Bamberg, Germany (Chap. 8)
- Tim Verwaart, LEI Wageningen, the Netherlands (Chap. 7)
- Ubbo Visser, TZI, University of Bremen, Germany (Chap. 1, 2, 8 and 9)
- Thomas Voegele, TZI, University of Bremen, Germany (Chap. 1, 2, 8 and 9)
- Holger Wache, TZI, University of Bremen, Germany (Chap. 2, 6 and 9)

Some of the work has been supported by the European Union under contracts IST-2001-33052 (WonderWeb) and IST-2001-34103 (SWAP). A significant part of the work has been carried out by the first author during his appointment at the Artificial Intelligence Group (Prof. Herzog) at the University of Bremen, Germany.

Amsterdam,   *Heiner Stuckenschmidt*
January 2004   *Frank van Harmelen*

Contents

Part II Creating ontologies and metadata

Part I

Information sharing and ontologies

1

Semantic integration

Summary. The goal of this chapter is to give an extended motivation for the problem of information sharing and the role of information semantics in this context. We address the problem of heterogeneity and argue that explicit representations of information semantics are needed in a weakly structured environment. In order to support this claim, we give a hypothetical application example illustrating the benefits of explicit semantics.

The problem of providing access to information has been largely solved by the invention of large-scale computer networks (i.e. the World Wide Web). The problem of processing and interpreting retrieved information, however, remains an important research topic called intelligent information integration [Wiederhold, 1996, Fensel, 1999]. Problems that might arise due to heterogeneity of the data are already well known within the distributed database systems community (e.g. [Kim and Seo, 1991, Kashyap and Sheth, 1997]). In general, heterogeneity problems can be divided into three categories:

1. syntax (e.g. data format heterogeneity),
2. structure (e.g. homonyms, synonyms or different attributes in database tables),
3. semantics (e.g. intended meaning of terms in a special context or application).

Throughout this book we will focus on the problem of semantic integration and content-based filtering, because sophisticated solutions to syntactic and structural problems have been developed. On the syntactical level, standardization is an important topic. Many standards have evolved that can be used to integrate different information sources. Beside the classical database interfaces like ODBC, Web standards like HTML [Ragget et al., 1999], XML [Yergeau et al., 2004] and RDF [Manola and Miller, 2004] gain importance (see http://www.w3c.org). As the World Wide Web offers the greatest potential for sharing information, we will base our work on these evolving standards that will be briefly introduced in the next section. We then discuss problems that arise from the heterogeneity of information on a structural and semantic level. We argue that these problems still occur when syntactic standards are used and make it difficult to share information in a meaningful way. As this book focusses on semantic problems in information sharing, we briefly review common ways of dealing with information semantics. We argue for the need of explicit representations of information semantics and discuss different ways of representing and comparing semantics. We conclude with a small example that sketches how explicit representations of information semantics can be used to share ad reuse information.

1.1 Syntactic standards

Due to the extended use of computer networks, standard languages proposed by the W3C committee are rapidly gaining importance. Some of these standards are reviewed in the context of information sharing. Our main focus is on the extensible markup language XML and the Resource Description Format RDF. However, we briefly discuss the hypertext markup language for motivation.

1.1.1 HTML: visualizing information

Creating a web page on the Internet was the first, and currently the most frequently and extensively used, technique for sharing information. These pages contain information with both free and structured text, images and possibly audio and video sequences. The hypertext markup language is used to create these pages. The language provides primitives called tags that can be used to annotate text or embedded files in order to determine the order in which they should be visualized. The tags have a uniform syntax enabling browsers to identify them as layout information when parsing a page and generating the layout:

```
<tag-name> information (free text) </tag-name>
```

It is important to note that the markup provided by HTML does not refer to the content of the information provided, but only covers the way it should be structured and presented on the page. On one hand, this restriction of visual features is a big advantage, because it enables us to share highly heterogeneous knowledge, namely arbitrary compositions of natural-language texts and digital media. On the other hand, it is a big disadvantage, because the process of understanding the content and assessing its value for a given task is mostly left to the user.

HTML was created to make information processable by machines, but not understandable. The conception of HTML, offering freedom of saying anything about any subject, led to a wide acceptance of the new technology. However, the Internet has a most challenging problem, its inherent heterogeneity. One way to cope with this problem appears to be an extensive use of support technology for browsing, searching and filtering of information based on techniques that do not rely on fixed structures. In order to build systems that support access to this information we have to find ways to handle the heterogeneity without reducing the "freedom" too much. This is accomplished by providing machine-readable and/or machine-understandable information about the content of a Web page.

1.1.2 XML: exchanging information

In order to overcome the fixed annotation scheme provided by HTML that does not allow us to define data structures, XML was proposed as an extensible language allowing the user to define his own tags in order to indicate the type of content annotated by the tag. First intended for defining document structures in the spirit of the SGML document definition language [ISO-8879, 1986] (XML is a subset of SGML), it turned out that the main benefit of XML actually lies in the opportunity to exchange data in a structured way. Recently, XML schemas were introduced [Fallside, 2001] that could be seen as a definition language for data structures emphasizing this idea. In the following we sketch the idea behind XML and describe XML schema definitions and their potential use for data exchange.

A data object is said to be an XML document if it follows the guidelines for well-formed documents provided by the W3C. The specification provides a formal grammar used in well-formed documents. In addition to general grammar, the user can impose further grammatical constraints on the structure of a document using a Document Type Definition (DTD). An XML document is then valid if it has an associated type definition and complies with the grammatical constraints of that definition. A DTD specifies elements that can be used within an XML document. In the document, the elements are delimited by start and end tags. Furthermore, each element has a type and may have a set of attribute specifications consisting of a name and a value. The additional constraints in a DTD refer to the logical structure of the document. This specifically includes the nesting of tags inside the information body that is allowed and/or required. Further restrictions that can be expressed in a document-type definition concern the types of attributes and the default values to be used when no attribute value is provided. At this point, we ignore the original way a DTD is defined, because XML schemas, which are described next, provide a much more comprehensible way of defining the structure of an XML document.

An XML schema is itself an XML document defining the valid structure of an XML document in the spirit of a DTD. The elements used in a schema definition are of the type "element" and have attributes that define the restrictions already mentioned. The information within such an element is simply a list of further element definitions that have to be nested inside the defined element:

```
<element name="value" type="value" ...>
    <element name="value" minOccurs="value" ... />
        ...
</element>
```

Additionally, XML schemas have other features that are very useful for defining data structures:

- support for basic data types [Biron and Malhotra, 2001]
- constraints on attributes (e.g. occurrence constraints)
- sophisticated structures [Thompson et al., 2001] (e.g. definitions derived by extending or restricting other definitions)
- a name space mechanism allowing the combination of different schemas

We will not be discussing these features in detail. However, it should be mentioned that the additional features make it possible to encode rather complex data structures. This enables us to map the data models of applications, whose information we wish to share with others, on an XML schema [Decker et al., 2000]. Once mapped, we can encode our information in terms of an XML document and make it (combined with the XML schema document) available over the Internet. The exchange of information is mediated across different formats in the following way:

$$\text{Application data model} \leftrightarrow \text{XML schema} \rightarrow \text{XML document}$$

This method has great potential for the actual exchange of data. However, the user must commit to our data model in order to make use of the information. As subsequently and previously mentioned, an XML schema defines the structure of data and provides no information about the content or the potential use of the data. Therefore, it lacks an important advantage of meta-information, which is now discussed in the next section.

1.1.3 RDF: a data model for meta-information

Previously, we stated that XML is designed to provide an interchange format for weakly structured data by defining the underlying data model in a schema and using annotations from the schema in order to relate information items to the schema specification. We have to notice that:

- XML is purely syntactic/structural in nature,

- XML describes data on the object level,
- XML often encodes an application-specific data model.

Consequently, we have to look for further approaches if we want to describe information on the meta-level and define its meaning. In order to fill this gap, the RDF standard has been proposed as a data model for representing metadata about Web pages and their content using XML syntax.

The basic model underlying RDF is very simple. Every type of information about a resource, which may be a Web page or an XML element, is expressed in terms of a triple:

> `(subject, predicate, object)`

Thereby, the predicate (also called property) is a two-placed relation that connects the subject (or resource) to a certain object. The object can be a data type, another resource or an untyped value called literal. Additionally, the value can be replaced by a variable representing a resource that is further described by linking triples making assertions about the properties of the resource that is represented by the variable:

> `(resource, property, X)`
> `    (X, property_1, value_1)`
> `        ...`
> `    (X, property_n, value_n)`

Another feature of RDF is its reification mechanism that makes it possible to use an RDF triple as a value for the property of a resource. Using the reification mechanism we can make statements about facts. Reification is expressed by nesting triples:

> `(resource_1, property_1, placeholder)`
> `(placeholder subject resource_2`
> `(placeholder predicate property_2`
> `(placeholder, object, value)`

Further, RDF allows multiple values for single properties. For this purpose, the model contains three built-in data types called collections, namely unordered lists (bag), ordered lists (seq) and sets of alternatives (alt) providing some kind of an aggregation mechanism.

A further problem arising from the nature of the Web is the need to avoid name clashes that might occur when referring to different Web sites that might use different RDF-models to annotate metadata. RDF uses name spaces that are provided by XML in order to overcome this problem. They are defined once by referring to a Unique Resourse Identifier (URI) that provides the name and connects it to a source ID that is then used to annotate each name in an RDF specification defining the origin of that particular name:

```
source_id:name
```

A standard syntax has been defined to write down RDF statements, making it possible to identify the statements as metadata, thereby providing a low level language for expressing the intended meaning of information in a machine-processable way.

1.1.4 The roles of XML and RDF

Both XML and RDF play an important role with respect to our aim of facilitating information sharing. XML is a universal meta-language for defining markup. It provides a uniform framework, and a set of tools like parsers, for interchange of data and metadata between applications. However, XML does not provide any means of talking about the *semantics* (meaning) of data. For example, there is no intended meaning associated with the nesting of tags; it is up to each application to interpret the nesting. Let us illustrate this point using an example. Suppose we want to express the following fact:

David Billington is a Lecturer of Discrete Mathematics.

There are various ways of representing this sentence in XML. Three possibilities are

```
<course name="Discrete Mathematics">
  <lecturer>David Billington</lecturer>
</course>

<lecturer name="David Billington">
  <teaches>Discrete Mathematics</teaches>
</lecturer>

<teachingOffering>
  <lecturer>David Billington</lecturer>
  <course>Discrete Mathematics</course>
</teachingOffering>
```

Note that the first two formalizations include essentially an opposite nesting although they represent the same information. So there is no standard way of assigning meaning to tag nesting.

Although often called a "language", RDF is essentially a *data model*. Its basic building block is a *statement*. The preceding sentence about Billington is such a statement. Of course, an abstract data model needs a concrete syntax in order to be represented and transmitted, and RDF has been given a syntax in XML. As a result, it inherits the benefits associated with XML. However, it is important to understand that other syntactic representations of RDF, not based on XML, are also possible; XML-based syntax is not a necessary component of the RDF model. RDF is domain independent in that no assumptions about a particular domain of use are made. It is up to users to define their own terminology in a schema language called *RDF Schema* (*RDFS*). The name RDF Schema is now widely regarded as an unfortunate choice. It suggests that RDF Schema has a similar relation to RDF as XML schema has to XML, but in fact this is not the case. XML Schema constrains the *structure* of XML documents, whereas RDF Schema defines the *vocabulary* used in RDF data models. In RDFS we can define the vocabulary, specify which properties apply to which kinds of objects and what values they can take, and describe the relationships between objects. For example, we can write

Lecturer is a subclass of *academic staff member.*

This sentence means that all lecturers are also academic staff members. It is important to understand that there is an intended meaning associated with "is a subclass of". It is not up to the application to interpret this term; its intended meaning must be respected by all RDF processing software. Through fixing the semantics of certain ingredients, RDF/RDFS enables us to model particular domains.

We illustrate the importance of RDF Schema with an example. Consider the following XML elements:

```
<academicStaffMember>Grigoris Antoniou</academicStaffMember>

<professor>Michael Maher</professor>

<course name="Discrete Mathematics">
  <isTaughtBy>David Billington</isTaughtBy>
</course>
```

Suppose we want to collect all academic staff members. We can do this using the Xpath language [Clark and DeRose, 1999]. A path expression in Xpath might be

```
//academicStaffMember
```

The result is only Grigoris Antoniou. While correct from the XML viewpoint, this answer is *semantically* unsatisfactory. Human readers would have also included Michael Maher and David Billington in the answer because

- All professors are academic staff members (that is, `professor` is a subclass of `academicStaffMember`).
- Courses are only taught by academic staff members.

This kind of information makes use of the *semantic model* of the particular domain, and cannot be represented in XML or in RDF but is typical of knowledge written in RDF Schema. Thus *RDFS makes semantic information machine accessible*, in accordance with the Semantic Web vision. In the following, we discuss the problem of providing semantic descriptions in more details.

1.2 The Problem of Heterogeneity

The existence of the syntactic standards mentioned in the last section enables us to represent and structure information on the World Wide Web in a uniform way. This uniformity makes it easier to automatically process not only local but also information obtained from other sources. This syntactic homogeneity is an important enabler of information sharing. Experiences from the database area, however, have shown that the existence of syntactic standards is not enough. Even in almost completely homogeneous environments such as relational databases, the exchange of information is a problem, because heterogeneity in the way information is structured and interpreted lead to conflicts when information from different sources makes it difficult to combine the information.

Different attempts have been made to characterize this kind of heterogeneity in terms of conflicts that can occur on the structural and the semantic level. One of the latest and most complete classification of different kinds of conflicts can be found in [Wache, 2003]. On the Semantic Web we are likely to be confronted with many if not all of these conflicts. In the following, we summarize the different kinds of conflicts mentioned by Wache. Thereby we assume that the information to be integrated is represented in RDF.

1.2.1 Structural Conflicts

According to Wache, we can distinguish three general ways in which conflicts can occur as a result of the way information is structured. These conflicts amount to the fact that the same objects and facts in the world can be described in different ways using the structures provided by RDF. We consider an example from the tourism domain where different sources could provide information about available accommodations. Consider the following representation:

```
(http://www.hotels.com#42 name "Amstel Hotel")
(http://www.hotels.com#42 category luxury)
(http://www.hotels.com#42 location "Amsterdam, Netherlands")
(http://www.hotels.com#42 priceSingle 250)
(http://www.hotels.com#42 priceDouble 350)
```

Bilateral Conflicts

The first type of conflicts are conflicts that only involve one element in the structures found in different information sources. Being concerned with RDF, these basic elements are resources, properties or data type, respectively. Other representations of the same accommodation from the example above can lead to bilateral conflicts with this representation in the following ways:

- *Integrity Conflicts.* In RDF resources are referred to by a unique ID in terms of an URI that serves as a kind of key value for accessing the resource. Different representations of the same object can be identified by a different key value, for example by a resource referred to as http://www.vacation.org/hotels#666. The use of different identifiers for the same objects makes it difficult to merge information about the object from different sources.
- *Data Type Conflicts.* In its latest version, RDF supports the use of XML schema datatypes for representing the values assigned to an object. This provides hints for efficient computation with these values, but causes a problem in cases where different datatypes are used for the same value. The price of the accommodation above can for example be represented by an integer, a real number or even by a string. If we want to compare this data, for example to find the best offer, the use of different data types is a problem, because comparison operators normally operate on two values of the same type.
- *Naming Conflicts.* The type on conflicts referred to as naming conflicts summarizes all cases where sources use different names for the same real world objects. The typical case is the use of different names for attributes in relational databases. Similar conflicts can occur in RDF. In our example, other sources might use different refer to the category of a hotel. Instead of the term category, properties called *class* or *stars* could be used. In the case of RDF, naming conflicts are actually equivalent to a special kind of integrity conflict as described above. The reason is that in RDF all modelling elements (except for literals) are also resources with a unique URI different names therefore amount to different keys.

Multilateral Conflicts

Besides conflicts that occur when trying to compare single elements in a representation, structural heterogeneity can also lead to conflicts that involve more than one element in each representation. In general, these conflicts occur when information represented in a single element in one source can only partially be found in the other source when only looking at a single element. So looking at a single statement from our example, the following multilateral conflicts can occur when trying to combine with information from a different source.

- *Multilateral Attribute Correspondences.* A multilateral attribute correspondence is present if the same information that is linked to a resource using a single property is liked using more than one property in another source. In our example information about the city and the country the accommodation is located in is pointed to using the property *location*. We can think of situations where two different properties *city* and *country* is used. If we we are looking for accommodations in a certain place now, we either have to split up the location information or combine the city and country information to make them comparable.

- *Multilateral Entity Correspondences.* A similar situation can occur with respect to the use of a single or multiple resources to model a certain piece of information. In our example, information about the accommodation and its location is clustered in the description of a single resource (the location is given by a literal value). In other sources, special resources could be used as unique representations of location such as cites or countries. We might find statements like:

      (http://www.locations.com/cities\#amsterdam lies_in
      http://www.locations.com/countries\#netherlands)
      (http://www.hotels.com#42 location
      http://www.locations.com/cities\#amsterdam)

- *Missing Values.* In addition to problems caused by information being split amongst different representation elements. There are also cases, where parts of the information contained in one source is simply missing in the other one. Our example contains information about prices for single and for double rooms. Other sources might only give the price for a double room. This might mean that there are no single rooms, that the price of a single room is the same as for a double room, or simply that this information has not been added to the representation. Thus if we want to compare prices in this case we have to guess the price for a single room.

Meta-Level Conflicts

The last type of conflict on the structural level is concerned with the use of different modelling elements to represent the same kind of information. In conceptual data models these basic elements are entities, attributes and data. The classification given by Wache uses this terminology to distinguish different types of meta-level conflicts. The modelling elements we have in RDF are resources, properties (actually a special kind of resource) and literals/datatypes respectively. In the previous paragraph we already discussed the possibility of representing the location information either as a literal or as a resource. Further, we sometimes find the situation where equivalent information that is encoded in explicit relations in one source (netherlands part-of Europe) are implicitly modelled in the type of the resource in another source (netherland type European Country).

1.2.2 Semantic Conflicts

The problem of structural heterogeneity has been addressed extensively in the database literature (see for example references in Chap. 2) and solutions have been developed for dealing with these conflicts. A problem that is still not completely solved is heterogeneity of the intended interpretation of information. In real world applications, we often have situations where systems that work on data that has been integrated at the structural level produce wrong or at least unexpected results, because the intended interpretation of the representations differs across the sources. We can roughly distinguish conflicts on the semantic level into conflicts that occur due to the use of different encodings and conflicts due to a different conceptualization of the domain.

Data Conflicts

In order to achieve compact and compact and comparable representations of a domain, information sources often use special type value systems for talking about the properties of an object. These are often based on abstractions of the concrete value. Different choices with respect to these value systems lead to the following data-related conflicts

- *Different Scales.* Especially numerical values like the price of an accommodation can be based on different scales. A popular example is the use of different currencies for stating the price of a room. When we want to compare prices it makes a difference whether we are talking about Euro, Dollar or German Mark. In some cases, the relation between scales is fixed (e.g. the exchange between Euro and German Mark), but sometimes the relation changes like the exchange rate of Euro and Dollar.
- *Different Value Ranges.* In cases where abstractions from concrete values are used we face the problem that different sources often introduce different abstractions of the same underlying scale. An example is the encoding of the quality of an accommodation. While in central Europe a scale of one to five stars is used while in Spain for example, the notion of "keys" are used to refer to the quality. The example of quality also illustrates the problem of comparing these abstractions because often the underlying scale is not known.
- *Surjective Mappings.* A specific problem with respect to the use of abstractions of the same scale are cases where the two value systems used as abstractions do not have the same number of values. In these cases, more than one value of one source map to more than one value in the other source. In our example, this problem might occur, because the accommodation is classified as *luxury* which probably corresponds to five or four stars in other sources. The most severe problem in this case is that it is not possible to decide whether the classification should be interpreted as five or as four stars.

Domain Conflicts

Usually, abstraction mechanisms are not only applied to data values but, earlier in the design process, also to domain objects to be represented. Normally, objects are grouped into classes of objects that share some properties. As the shared properties of these objects are normally not explicitly represented any more (the purpose of this abstraction is to reduce the amount of information to be considered), we again face the problem of having to find relations between these categorizations.

- *Subsumption.* The term subsumption describes the situation where one class of objects contains all the objects contained in another class. An example are the classes *accommodation* that contains all accommodation objects and the class *hotels*. It is clear that all hotels are accommodations as well. Consequently, we want to find all members of that class when we are looking for a place to stay. If we are not explicitly looking for hotels as well, this information might not be found.
- *Overlap.* A more complicated case is the one where two classes partially overlap each other. This is the case for the two classes *hotels* and *hostels* as some hostels can also be seen as cheap hotels and vice versa while some hotels are definitely not hotels and some hostels would hardly qualify as a hotel. In these cases it is difficult to share the information, because additional criteria are needed to decide which parts of the instances the concepts share and which not.
- *Inconsistency.* Conversely, it is not only important for a meaningful exchange of information to know when two classes share members. Sometimes, classes of objects are disjoint by definition. An example from the accommodation domain are the classes *hotel* and *camp-site*. This information is important, because it can lead to unwanted results if not payed attention to.
- *Aggregation.* Another potential conflict on the domain level is due to different levels of abstraction leading to a situation where data is present in an aggregated form. One information source might group city according to the country they lie in, another source according to the continent. We have to note that in many cases, this situation is similar to the subsumption case, because the class *Dutch City* is subsumed by the concept *European City*.

Throughout this book we focus on the semantic conflicts discussed above and more or less ignore structural conflicts that might occur when trying to share information. We made this choice, because most structural conflicts can be successfully solved using existing system like the Mecota Mediator [Wache, 2003].

1.3 Handling information semantics

In the following, we use the term *semantic integration* or *semantic translation* to denote the resolution of semantic conflicts that occur between heterogeneous information systems in order to achieve semantic interoperability . For this purpose, the systems have to agree on the *meaning* of the information that is interchanged. Semantic conflicts occur whenever two systems do not use the same interpretation of the information. The simplest forms of disagreement in the interpretation of information are homonymy (the use of the same word with different meanings) and synonymy (the use of different words with the same meaning). However, these problems can be solved by one-to-one structural mappings. Therefore, most existing converter and mediator systems are able to solve semantic conflicts of this type. More interesting are conflicts where one-to-one mappings do not apply. In this case, the semantics of information has to be taken into account in order to decide how different information items relate to each other. Many attempts have been made in order to access information semantics. We will discuss general approaches to this problem with respect to information sharing.

1.3.1 Semantics from structure

A common approach to capture information semantics is in terms of its structure. The use of conceptual models of stored information has a long tradition in database research. The most well-known approach is the Entity Relationship approach [Chen, 1976]. Such conceptual models normally have a tight connection to the way the actual information is stored, because they are mainly used to structure information about complex domains. This connection has significant advantages for information sharing, because the conceptual model helps to access and validate information. The access to structured information resources can be provided by wrappers derived from the conceptual model [Wiederhold, 1992]. In the presence of less structured information sources, e.g. HTML pages on the Web, the problem of accessing information is harder to solve. Recently, this problem has been successfully tackled by approaches that use machine-learning techniques for inducing wrappers for less structured information. One of the most prominent approaches is reported in [Freitag and Kushmerick, 2000]. The result of the learning process is a set of extraction rules that can be used to extract information from Web resources and insert it into a newly created structure that is used as a basis for further processing.

While wrapper induction provides a solution for the problem of extracting information from weakly structured resources, the problem of integrating information from different sources remains largely unsolved because extraction rules are solely defined on the structural level. In order to achieve an integration on the semantic level as well, a logical model has to be built on top of the information structure. We find two different approaches in the literature.

Structure resemblance

A logical model is built that is a one-to-one copy of the conceptual structure of the database and encoded in a language that makes automated reasoning possible. The integration is then performed on the copy of the model and can easily be tracked back to the original data. This approach is implemented in the SIMS mediator [Arens et al., 1993] and also by the TSIMMIS system [Garcia-Molina et al., 1995]. A suitable encoding of the information structure can already be used in order to generate hypotheses about semantically related structures in two information sources.

Structure enrichment

A logical model is built that resembles the structure of the information source and contains additional definitions of concepts. A detailed discussion of this kind of mapping is given in [Kashyap and Sheth, 1996]. Systems that use structure enrichment for information integration are OB-SERVER [Kashyap and Sheth, 1997] , KRAFT [Preece et al., 1999], PICSEL [Goasdoue and Reynaud, 1999] and DWQ [Calvanese et al., 1998b]. While OBSERVER uses description logics for both structure resemblance and additional definitions, PICSEL and DWQ define the structure of the information by (typed) horn rules. Additional definitions of concepts mentioned in these rules are done by a description-logic model. KRAFT does not commit to a specific definition scheme.

The approaches are based on the assumption that the structure of the information already carries some semantics in terms of the domain knowledge of the database designer. We therefore think that the derivation of semantics from information structures is not applicable in an environment where weakly structured information has to be handled, because in most cases a conceptual model is not available.

1.3.2 Semantics from text

An alternative approach for extracting semantic information from the structure of information resources is the derivation of semantics from text. This approach is attractive on the World Wide Web, because huge amounts of free text resources are available. Substantial results in using natural-language processing come from the area of information retrieval [Lewis, 1996]. Here the task of finding relevant information on a specific topic is tackled by indexing free-text documents with weighted terms that are related to their contents. There are different methods for matching user queries against these weighted terms. It has been shown that statistical methods outperform discrete methods [Salton, 1986]. As in this approach the semantics of a document is contained in the indexing terms, their choice and generation is the crucial step in handling information semantics. Results of experiments have shown that document retrieval using stemmed natural-language terms taken from a document for indexing is comparable to the use of controlled languages [Turtle and Croft, 1991]. However, it is argued that the use of compound expressions or propositional statements (very similar to RDF) will increase precision and recall [Lewis, 1996].

The crucial task in using natural language as a source of semantic information is the analysis of documents and the generation of indexing descriptions from the document text. Straightforward approaches based on the number of occurrences of a term in the document suffer from the problem that the same term may be used in different ways. The same word may be used as a verb or as an adjective (*fabricated units* vs. *they fabricated units*) leading to different degrees of relevance with respect to a user query. Recent work has shown that retrieval results can be improved by making the role of a term in a text explicit [Basili et al., 2001]. Further, the same natural language term may have different meanings even within the same text. The task of determining the intended meaning is referred to as word-sense disambiguation. A prominent approach is to analyze the context of a term under consideration and decide between different possible interpretations based on the occurrence of other words in this context that provide evidence for one meaning. The exploitation of these implicit structures is referred to as latent semantic indexing [Deerwester et al., 1990]. The decision for a possible sense is often based on a general natural-language thesaurus (see e.g. [Yarowsky, 1992]). In the case where specialized vocabularies are used in documents, explicit representations of relations between terms have to be used. These are provided by domain-specific thesauri [Maynard and Ananiadou, 1998] or semantic networks [Gaizauskas and Humphreys, 1997]. Extracting more complex indexing information such as propositional statements is mostly unexplored. Ontologies, which will be discussed later, provide possibilities for using such expressive annotations.

Despite the progress made in natural language processing and the its successful application to information extraction and information retrieval, there are still many limitations due to the lack of explicit semantic information. While many ambiguities in natural language can be resolved by the use of contextual information, artificially invented terms cause problems, because their meaning can often not be deduced from everyday language, but depends on the specific use of the information source. In this case we have to rely on the existence of corresponding background information.

1.3.3 The need for explicit semantics

In the last section we reviewed approaches for capturing information semantics. We concluded that the derivation of semantics from structures does not easily apply to weakly structured information. The alternative of using text-understanding techniques on the other hand works quite well for textual information that contains terms from everyday language, for in this case existing linguistic resources can be used to disambiguate the meaning of single words. The extraction of more complex indexing expressions is less well investigated. Such indexing terms, however, can be easily derived from explicit models of information semantics. A second shortcoming of approaches that purely rely on the extraction of semantics from texts is the ability to handle special terminology as it is used by scientific communities or technical disciplines.

The problems of the approaches mentioned above all originated from the lack of an explicit model of information semantics. Recently, the need for a partial explication of information semantics has been recognized in connection with the World Wide Web. Fensel identifies a three-level solution to the problem of developing intelligent applications on the web [Fensel and Brodie, 2003]:

- *Information extraction.* In order to provide access to information resources, information extraction techniques have to be applied providing wrapping technology for a uniform access to information.
- *Processable semantics.* Formal languages have to be developed that are able to capture information structures as well as meta-information about the nature of information and the conceptual structure underlying an information source.
- *Ontologies.* The information sources have to be enriched with semantic information using the languages mentioned in step two. This semantic information has to be based on a vocabulary that reflects a consensual and formal specification of the conceptualization of the domain, also called an ontology.

The first layer directly corresponds to the approaches for accessing information discussed at the beginning of this section. The second layer partly corresponds to the use of the annotation languages XML and RDF mentioned in connection with the syntactic and structural approaches. The third layer, namely the enrichment of information sources with additional semantic information and the use of shared term definitions, has already been implemented in recent approaches for information sharing in terms of meta-annotations and term definitions. We would like to emphasize that the use of explicit semantics is no contradiction to the other approaches mentioned above. Using explicit models of information semantics is rather a technique to improve or enable the other approaches. However, we think that large-scale information sharing requires explicit semantic models.

In information sources, specialized vocabularies often occur in terms of classifications and assessments used to reduce the amount of data that has to be stored in an information source. Instead of describing all characteristics of an object represented by a dataset a single term is used that relates the object to a class of objects that share a certain set of properties. This term often corresponds to a classification that is specified outside the information source. The use of product categories in electronic commerce or the relation to a standard land-use classification in geographic information systems are examples for this phenomenon. A special kind of classification is the use of terms that represent the result of an assessment of the object described by the dataset. In e-commerce systems, for example, customers might be assigned to different target groups, whereas the state of the environment is a typical kind of assessment stored in geographic information systems.

We believe that classifications and assessments, which can be seen as a special case of a classification, play a central role in large-scale information sharing, because their ability to reduce the information load by abstracting from details provides means to handle very large information networks like the World Wide Web. Web directories like Yahoo! (http://www.yahoo.com) or the Open Directory project (http://dmoz.org) organize millions of web pages according to a fixed classification hierarchy. Beyond this, significant success has been reached in the area of document and Web-page classification (see [Pierre, 2001] or [Boley et al., 1999]). Apart from the high relevance for information sharing on the World Wide Web, being able to cope with heterogeneous classification schemes is also relevant for information integration in general. In the following we give two examples of the use of specific classifications in conventional information systems and illustrate the role of explicit semantic models in providing interoperability between systems.

1.4 Representing and comparing semantics

Being able to compare information on a semantic level is crucial for information integration. More specifically, we need to be able to compare the meaning of terms that are used as names of schema elements and as values for data entries. Semantic correspondences between these terms are the basis for schema integration and transformation of data values. As already mentioned in Sect. 1.3.2 this is complicated by the fact that there is no one-to-one relation between terms and intended meanings. This already becomes clear when we look up the meaning of a term in a dictionary. The example below shows a dictionary entry for the term "trip".

```
trip n. 1. (659) trip -- (a journey for some purpose (usually
including the return);
        "he took a trip to the shopping center")
2. (5) trip -- (a hallucinatory experience induced by drugs;
        "an acid trip")
3. slip, trip -- (an accidental misstep threatening (or causing) a
fall;
        "he blamed his slip on the ice";
        "the jolt caused many slips and a few spills")
4. tripper, trip -- (a catch mechanism that acts as a switch;
        "the pressure activates the tripper and releases the water")
```

```
5. trip -- (a light or nimble tread;
        "he heard the trip of women's feet overhead")
6. trip, stumble, misstep -- (an unintentional but embarrassing
blunder;
        "he recited the whole poem without a single trip";
        "confusion caused his unfortunate misstep")
```

As we can see, the simple term "trip" has six different possible interpretations depending on the context it is used in. Conversely, there are many different words that have the same or at least a very similar meaning as "trip" such as "journey" or "voyage". Both effects have a negative impact on information sharing. In the first case where a single term has different possible interpretations (homonymy) we might receive irrelevant answers when asking for information about trip. In the latter case where different terms have the same meaning (synonymy), we will miss relevant information that is described using one of the other terms. In order to overcome these problems, a number of approaches for describing and comparing the intended meanings of terms have been developed. In the following, we give a brief overview of some basic approaches.

1.4.1 Names and labels

Mostly in the area of information retrieval, a number of methods have been developed that aim at providing more information about the intended meaning of a term using other terms for clarifying the context. A well-known approach is the use of synonym sets instead of single terms. A synonym set contains all terms that share a particular meaning. In our example "trip" and "journey" will be in a synonym set making clear that the meaning of the term "trip" intended here is the first in the list above, while the synonym set representing the second possible interpretation will contain the terms "trip" and "hallucination".

Rodriguez and Egenhofer [Rodriguez and Egenhofer, 2003] have shown that synonym sets also provide a better basis for determining the similarity of terms based on string matching. They propose a similarity measure that takes into account all members of the synonym sets of two terms to be compared. This leads to a higher chance of finding terms with a similar meaning because their synonym sets will share some terms. It also avoids matches between terms that do not have a similar meaning because their synonym sets will be largely disjoint.

1.4.2 Term networks

The notion of synonym set only used a single relation between terms as a means for describing intended meaning. In order to obtain a more precise and complete description, other kinds of relations to other terms can be used. Examples of such relations are:

1. hypernyms (terms with a broader meaning),
2. hyponyms (terms with a narrower meaning),
3. holonyms (terms that describe a whole the term is part of),
4. mereonyms (terms describing parts of the term).

Together with the terms they connect, these relations form networks of terms and their relations. In such a network, the intended meaning of a term is described by its context (the terms it is linked to via the different relations). The most common form of such networks are thesauri that mainly use the broader term and narrower term relations to build up term hierarchies.

A number of methods have been proposed to determine the similarity of terms in a term network. Hirst and St Onge [Hirst and St-Onge, 1998] use the length of the path connecting two terms in the network as a basis for their similarity measure. Leacock and Chodorow [Leacock and Chodorow, 1998] use the length of the path consisting only of hypernym and hyponym relations and normalize it by the height of the hierarchy. Other approaches also use statistical information about the probability of finding the most narrow broader term of two terms [Resnik, 1995] or variations of this strategy.

1.4.3 Concept lattices

A problem with the use of term networks lies in the fact that there is no formal principle the hierarchy is built upon. As a result, we still have the situation where the different possible interpretations of a term share a place in the hierarchy. Consequently, "trek" as well as "tumble" will be narrower terms with respect to the term "trip". In order to overcome this problem, the notion of concept is used to refer to the intended meaning of a term. Instead of using a hierarchy of terms for describing their meaning, a hierarchy of concepts (intended meanings) is used. This hierarchy, also referred to as a concept lattice is now based on the principle that every concept in the hierarchy inherits and is defined by the properties of its ancestors in the hierarchy. A prominent method following this principle is formal concept analysis (FCA) [Ganter and Wille, 1999]. The idea of FCA is to automatically construct a concept lattice based on a specification of characteristic properties of the different concepts. The use of FCA for semantic integration is reported in [Stumme and Maedche, 2001].

The advantage of this rigid interpretation of a hierarchy is the fact that we can also use inherited definitions when comparing the meaning of two concepts, which provides us with much richer and more accurate information. Consider the two hierarchies in Fig. 1.1. Just looking at the labels "morning"

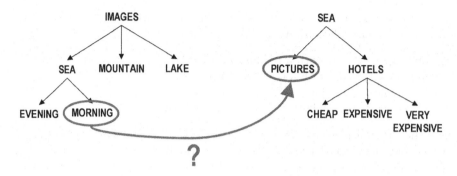

Fig. 1.1. Matching with concept lattices

and "pictures" of the two concepts we want to match it seems that they are completely different. When also taking into account the inherited information, however, we see that we are actually comparing the concepts "images of the sea in the morning" and "pictures of the sea". We can find that images and pictures actually have the same meaning by looking at their synonym sets and then conclude that the former concept is a special case of the latter (compare [Giunchiglia and Shvaiko, 2003]).

1.4.4 Features and constraints

The use of concept lattices is often combined with a description of features or constraints the instances of a concept show or adhere to. In our example we could for example define that each trip has certain attributes such as a destination and a duration, that a trip may consist of different parts (stages, legs) and that it may serve certain functions such as "visit".

There are many different approaches for modelling features and constraints that restrict the possible interpretation of a concept. The approaches range from simple attribute–value pairs to complex axiomatizations in first order logic. Besides these extreme cases, a number of specialized representation formalisms have been developed that provide epistemological primitives for defining concepts in terms of features of their instances. The most frequently used ones are frame-based representations [Karp, 1993] and description logics [Baader et al., 2002]. While frame-based systems define a rather fixed structural framework for describing the properties of instances of certain concepts, description logics provide a flexible logical language for defining necessary and sufficient conditions for instances to belong to a concept.

All the mentioned approaches for describing semantics based on features of instances can be used to compare the intended meaning of information. In the area of case-based reasoning, similarity measures have been defined that allow the comparison of concepts represented as "cases" based on attribute–value pairs [Richter, 1995]. For frame-based languages, matching algorithms have been proposed that exploit the structure of the concept expressions to determine semantic correspondences [Noy and Musen, 2004]. In the case of first-order axiomatizations, we can use logical reasoning to determine whether one axiomatization implies another one or whether two axiomatizations are equivalent and therefore represent the same intended meaning. As this kind of comparing semantics based on general deduction is often intractable, description logics provide specialized reasoning services for determining whether the definition of one concept is a special case of (is subsumed by) another[Donini et al., 1996]. This possibility make description logics a powerful tool for describing and comparing semantics with the goal of information sharing. Its concrete use will be discussed in other parts of this work.

1.5 Conclusion

Interoperability between different information sources is an important topic with regard to the efficient sharing and use of information across different systems and applications. While many syntactical and structural problems of the integration process that is essential for achieving interoperability have been solved, the notion of *semantic interoperability* still bears serious problems. Problems on the semantic level occur due to the inherent context dependency of information that can only be understood in the context of their original source and purpose. The main problem with context dependency with respect to semantic interoperability is the fact that most of the contextual knowledge that is necessary for understanding the information is hidden in the documentation and specification of an information source: it remains implicit from the view of the actual information. The only way to overcome this problem is the use of an explicit context model that can be used to re-interpret information in the context of a new information source and a new application.

Further Reading

A more detailed discussion of the role of XML and RDF in the Semantic Web can be found in [Decker et al., 2000]. The related areas of information integration and information retrieval are presented in [Wiederhold, 1996] and [Frakes and Baeza-Yates, 1992], respectively. The idea of using explicit semantics to support information sharing on the Web is discussed in [Fensel and Brodie, 2003]. The leading approaches for an explicit representation of information semantics, namely frame-based systems and description logics are presented in [Karp, 1993] and [Baader et al., 2002].

2

Ontology-based information sharing

Summary. In the last chapter we introduced the general problem of information sharing in the presence of heterogeneous data. In this chapter, we introduce ontologies as a means of dealing with semantic heterogeneity. We discuss the nature and applications of ontologies and review existing approaches that use ontologies for dealing with heterogeneous data. We also identify the state of the art in ontology-based information integration and identify open problems that will be addressed in the remainder of the book.

As we have seen in the last chapter, intelligent information sharing needs explicit representations of information semantics. We reviewed different approaches for capturing semantics that have been developed in different scientific communities. In this section we discuss ontologies as a general mechanism for representing information semantics that can be implemented using the approaches mentioned in Chap. 1. We start with a general introduction to the notion of ontologies and argue for their benefits for information integration and retrieval making them suitable as a tool for supporting information sharing. We also review the use of ontologies in the information-integration literature identifying ontology-based architectures for information sharing. Based on the review of integration architectures we present a general framework for supporting information sharing on the semantic web that summarizes the work reported in the remainder of the book. We relate the framework to existing work and give pointers to the different chapters of the book. Finally, we describe the representational infrastructure that is the core feature of the framework.

2.1 Ontologies

In this section we argue for ontologies as a technology for approaching the problem of explicating semantic knowledge about information. We first give a general overview of the nature and purpose of ontologies that already reveals a great potential with respect to our task. Afterwards we sketch the idea of how ontologies could be used in order to support the semantic translation process. The idea presented will be elaborated in the remainder of the book.

The term "ontology" has been used in many ways and across different communities [Guarino and Giaretta, 1995]. If we want to motivate the use of ontologies for geographic information processing we have to make clear what we have in mind when we refer to ontologies. Thereby we mainly follow the description given in [Uschold and Gruninger, 1996]. In the following sections we will introduce ontologies as an explication of some shared vocabulary or conceptualization of a specific subject matter. We will briefly describe the way an ontology explicates concepts and their properties and argue for the benefit of this explication in different typical application scenarios.

2.1.1 Shared vocabularies and conceptualizations

In general, each person has her individual views on the World and the things she has to deal with every day. However, there is a common basis of understanding in terms of the language we use to communicate with each other. Terms from natural language can therefore be assumed to be a shared vocabulary relying on a (mostly) common understanding of certain concepts with only little variety. This common understanding relies on the idea of how the World is organized. We often call this idea a "conceptualization" of the World. Such conceptualizations provide a terminology that can be used for communication.

The example of natural language already shows that a conceptualization is never universally valid, but rather for a limited number of persons committing to that conceptualization. This fact is reflected in the existence of different languages which differ more or less. For example, Dutch and German share many terms; however, Dutch contains far more terms for describing bodies of water, due to the great importance of water in the life of people. Things get even worse when we are not concerned with everyday language but with terminologies developed for special areas. In these cases we often find situations where the same term refers to different phenomena. The use of the term "ontology" in philosophy and its use in computer science may serve as an example. The consequence is a separation into different groups that share a terminology and its conceptualization. These groups are also called information communities [Kottmann, 1999] or ontology groups [Fensel et al., 1997]. An example of such a community is the $(KA)^2$ initiative [Benjamins and Fensel, 1998].

The main problem with the use of a shared terminology according to a specific conceptualization of the World is that much information remains implicit.

When a mathematician talks about the binomial $\binom{n}{k}$ he has much more in mind than just the formula itself. He will also think about its interpretation (the number of subsets of a certain size) and its potential uses (e.g. estimating the chance of winning in a lottery). Ontologies have set out to overcome the problem of implicit and hidden knowledge by making the conceptualization of a domain (e.g. mathematics) explicit. This corresponds to one of the definitions of the term ontology most popular in computer science [Gruber, 1993]:

"An ontology is an explicit specification of a conceptualization."

An ontology is used to make assumptions about the meaning of a term available. It can also be seen as an explication of the context a term is normally used in. Lenat [Lenat, 1998] for example describes context in terms of 12 independent dimensions that have to be known in order to understand a piece of knowledge completely and shows how these dimensions can be explicated using the Cyc ontology.

2.1.2 Specification of context knowledge

There are many different ways in which an ontology may explicate a conceptualization and the corresponding context knowledge. The possibilities range from a purely informal natural-language description of a term corresponding to a glossary up to strictly formal approaches with the expressive power of full first-order predicate logic or even beyond (e.g. ONTOLINGUA [Gruber, 1991]). Jasper and Uschold distinguish two ways in which the mechanisms for the specification of context knowledge by an ontology can be compared [Jasper and Uschold, 1999]:

Level of formality

The specification of a conceptualization and its implicit context knowledge can be done at different levels of formality. As already mentioned above, a glossary of terms can also be seen as an ontology despite its purely informal character. A first step to gain more formality is to prescribe a structure to be used for the description. A good example for this approach is the new standard Web annotation language XML [Yergeau et al., 2004]. XML offers the possibility to define terms and organize them in a simple hierarchy according to the expected structure of the Web document to be described in XML. However, the rather informal character of XML encourages its misuse. While the hierarchy of an XML specification was originally designed to describe layout it can also be exploited to represent subtype hierarchies [van Harmelen and Fensel, 1999], which may lead to confusion. This problem can be solved by assigning formal semantics to the structures used for the description of the ontology. An example is the conceptual modelling language CML [Schreiber et al., 1994]. CML offers primitives to describe a domain that can be given a formal semantics in terms of first order logic [Aben, 1993]. However, a formalization is only available for the structural part of a specification. Assertions about terms and the description of dynamic knowledge are not formalized, offering total freedom for the description. On the other extreme there are also specification languages which are completely formal. A prominent example is ONTOLIN-GUA (see above), one of the first Ontology languages which is based on the knowledge interchange format KIF [Genesereth and Fikes, 1992] which was designed to enable different knowledge-based systems to exchange knowledge.

Extent of Explication

The other comparison criterion is the extent of explication that is reached by the ontology. Jasper and Uschold [Jasper and Uschold, 1999] refer to "lightweight" vs. "heavyweight" ontologies to described differences in the extend of explication. This criterion is strongly connected with the expressive power of the specification language used. We can generalize this by saying that the least expressive specification of an ontology consists of an organization of terms in a network using two-placed relations. This idea goes back to the use of semantic networks. Many extensions of the basic idea have been proposed. One of the most influential was the use of roles that could be filled out by entities showing a certain type [Brachman, 1977]. This kind of value restriction can still be found in recent approaches. RDF Schema descriptions [Brickley and Guha, 2004] (see Chap. 3 which is the new standard for the semantic descriptions of Web pages, is an example. An RDF Schema contains class definitions with associated properties that can be restricted by so-called constraint-properties. However, default values and value-range descriptions are not expressive enough to cover all possible conceptualizations. A greater expressive power can be provided by allowing classes to be specified by logical formulas. These formulas can be restricted to a decidable subset of first order logic. This is the approach of so-called description logics [Donini et al., 1996]. This trade-off between expressiveness and decidability is also reflected in the development of the Web Ontology Language OWL which is described in more details in Chap. 3 where the language subset that corresponds to description logics is explicitly distinguished. Nevertheless, there are also approaches allowing for more expressive descriptions. In ONTOLINGUA, for example, classes can be defined by arbitrary KIF expressions. Beyond the expressiveness of full first-order predicate logic there are also special purpose languages that have an extended expressiveness to cover specific needs of their application area. The latest example is OWL, where the complete language (OWL full) is undecidable[1] as it combines description logics with meta-level features.

---

[1] undecidability still has to be proven formally, but there are no doubts about this fact

2.1.3 Beneficial applications

Ontologies are useful for many different applications that can be classified into several areas [Jasper and Uschold, 1999]. Each of these areas has different requirements on the level of formality and the extent of explication provided by the ontology. The common idea of all of these applications is to use ontologies in order to reach a common understanding of a particular domain. In contrast to syntactic standards, the understanding is not restricted to a common representation or a common structure. The use of ontologies also helps to reach a common understanding of the *meaning* of terms. Therefore, ontologies are a promising candidate in order to support semantic interoperability. We will shortly review some common application areas, namely the support of communication processes, the specification of systems and information entities and the interoperability of computer systems.

Communication

Information communities are useful, because they ease communication and cooperation among their members by the use of a shared terminology with a well-defined meaning. On the other hand, the formation of information communities makes communication between members from different information communities very difficult, because they do not agree on a common conceptualization. They may use the shared vocabulary of natural language. However, most of the vocabulary used in their information communities is highly specialized and not shared with other communities. This situation demands an explication and explanation of the terminology used. Informal ontologies with a large extent of explication are a good choice to overcome these problems. While definitions have always played an important role in scientific literature, conceptual models of certain domains are rather new. However, nowadays systems analysis and related fields like software engineering rely on conceptual modelling to communicate structure and details of a problem domain as well as the proposed solution between domain experts and engineers. Prominent examples of ontologies used for communication are entity-relationship diagrams [Chen, 1976] and object-oriented modelling languages like UML [Rumbaugh et al., 1998].

Systems engineering

Entity-relationship diagrams as well as UML are not only used for communication, they also serve as building plans for data and systems guiding the process of building (engineering) the system. The use of ontologies for the description of information and systems has many benefits. The ontology can be used to identify requirements as well as inconsistencies in a chosen design. It can help to acquire or search for available information. Once a systems component has been implemented its specification can be used for maintenance and extension purposes. Another very challenging application of ontology-based specification is the re-use of existing software. In this case the specifying ontology serves as a basis to decide if an existing component matches the requirements of a given task [Motta, 1999]. Depending on the purpose of the specification, ontologies of different formal strength and expressiveness are to be used. While the process of communicating design decisions and the acquisition of additional information normally benefit from rather informal and expressive ontology representations (often graphical), the directed search for information needs a rather strict specification with a limited vocabulary to limit the computational effort. At the moment, the support of semi- automatic software re-use seems to be one of the most challenging applications of ontologies, because it requires expressive ontologies with a high level of formal strength (see for example [van Heijst et al., 1997]).

Interoperability

The above considerations might provoke the impression that the benefits of ontologies are limited to systems analysis and design. However, an important application area of ontologies is the integration of existing systems. The ability to exchange information at run time, also known as interoperability, is an important topic. The attempt to provide interoperability suffers from problems similar to those associated with the communication amongst different information communities. The important difference is that the actors are not persons able to perform abstraction and common sense reasoning about the meaning of terms, but machines. In order to enable machines to understand each other we also have to explicate the context of each system, but on a much higher level of formality in order to make it machine understandable (the KIF language was originally defined for the purpose of exchanging knowledge models between different knowledge-based systems). Ontologies are often used as interlinguas for providing interoperability [Uschold and Gruninger, 1996]: they serve as a common format for data interchange. Each system that wants to interoperate with other systems has to transfer its information into this common framework.

Information Retrieval

Common information-retrieval techniques either rely on a specific encoding of available information (e.g. fixed classification codes) or simple full-text analysis. Both approaches suffer from severe shortcomings. First of all, both completely rely on the input vocabulary of the user, which might not be completely consistent with the vocabulary of the information. Second, a specific encoding significantly reduces the recall of a query, because related information with a slightly different encoding is not matched. Full-text analysis on the other hand reduces precision, because the meaning of the words might be ambiguous.

Using an ontology in order to explicate the vocabulary can help overcome some of these problems. When used for the description of available information as well as for query formulation, an ontology serves as a common basis for matching queries against potential results on a semantic level. The use of rather informal ontologies like WordNet [Fellbaum, 1998] increases the recall of a query by including synonyms in the search process. The use of more formal representations like conceptual graphs [Sowa, 1999] further enhances the retrieval process, because a formal representation can be used to increase recall by reasoning about inheritance relationships and precision by matching structures. To summarize, information retrieval benefits from the use of ontologies. Ontologies help to decouple description and query vocabularies and increase precision as well as recall [Guarino et al., 1999].

2.2 Ontologies in information integration

We analyzed about 25 approaches to intelligent information integration including SIMS [Arens et al., 1993], TSIMMIS [Garcia-Molina et al., 1995], OBSERVER [Mena et al., 2000a] , CARNOT [Collet et al., 1991], Infosleuth [Nodine et al., 1999], KRAFT [Preece et al., 1999], PICSEL [Levy et al., 1996], DWQ [Calvanese et al., 1998b], Ontobroker [Fensel et al., 1998] , SHOE [Heflin et al., 1999] and others with respect to the role and use of ontologies. While all of the systems used ontologies to describe the meaning of information, the role and use of these descriptions differ between the approaches. In the following we discuss the different roles ontologies can play in information integration.

2.2.1 Content explication

In nearly all ontology-based integration approaches ontologies are used for the explicit description of the information-source semantics. But there are different ways of how to employ the ontologies. In general, three different directions can be identified: *single-ontology approaches*, *multiple-ontology approaches* and *hybrid approaches*. Fig. 2.1 gives an overview of the three main architectures.

The integration based on a single ontology seems to be the simplest approach because it can be simulated by the other approaches. Some approaches provide a general framework where all three architectures can be implemented (e.g. DWQ [Calvanese et al., 1998b]). The following paragraphs give a brief overview of the three main ontology architectures.

Single-ontology approaches

Single-ontology approaches use one global ontology providing a shared vocabulary for the specification of the semantics (see Fig. 2.1a). All information

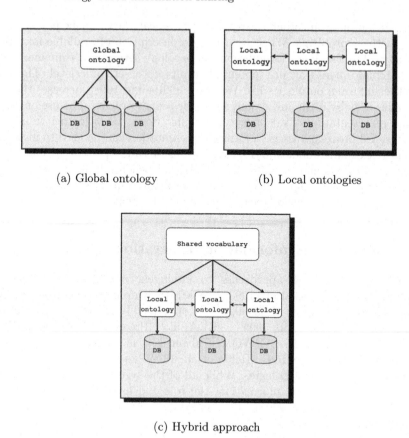

(a) Global ontology   (b) Local ontologies

(c) Hybrid approach

Fig. 2.1. The three possible ways for using ontologies for content explication

sources are related to the one global ontology. A prominent approach of this kind of ontology integration is SIMS [Arens et al., 1993]. SIMS model of the application domain includes a hierarchical terminological knowledge base with nodes representing objects, actions and states. An independent model of each information source must be described for this system by relating the objects of each source to the global domain model. The relationships clarify the semantics of the source objects and help to find semantically corresponding objects. The global ontology can also be a combination of several specialized ontologies. A reason for the combination of several ontologies can be the modularization of a potentially large monolithic ontology. The combination is supported by ontology-representation formalisms, i.e. importing other ontology modules (cf. ONTOLINGUA [Gruber, 1991]).

Single-ontology approaches can be applied to integration problems where all information sources to be integrated provide nearly the same view of a domain. But if one information source has a different view of a domain, e.g. by providing another level of granularity, finding the minimal ontology commitment [Gruber, 1995] becomes a difficult task. For example, if two information sources provide product specifications but refer to absolute heterogeneous product catalogues which categorize the products, the development of a global ontology which combines the different product catalogues becomes very difficult. Information sources with reference to similar product catalogues are much easier to integrate. Also, single-ontology approaches are susceptible to changes in the information sources, which can affect the conceptualization of the domain represented in the ontology. Depending on the nature of the changes in one information source it can imply changes in the global ontology and in the mappings to the other information sources. These disadvantages led to the development of multiple-ontology approaches.

Multiple ontologies

In multiple-ontology approaches, each information source is described by its own ontology (Fig. 2.1b). For example, in OBSERVER [Mena et al., 2000a], the semantics of an information source is described by a separate ontology. In principle, the "source ontology" can be a combination of several other ontologies but it cannot be assumed that the different "source ontologies" share the same vocabulary.

At a first glance, the advantage of multiple-ontology approaches seems to be that no common and minimal ontology commitment [Gruber, 1995] about one global ontology is needed. Each source ontology could be developed without reference to the other sources or their ontologies, no common ontology with the agreement of all sources is needed. This ontology architecture can simplify the change, i.e. modifications in one information source or the adding and removing of sources. But in reality the lack of a common vocabulary makes it extremely difficult to compare different source ontologies. To overcome this problem, an additional representation formalism defining the mapping is provided. The mapping identifies semantically corresponding terms of different source ontologies, e.g. which terms are semantically equal or similar. But the mapping also has to consider different views of a domain, e.g. different aggregation and granularity of the ontology concepts. We believe that in practice the mapping is very difficult to define, because of the many semantic heterogeneity problems which may occur.

Hybrid approaches

To overcome the drawbacks of the single- or multiple-ontology approaches, hybrid approaches were developed (Fig. 2.1c). Similar to multiple-ontology approaches the semantics of each source is described by its own ontology.

But in order to make the source ontologies comparable to each other they are built upon one global shared vocabulary [Wache et al., 1999, Goh, 1997]. The shared vocabulary contains basic terms (the primitives) of a domain. In order to build complex terms of a source ontology the primitives are combined by some operators. Because each term of a source ontology is based on the primitives, the terms become easier comparable than in multiple-ontology approaches. Sometimes the shared vocabulary is also an ontology [Stuckenschmidt and Wache, 2000].

In hybrid approaches the interesting point is how the local ontologies are described, i.e. how the terms of the source ontology are described by the primitives of the shared vocabulary.

- In COIN [Goh, 1997], the local description of an information, the so-called context, is simply an attribute value vector. The terms for the context stems from the common shared vocabulary and the data itself.
- In MECOTA [Wache, 1999], each source information is annotated by a label which indicates the semantics of the information. The label combines the primitive terms from the shared vocabulary. The combination operators are similar to the operators known from the description logics, but are extended for the special requirements resulting from integration of sources, e.g. by an operator which indicates that an information aggregates several different information items (e.g. a street name together with a number).
- In BUSTER [Visser et al., 2002], the shared vocabulary is a (general) ontology, which covers all possible refinements. The general ontology may define the attribute value ranges of its concepts. A source ontology is one (partial) refinement of the general ontology, e.g. it restricts the value range of some attributes. Since the source ontologies only use the vocabulary of the general ontology, they remain comparable.

The advantage of a hybrid approach is that new sources can easily be added without the need of modification in the mappings or in the shared vocabulary. It also supports the acquisition and evolution of ontologies. The use of a shared vocabulary makes the source ontologies comparable and avoids the disadvantages of multiple-ontology approaches. The drawback of hybrid approaches , however, is that existing ontologies cannot be re-used easily, but have to be re-developed from scratch, because all source ontologies have to refer to the shared vocabulary. Table 2.1 summarizes the benefits and drawbacks of the different ontology approaches.

2.2.2 Additional roles of ontologies

Some approaches use ontologies not only for content explication, but also either as a global query model or for the verification of the (user-defined or

Table 2.1. Comparison of ontology-based integration approaches

	Single-ontology approaches	Multiple-ontology approaches	Hybrid approaches
Implementation effort	Straight-forward	Costly	Reasonable
Semantic heterogeneity	Similar views of a domain	Supports heterogeneous views	Supports heterogeneous views
Adding/ removing sources	Need for some adaption in the global ontology	Providing a new source ontology; relating to other ontologies	Providing a new source ontology
Comparing multiple ontologies	—	Difficult because of the lack of a common vocabulary	Simple because ontologies use a common vocabulary

system-generated) integration description. In the following, these additional roles of ontologies are considered in more detail.

Query model

Integrated information sources normally provide an integrated global view. Some integration approaches use the ontology as the global query schema. For example, in SIMS [Arens et al., 1996] the user formulates a query in terms of the ontology. Then SIMS reformulates the global query into subqueries for each appropriate source, collects and combines the query results and returns the results. The use of ontologies as query models is independent of the use of a global ontology. In OBSERVER, for example, the user can pose queries using terms from the ontology of the local source.

Using an ontology as a query model has the advantage that the structure of the query model should be more intuitive for the user because it corresponds more to the user's appreciation of the domain. But from a database point of view this ontology only acts as a global query schema. If a user formulates a query, he has to know the structure and the contents of the ontology; he cannot formulate the query according to a schema he would prefer personally. Therefore, it is questionable whether the global ontology is an appropriate query model.

Verification

During the integration process several mappings must be specified from a global schema to the local source schema. The correctness of such mappings can be considered ably improved if these can be verified automatically. A subquery is correct with respect to a global query if the local subquery provides a part of the queried answers, i.e. the subqueries must be contained in the global query (query containment) [Goasdoue et al., 2000, Calvanese et al., 1998a]. Since an ontology contains a (complete) specification of the conceptualization, the mappings can be validated with respect to the ontologies. Query containment means that the ontology concepts corresponding to the local sub-queries are contained in the ontology concepts related to the global query.

In DWQ [Calvanese et al., 1998b], each source is assumed to be a collection of relational tables. Each table is described in terms of its ontology with the help of conjunctive queries. A global query and the decomposed subqueries can be unfolded to their ontology concepts. The subqueries are correct, i.e. are contained in the global query, if their ontology concepts are subsumed by the global ontology concepts. The PICSEL project [Goasdoue et al., 2000] can also verify the mapping, but in contrast to DWQ it can also generate mapping hypotheses automatically which are validated with respect to a global ontology.

The quality of the verification task strongly depends on the completeness of an ontology. If the ontology is incomplete, the verification result can erroneously imagine a correct query subsumption. Since in general the completeness cannot be measured, it is impossible to make any statements about the quality of the verification.

2.3 A framework for information sharing

In this book, we describe different components of a framework for information sharing on the Semantic Web. The design of the framework is motivated by the potential roles of ontologies in information integration. In particular, we use ontologies to represent the intended interpretation of contents different information sources. We adopt the hybrid approach because it provides a good trade-off with respect to development costs and maintainability. We assume that a shared vocabulary provides the foundation for query formulation, for translations between the ontologies describing different information sources and for the verification of metadata as well as mappings between sources. Taking the hybrid approach as a starting point, our framework contains three main components whose relations are sketched in Fig. 2.2. In the following, we briefly describe the different components, their relations and related them to parts of the book.

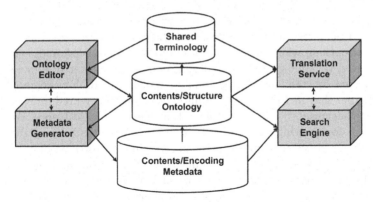

Fig. 2.2. A framework for ontology-based information sharing

Representational Infrastructure

The representational infrastructure we use to facilitate information sharing consists of three layers. On the lowest level, metadata describes the content of information sources. We assume that this metadata is represented using RDF as a common language. On the highest level, a common vocabulary defines terms that are assumed to have the same meaning across all information sources. This shared vocabulary mostly consists of concept hierarchies and relations between concepts in these hierarchies. We use RDF Schema to represent this information. Unlike most current work in the semantic web area, we do not directly layer RDF Schema models on top of the RDF metadata. Instead we insert an additional layer consisting of ontologies that describe the conceptualizations and structures specific to a certain source of information. The definitions in these ontologies are built using terms from the shared vocabulary. We encode these source-specific ontologies using the web ontology language OWL. The expressive power of OWL allows us to accurately define the intended meaning of the modelling elements and the data values used in the different sources. After providing a more detailed description of this layering in the remainder of this chapter, we introduce RDF Schema and OWL in Chap. 3. We also present an extension to OWL that allows the definition of direct mappings between source ontologies in Chap. 10 and describe source ontologies and metadata models for special data sources, more specifically for statistical (Chap. 7) and for spatially-related information (Chap. 8).

Development and Maintenance

In order to be able to share information from different sources it is not enough to described the representational infrastructure needed, we also have to address the problem of creating the infrastructure. In particular, this includes the selection of a shared vocabulary, the definition of source ontologies as well as the generation of metadata description for the concrete information in a source. We envision this process to start with the analysis of the information sources to be shared and the conceptual choices made therein. Based on the these conceptualizations and the kind of information to be shared, candidates for a shared vocabulary are selected and refined in an iterative process which is supported by standard editing tools for OWL and RDF Schema. We further assume that metadata for the different sources is created independently of each other using the source ontology that has been build before. We developed tools for creating metadata by discovering patterns in the structure of information sources and link them to concepts in the source ontology. Finally, we describe a framework for managing the evolution of ontologies that are linked by mappings in order to react to changes in the information. We discuss the creation of source ontologies and shared vocabulary along with the detailed description of their connection in Chap. 4. The automatic creation of metadata based on the result of this process is described in Chap. 5. Evolution management for interrelated ontologies is the topic of Chap. 11.

Retrieval and Integration

The ultimate goal of our framework is to enable people to share information across different sources in a meaningful way. The representational infrastructure for describing information semantics and the methods for building and maintaining these representations are a necessary pre-condition for approach this goal. Based on this infrastructure our framework provides two principled mechanisms for supporting information sharing: Methods for content-based retrieval of information from remote sources and methods for translating between the conceptualizations of different sources. The translation services, we describe in this book are mainly concerned with domain conflicts by detecting and resolving conflicts between the the definition of object classes. Our methods exploit the existence of a shared vocabulary and uses existing reasoning systems for OWL and RDF schema to automatically compute subsumption relations between from different ontologies. The translation and the retrieval methods are tightly integrated as translation is needed during the retrieval process in order to find relevant information and for actually translating retrieved data items into the terminology used by the user. The retrieval and integration methods are described in Chap. 6. Large parts of these methods have been implemented in the BUSTER system which follows the schema in Fig. 2.2. On the other hand, similar methods are found in other existing systems. Three of these systems that all more or less implement parts of the framework are described in Chap. 9.

2.4 A translation approach to ontology alignment

The core idea of the information framework sketched above is the use of a shared vocabulary as a basis for comparing the conceptualizations of different information sources. The existence of such a shared vocabulary makes it possible to translate between different information on a semantic level. On the Semantic Web, it will frequently happen that information sources are added or removed. Further, the number of information sources will be considerably high. Based on these observations, we conclude that an on-demand translation of information semantics is most adequate for our purposes. Therefore, we will use the idea of integration by translation as a guideline for the remainder of the book.

2.4.1 The translation process

The proposed translation process is sketched below describing actors, supporting tools and knowledge items (i.e. ontologies) involved. Notice that although the approach described above translates only between two sources at a time, it is not limited to bilateral integration.

Authoring of shared terminology

Our approach relies on the use of a shared terminology in terms of properties used to define different concepts. This shared terminology has to be general enough to be used across all information sources to be integrated but specific enough to make meaningful definitions possible. Therefore the shared terminology will normally be built by an independent domain expert who is familiar with typical tasks and problems in a domain, but who is not concerned with a specific information source. As building a domain ontology is a challenging task, sufficient tool support has to be provided to build that ontology. A growing number of ontology editors exist [Duineveld et al., 1999]. The choice of a tool has to be based on the special needs of the domain to be modelled and the knowledge of the expert.

Annotation of information sources

Once a common vocabulary exists, it can be used to annotate different information sources. In this case annotation means that the inherent concept hierarchy of an information source is extracted and each concept is described by necessary and sufficient conditions using the terminology built in step one. The result of this annotation process is an ontology of the information source to be integrated. The annotation will normally be done by the owner of an information source who wants to provide better access to his or her information. In order to enable the information owner to annotate his information he has to know about the right vocabulary to use. It will also be beneficial to provide tool support also for this step. We need an annotation tool with different repositories of vocabularies according to different domains of interest.

Semantic translation of information entities

The only purpose of the steps described above was to lay a base for the actual translation step. The existence of ontologies for all information sources to be integrated enables the translator to work on these ontologies instead of treating real data. This way of using ontologies as surrogates for information sources has already been investigated in the context of information retrieval [Visser and Stuckenschmidt, 1999]. In that paper we showed that the search for interesting information can be enhanced by ontologies. Concerning semantic translation the use of ontologies as surrogates for information sources enables us to restrict the translation to the transformation of type information attached to an information entity by manipulating concept terms indicating the type of the entity.

The new concept term describing the type of an information entity in the target information source is determined automatically by an inference engine that uses ontologies of source and target structures as classification knowledge. This is possible, because both ontologies are based on the same basic vocabulary that has been built in the first step of the integration approach.

2.4.2 Required infrastructure

In order to enable a terminological reasoning system to actually relate concepts, we have to make assumptions about the knowledge represented. These assumptions directly refer to the two solutions to the explication dilemma mentioned above, because reasoning across ontologies requires a shared basic vocabulary (reduction to syntax) and the description of concepts in both ontologies in terms of logical expressions over these shared terms (reduction to logic).

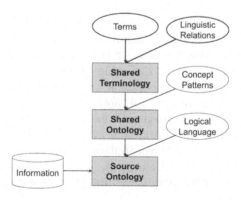

Fig. 2.3. Conceptual Architecture of the Translation Knowledge

We distinguish between shared terminology and shared ontology. The shared terminology consists of terms assumed to have a unique meaning across different classifications. These terms are structured by relations borrowed from linguistics, i.e. synonym (equivalent term), hypernym (broader term) and hyponym (more specialized term) relations. Formally, we define a shared terminology as a set of words and a partial function over pairs of words:

Definition 2.1 (shared terminology). *A shared terminology is a tuple* $\langle W, l \rangle$, *where* W *is a set of words and* $l : W \times W \rightarrow \{syno, hyper, hypo\}$ *is a partial function from the set of all pairs of terms into a set of identifiers specifying whether the first term is a synonym, a hypernym or a hyponym of the second.*

This shared terminology is linked to the specific integration problem using *structural patterns*. A structural pattern is a general specification of relations between objects denoted by the words in the shared terminology. In order to be able to apply these relations to information objects, the shared terminology is encoded in a simple logical structure consisting of a set of terms corresponding to words from the shared terminology relations between these terms and a set of axioms. The axioms define the synonym, hypernym and hyponym relations between terms in terms of the subsumption relation.

Definition 2.2 (shared ontology). *A shared ontology is a tuple* $\langle ST, T, R, A \rangle$, *where* $ST = \langle W_L, l_L \rangle$ *is a shared terminology,* T *is a basic set of terms,* R *is a set of relations* $R \subseteq T \times T$ *and* A *is a set of axioms of the form* $T_i \sqsubseteq T_j$ *if the following conditions hold:*

- $T \subseteq W_L$,
- *for each pair of words* (W_i, W_j),
  - *if* $l((W_i, W_j)) = hyper$ *then* $W_j \sqsubseteq W_i$ *is in* A,
  - *if* $l((W_i, W_j)) = hypo$ *then* $W_i \sqsubseteq W_j$ *is in* A,
  - *if* $l((W_i, W_j)) = syno$ *then* $W_i \sqsubseteq W_j$ *and* $W_j \sqsubseteq W_i$ *are in* A.

From the point of expressiveness, this shared ontology is very similar to a model in RDF Schema, because it defines a hierarchy of terms (classes in RDF Schema) as well as a set of relations (properties) with corresponding range and domain restrictions. This correspondence enables us to use RDF Schema in order to encode shared ontologies as a basis for defining information semantics.

Shared ontologies provide us with a vocabulary we can use in order to specify the semantics of information in different sources. This semantics, however, has to be defined individually for different information sources. In order to capture the semantics of types or assessments used in an information source, we need a richer language, because their meaning almost never directly corresponds to a term in the shared ontology. We therefore define a source ontology, an ontology that defines the meaning of specific classifications used in the source, to consist of a set of class definitions. These definitions are legal expressions over terms from the shared ontology built using a terminological language that defines operators for the relations also defined in the shared ontology:

Definition 2.3 (source ontology). *A source ontology is a tuple $\langle S, C, d \rangle$, where $S = \langle ST_S, T_S, R_S, A_S \rangle$ is a shared ontology, C is a set of class names not from the set of terms in S, L is a terminological language and d is a function that assigns expressions δ_i to class names C_i in C such that:*

- *δ_i only refers to relations in R_S,*
- *L is defined over T_S.*

In the following we refer to δ_i as the definition of C_i, which is denoted by $d(C_i)$.

Given a source ontology we can perform terminological reasoning over the definition of classes contained therein by considering the set of axioms from the shared ontology, the definitions of relations and the set of class definitions. Together, these elements form a terminological knowledge-base that can be used by suitable description-logic reasoners in order to provide standard inference services such as classification and retrieval. How these inference services are used for retrieval and integration will be discussed in Chap. 6.

2.5 Conclusions

The use of ontologies is a straightforward and promising approach in order to explicate contextual information and to make a semantics-preserving translation possible. Especially, ontologies could be used for the specification of a source-independent shared vocabulary (domain ontology) whose concepts are used to describe the specific contextual information of different information sources to be integrated (application ontologies). The use of a common vocabulary as a basis for the context specifications is assumed to enable us to perform (semi-)automatic translations between different contexts that preserve the intended meaning of the translated terms to a large extent.

The central question is how to actually capture information semantics in ontologies. A strategy is needed that determines what kinds of ontologies are needed and how they can be built. This strategy has to trade-off globalized representations that provide a common basis for defining and comparing information semantics and local representations that capture the specific conceptual choices made in the design of individual information sources. In order to be comparable, these local definitions should be based on terms defined globally. Linguistic resources and top-level ontologies provide guidance in the choice for a global vocabulary. The representational framework defined in the first part of this book then provides operators for composing these basic terms into more complex concept definitions and to perform terminological reasoning.

State of the research

The typical information-integration system uses ontologies to explicate the contents of an information source, mainly by describing the intended meaning of table- and data-field names. For this purpose, each information source is supplemented by an ontology which resembles and extends the structure of the information source. In a typical system, integration is done at the ontology level using either a common ontology all source ontologies are related to or fixed mappings between different ontologies. The ontology language of the typical system is based on description logics, and subsumption reasoning is used in order to compute relations between different information sources and sometimes to validate the result of an integration. The process of building and using ontologies in the typical system is supported by specialized tools in terms of editors.

Open questions

The description of the typical integration system shows that reasonable results have been achieved on the technical side of using ontologies for intelligent information integration. Only the use of mappings is an exception. It seems that most approaches still use ad hoc or arbitrary mappings especially for the connection of different ontologies. There are approaches that try to provide well-founded mappings, but they either rely on assumptions that cannot always be guaranteed or they face technical problems. We conclude that there is a need to investigate mappings on a theoretical and an empirical basis.

Beside the mapping problem, we found a striking lack of sophisticated methodologies supporting the development and use of ontologies. Most systems only provide tools. If there is a methodology it often only covers the development of ontologies for a specific purpose which is prescribed by the integration system. The comparison of different approaches, however, revealed that requirements concerning ontology language and structure depend on the kind of information to be integrated and the intended use of the ontology. We therefore think that there is a need to develop a more general methodology that includes an analysis of the integration task and supports the process of defining the role of ontologies with respect to these requirements. We think that such a methodology has to be language independent, because the language should be selected based on the requirements of the application and not the other way round. A good methodology also has to cover the evaluation and verification of the decisions made with respect to language and structure of the ontology. The development of such a methodology will be a major step in the work on ontology-based information integration because it will help to integrate results already achieved on the technical side and to put these techniques to work in real-life applications.

Further reading

The first widely accepted definition of ontologies from a computer science perspective is given by Gruber [Gruber, 1993] in his seminal work. Uschold and Gruninger give excellent overview over the nature as use of ontologies [Uschold and Gruninger, 1996]. Guarino and Giaretta discuss the special character of ontologies that distinguish them from other knowledge models [Guarino and Giaretta, 1995]. We give an overview of ontology-based information integration systems in [Wache et al., 2001]. An overview of the use of ontologies at different levels of formality and extends of explication is [McGuinness, 2002].

3

Ontology languages for the Semantic Web

Summary. The role of this chapter is to give a general introduction to some of the ontology languages that play a prominent role on the Semantic Web. These languages will be the main carriers of the information that we will want to share and integrate.

We first give a general and abstract model of ontologies and the logical inferences that they support (in section 3.1). We then describe a stack of ever more expressive Web-based ontology languages: RDF Schema, OWL Lite, OWL DL and OWL Full (sections 3.2.1–3.2.4). We conclude this chapter with a brief comparison with other ontology languages (section 3.3).

3.1 An abstract view

In order to get a general notion of ontological knowledge, we define the general structure of a terminological knowledge base (ontology) and its instantiation independent of a concrete language.

Definition 3.1 (terminological knowledge base).
A terminological knowledge base T is a triple

$$T = \langle \mathcal{C}, \mathcal{R}, \mathcal{O} \rangle,$$

where $\mathcal{C}$ is a set of class definitions, $\mathcal{R}$ is a set of relation definitions and $\mathcal{O}$ is a set of object definitions.

Terminological knowledge usually groups objects of the World that have certain properties in common (e.g. cities or countries). A description of the shared properties is called a class definition. Concepts can be arranged into a subclass–superclass relation in order to be able to further discriminate objects into subgroups (e.g. capitals or European countries). A class can be defined in two ways, by enumeration of its members or by stating that it is a refinement of a complex logical expression. The specific logical operators to express such logical definitions can vary between ontology languages; the general definitions we give here abstract from these specific operators.

Definition 3.2 (class definitions). *A class definition is an axiom of one of the following forms:*

- $c \equiv (o_1, ..., o_n)$ *where c is a class definition and $o_1, ..., o_n$ are object definitions.*
- $c_1 \sqsubseteq c_2$, *where c_1 and c_2 are class definitions.*

Further, there is the universal class denoted as $\top$.

Objects of the same type normally occur in similar situations where they have a certain relation to each other (cities lie in countries, countries have a capital). These typical relations can often be specified in order to establish structures between classes. Terminological knowledge considers binary relations that can either be defined by restricting their domain and range or by declaring the relation to be a subrelation of an existing one.

Definition 3.3 (relation definitions). *A relation definition is an axiom of one of the following forms:*

- $r \sqsubseteq (c_1, c_2)$, *where r is a role definition and c_1 and c_2 are class definitions.*
- $r_1 \sqsubseteq r_2$, *where r_1 and r_2 are role definitions.*

The universal role is defined as $\top \times \top$.

Sometimes single objects (e.g. the continent of Europe) play a prominent role in a domain of interest, or the membership of a concept is defined by the relation to a specific object (European countries are those contained in Europe). For this purpose ontology languages often allow us to specify single objects, also called instances. In our view of terminological knowledge, instances can be defined by stating their membership in a class. Further, we can define instances of binary relations by stating that two objects form such a pair.

Definition 3.4 (object definitions). *An object definition is an axiom of one of the following forms:*

- $o : c$, *where c is a class definition and o is an individual.*
- $(o_1, o_2) : r$, *where r is a relation definition and o_1, o_2 are object definitions.*

In the following, we will consider terminological knowledge bases that consist of such axioms. Of course, any specific ontology language will have to further instantiate these definitions to specify logical operators between classes, etc but for the purposes of this paper, these general definitions are sufficient. Further, we define the signature of a terminological knowledge base to be a triple $\langle \mathcal{CN}, \mathcal{RN}, \mathcal{IN} \rangle$, where $\mathcal{CN}$ is the set of all names of classes defined in $\mathcal{C}$, $\mathcal{RN}$ the set of all relation names and $\mathcal{IN}$ the set of all object names occurring in the knowledge base.

We can define semantics and logical consequences of a terminological knowledge base using an interpretation mapping $.^{\Im}$ into an abstract domain Δ such that:

- $c^{\Im} \subseteq \Delta$ for all class definitions c in the way defined above,
- $r^{\Im} \subseteq \Delta \times \Delta$ for all relation definitions r,
- $o^{\Im} \in \Delta$ for all object definitions o.

This type of denotational semantics is inspired by description logics [Donini et al., 1996]; however, we are not specific about operators that can be used to build class definitions which are of central interest of these logics. Using the interpretation mapping, we can define the notion of a model in the following way:

Definition 3.5 (model of a terminological knowledge base). *An interpretation $\Im$ is a model for the knowledge base $\mathcal{T}$ if $\Im \models A$ for every axiom $A \in (\mathcal{C} \cup \mathcal{R} \cup \mathcal{O})$, where $\models$ is defined as follows.*

- $\Im \models c \equiv (o_1, ..., o_n)$, *iff* $c^{\Im} = \{o_1^{\Im}, ..., o_n^{\Im}\}$
- $\Im \models c_1 \sqsubseteq c_2$, *iff* $c_1^{\Im} \subseteq c_2^{\Im}$
- $\Im \models r \sqsubseteq (c_1, c_2)$, *iff* $r^{\Im} \subseteq c_1^{\Im} \times c_2^{\Im}$
- $\Im \models r_1 \sqsubseteq r_2$, *iff* $r_1^{\Im} \subseteq r_2^{\Im}$
- $\Im \models o : c$, *iff* $o^{\Im} \in c^{\Im}$
- $\Im \models (o_1, o_2) : r$, *iff* $(o_1^{\Im}, o_2^{\Im}) \in r^{\Im}$

These definitions enable us to perform reasoning across different ontologies using the notion of logical consequence:

Definition 3.6 (logical consequence). *An axiom A logically follows from a set of axioms $\mathcal{S}$ if $\Im \models \mathcal{S}$ implies $\Im \models A$ for every model $\Im$. We denote this fact by $\mathcal{S} \models A$.*

In the following, we describe ontology languages in use on the semantic web and give examples of how the notion of logical consequence is used in the languages to derive implicit facts.

3.2 Two Semantic Web ontology languages

We now turn to a discussion of specific ontology languages that are based on the abstract view from the previous version: RDF Schema and OWL. Quite a few other sources already exist that give general introductions to these languages. Some parts of the RDF and OWL specifications are intended as such introductions (in particular [Manola and Miller, 2003],

[McGuinness and van Harmelen, 2003]   and   [Smith et al., 2003]),   and
also didactic material such as [Antoniou and van Harmelen, 2004] and
[Antoniou and van Harmelen, 2003].

Our presentation is structured along the layering of OWL: OWL Lite, OWL
DL and OWL Full. This layering is motivated by different requirements that
different users have for a Web ontology language:

- RDF(S) is intended for those users primarily needing a classification hierarchy
- OWL Lite adds the possibility to express (in)equalities and and simple
  constraints on such hierarchies
- OWL DL supports those users who want the maximum expressiveness
  while retaining computational completeness (all conclusions are guaranteed to be computable) and decidability (all computations will finish in
  finite time).
- OWL Full is meant for users who want maximum expressiveness and syntactic freedom with no computational guarantees.

Before discussing the language primitives of OWL Lite, we first discuss language elements from RDF and RDF Schema (RDF(S) for short). In order to
obtain a strict layering in our discussion, we will restrict our discussion of
RDF(S) to the case where the vocabulary is strictly partitioned, as described
in [Antoniou and van Harmelen, 2004][1]:

> "Any resource is allowed to be only a class, a data type, a data type
> property, an object property, an individual, a data value, or part of
> the built-in vocabulary, and not more than one of these. This means
> that, for example, a class cannot at the same time be an individual,
> [...]"

In terms of the abstract model of Sect. 3.1, this amounts to requiring that
the elements $\mathcal{C}, \mathcal{R}$ and $\mathcal{O}$ that make up a terminological knowledge base $\mathcal{T}$ in
Definition 3.1 are pairwise disjoint.

Under this restriction, we have the following strict inclusion-relationship[2]:

$$\text{RDF(S)} \subset \text{OWL Lite} \subset \text{OWL DL} \subset \text{OWL Full,}$$

where $\subset$ stands for both syntactic and semantic inclusion, in other words:
every syntactically correct RDF(S) statement is also a correct OWL Lite
statement, and every valid RDF(S) inference is also a valid OWL Lite
inference (and similarly for the other cases).

---

[1] Also called "type separation" in [McGuinness and van Harmelen, 2003]

[2] When dropping the restriction of a partitioned vocabulary for RDF(S), the first
inclusion relationship no longer holds

Before we discuss the different language primitives that we encounter along this set of inclusions, we first list some of our notational conventions.

We use the normative abstract syntax for OWL as defined in [Patel-Schneider et al., 2002b]. While this syntax in only meant for OWL itself, we use the same syntax for introducing RDF(S) in order to clarify the relation between the languages[3]. We will use symbols c_i for classes (i.e. corresponding to elements of $\mathcal{C}$ from Definition 3.1), e_i for instances of classes (i.e. corresponding to elements of $\mathcal{O}$ from Definition 3.1), p_i for properties between e_i (i.e. corresponding to elements of $\mathcal{R}$ from Definition 3.1) and o_i for ontologies. Whenever useful, we will prefix classes and instances with pseudo-namespaces to indicate the ontology in which these symbols occur, e.g. $o_1\, e_1$ and $o_2\, e_1$ are two different instances, the first occurring in ontology o_1, the second in ontology o_2.

3.2.1 RDF Schema

The most An elementary building block of RDF(S) is a class, which defines a group of individuals that belong together because they share some properties. The following states that an instance e belongs to a class c:

$$\texttt{Individual(e type(c))}\ (\textit{“e is of type c”}).$$

This corresponds to the first clause of Definition 3.4 of Sect. 3.1.

The second elementary statement of RDF(S) is the subsumption relation between classes: `subClassOf` (the second clause of Definition 3.2):

$$\texttt{subClassOf(c$_i$ c$_j$)}$$

In RDF, instances are related to other instances through properties:

$$\texttt{Individual(e$_i$ value(p e$_j$))}$$

(the second clause of Definition 3.4). Properties are characterized by their domain and range:

$$\texttt{ObjectProperty(p domain(c$_i$)range(c$_j$))}$$

(the first clause of Definition 3.3).

Finally, just as with classes, properties are organized in a subsumption hierarchy:

$$\texttt{SubPropertyOf(o$_1$: p$_i$ o$_2$: p$_j$)}$$

(the second clause of Definition 3.3).

---

[3] Note that the semantics of the same constructs in RDF(S) and OWL can differ

3.2.2 OWL Lite

One of the significant limitations of RDF Schema was the inability to make equality claims between individuals. Such equality claims are possible in OWL Lite:

$$\texttt{SameIndividual}(e_i\ e_j)$$

Besides equality between instances, OWL Lite also introduces constructions to state equality between classes and between properties. Although such equalities could already be expressed in an indirect way in RDF(S) [4], this can be done directly in OWL Lite:

$$\texttt{EquivalentClasses}(c_1\ c_j)$$
$$\texttt{EquivalentProperties}(p_1\ p_j)$$

Just as importantly, as making positive claims about equality or subsumption relationships, is stating negative information about inequalities. A significant limitation of RDF(S)[5] is the inability to state such inequalities. Since OWL does not make the unique name assumption, two instances e_i and e_j are not automatically regarded as different. Such an inequality must be explicitly stated, as:

$$\texttt{DifferentIndividuals}(e_i\ e_j)$$

Because inequality between individuals is an often occurring and important statement (in many ontologies, all differently named individuals are assumed to be different, i.e. they embrace the unique name assumption), OWL Lite provides an abbreviated form:

$$\texttt{DifferentIndividuals}(e_1\ ...\ e_4)$$

abbreviates the six `DifferentIndividuals` statements that would have been required for this.

Whereas the above constructions are aimed at mapping instances and classes, OWL Lite also has constructs specifically aimed at properties. An often occurring phenomenon is that two a propety can be modelled in two directions. Examples are *ownerOf* vs. *ownedBy*, *contains* vs. *isContainedIn*, *childOf* vs. *parentOf* and countless others. The relationship between such pairs of properties is established by stating

$$\texttt{ObjectProperty}(p_i\ \texttt{inverseOf}(p_j))$$

Other vocabulary in OWL Lite (namely `TransitiveProperty` and `SymmetricProperty` are modifying a single property, rather then establishing a relation between two properties:

---

[4] through a pair of mutual `Subclassof` or `SubPropertyOf` statements.

[5] but motivated by a deliberate design decision concerning the computational and conceptual complexity of the language

$$\texttt{ObjectProperty}(o_1 : p_i \texttt{ Transitive})$$
$$\texttt{ObjectProperty}(o_1 : p_i \texttt{ Symmetric})$$

Another significant limitation of RDF(S) is the inability to state whether a property is optional or required (in other words: should it have at least one value or not), and whether it is single- or multi-valued (in other words: is it allowed to have more than one value or not). Technically, these restrictions constitute 0/1-cardinality constraints on the property. The case where a property is allowed to have at most one value for a given instance (i.e. a max-cardinality of 1) has a special name: $\texttt{FunctionalProperty}$. The case where the value of a property uniquely identifies the instance of which it is a value (i.e. the inverse property has a max-cardinality of 1) is called $\texttt{InverseFunctionalProperty}$. These two constructions allow for some interesting derivations under the OWL semantics: If an ontology models that any object can only have a single "age":

$$(\texttt{ObjectProperty age Functional})$$

then different age-values for two instances e_i and e_j allow us to infer that

$$\texttt{DifferentIndividuals}(e_i \ e_j)$$

(if two objects e_i and e_j have a different age, they must be different objects). Similarly, if an ontology states that social security numbers uniquely identify individuals, i.e.

$$\texttt{ObjectProperty(hasSSN InverseFunctional)}$$

then the two facts

$$\texttt{Individual}(e_i \ \texttt{value(hasSSN 12345)})$$
$$\texttt{Individual}(e_j \ \texttt{value(hasSSN 12345)})$$

sanction the derivation of the fact

$$\texttt{SameIndividuals}(e_i \ e_j)$$

Although RDF(S) already allows to state domain and range restrictions, these are very limited. OWL Lite allows more refined version of these:

$$\texttt{Class}(c_i \texttt{restriction}(p_i \texttt{allValuesFrom}(c_j)))$$

says that all p_i-values *for members of* c_i must be members of c_j. This differs from the RDF(S) range restriction

$$\texttt{ObjectProperty}(p \texttt{ range}(c_j))$$

which says that all p_i-values must be members of c_j, irrespective of whether they are members of c_i or not. This allows us to use the same property-name

p_i with different range restrictions c_j depending on the class c_i to which p_i is applied. For example, take for p_i the property `Parent`. Then `Parent`s of cats are cats, while `Parent`s of dogs are dogs. An RDF(S) range restriction would not be able to capture this.

Similarly, although in RDF(S) we can define the range of a property, we cannot enforce that properties actually do have a value: we can state the authors write books:

$$\texttt{ObjectProperty(write domain(author)range(book))}$$

but we cannot enforce in RDF(S) that every author must have written at least one book. This is possible in OWL Lite:

$$\texttt{Class(authorrestriction(writesomeValuesFrom(book)))}$$

Technically speaking, these are just special cases of the general cardinality constraints allowed in OWL DL. The `someValuesFrom` corresponds to a min-cardinality constraint with value 1, and the functional property constraint mentioned above corresponds to a max-cardinality constraint with value 1. These can also be stated directly:

$$\texttt{Class(authorrestriction(writeminCardinality(1)))}$$

$$\texttt{Class(objectrestriction(agemaxCardinality(1)))}$$

When a property has a `minCardinality` and `maxCardinality` constraints with the same value, these can be summarised by a single exact `Cardinality` constraint.

3.2.3 OWL DL

With the step from OWL Lite to OWL DL, we obtain a number of additional language constructs. It is often useful to say that two classes are disjoint (which is much stronger than saying they are merely not equal):

$$\texttt{DisjointClasses(c}_i \texttt{ c}_j\texttt{)}$$

OWL DL allows arbitrary Boolean algebraic expressions on either side of an equality of subsumption relation. For example

$$\texttt{SubClassOf(c}_i \texttt{ unionOf(c}_j \texttt{ c}_k\texttt{))}$$

In other words: c_i is not subsumed by either c_j or c_k, but is subsumed by their union. Similarly

$$\texttt{EquivalentClasses(c}_i \texttt{ intersectionOf(c}_j\texttt{c}_k\texttt{))}$$

in other words: although c_i is subsumed by c_j and c_k (a statement already expressible in RDF(S)), stating that c_i is equivalent to their intersection is much stronger. An obvious example to think of here is "old men": "old men" are not just both old and men, but they are *exactly* the intersection of these two properties.

Of course, the `unionOf` and `intersectionOf` may be taken over more than two classes, and may occur in arbitrary Boolean combinations.

Besides disjunction (`unionOf`) and conjunction (`intersectionOf`), OWL DL completes the Boolean algebra by providing a construct for negation: `complementOf`:

$$\texttt{complementOf}(e_i \ e_j)$$

In fact, arbitrary class expressions can be used on either side of subsumption or equivalence axioms.

There are cases where it is not possible to define a class in terms of such algebraic expressions. This can be either impossible in principle. In such cases it is sometimes useful to simply enumerate sets of individuals to define a class. This is done in OWL DL with the `oneOf` construct (corresponding to the first clause of Definition 3.2):

$$\texttt{EquivalentClasses}(c_j \ \texttt{oneOf}(e_1 \ ... \ e_n))$$

Similar to defining a class by enumeration, we can define a property to have a specific value by stating the value:

$$\texttt{Class}(c_i \texttt{restriction}(p_j \texttt{hasValue} \ e_k)$$

The extension from OWL Lite to OWL DL also lifts the restriction on cardinality constraints to have only 0/1 values.

3.2.4 OWL Full

As explained in Sect. 3.2, OWL Lite and DL are based on a strict segmentation of the vocabulary: no term can be both an instance and a class, or a class and a property, etc. A somewhat less strict proposal is RDFS(FA) [Pan and Horrocks, 2003], which does allow a class to be an instance of another class, as long as this is done in a stratified fashion. Full RDF(S) is much more liberal still: a class c_1 can have both a `type` and a `subClassOf` relation to a class c_2, and a class can even be an instance of itself. In fact, the class `Class` is a member of itself. OWL Full inherits from RDF(S) this liberal approach.

Schreiber [Schreiber, 2002] argues that this is exactly what is needed in many cases of practical ontology integration. When integrating two ontologies, opposite commitments have often been made in the two ontologies on whether something is modelled as a class or an instance. This is less unlikely than it may sound: is "747" an *instance* of the class of all airplane-types made by Boeing or is "747" a *subclass* of the class of all airplanes made by Boeing, and are particular jet planes instances of this subclass? Both points of view are defensible. In OWL Full, it is possible to have equality statements between a class and an instance.

In fact, just as in RDF Schema, OWL Full allows us even to apply the constructions of the language to themselves. It is perfectly legal to (say) apply a max-cardinality constraint of 2 on the subClassOf relationship. Of course, building any efficient reasoning tools that support this very liberal self-application of the language is out of the question.

3.2.5 Computational Complexity

The layering in RDF(S), OWL Lite, OWL DL and OWL Full was motivated by different criteria, such as user requirements, difficulty of building tool support, and computational complexity. More recently, an interesting new "layer" in the OWL hierarchy has been identified, called OWL-DLP [Grosof et al., 2003]. This collection of OWL primitives has been carefully identified so as so enable the use of "off the shelve" implementation technology for inferencing and query-answering over OWL ontologies, in particular deductive database technology and Logic Programming[6] [Motik et al., 2004]. In a nutshell, DLP is the maximal fragment of OWL that can be converted to (disjunctive) logic programs. DLP is of particular interest in semantic integration problems: In Chap. 6 on semantic integration, we will make crucial use of the notion of a "conjunctive query" the same holds for the definition of mappings between distributed ontologies in Chap. 10. Such conjunctive queries can indeed be expressed in terms of the DLP fragment, and can be given an efficient implementation, based on the results in [Motik et al., 2003].

3.2.6 Simple relations between ontologies

Since the prime interest of this work is not in ontologies per se, but in ontologies for information sharing, we will illustrate how some of the language constructions of RDF(S) and OWL can be used for expressing simple mappings between different ontologies. This is of course somewhat unconventional: both RDF Schema and OWL are designed to express ontologies, and not primarily to express mappings between ontologies. Nevertheless, it will turn out that many useful mappings between OWL ontologies can be expressed in RDF Schema and OWL.

The general setting will be that o_1 and o_2 are two ontologies between which we want to establish mappings by writing a further set of OWL statements

---

[6] which explains the name: Description Logic Programs

involving terms from both ontologies. We will write with $o_i : e$ to denote an instance of ontology o_i

Multiple namespaces

Since RDF(S) allows the use of terms from different namespaces in a single RDF document, this can equally well be used to state the most elementary form of ontology mapping:

$$\texttt{Individual}(o_1 : e \ \texttt{type}(o_2 : c))$$

In other words: an instance from o_1 belongs (also) to a class from o_2. This allows us to state ontology mappings by simply enumerating such statements for as many $o_1 : e_i$ as possible.

SubclassOf

Although a trivial observation, even the simple mechanism of SubClassOf has turned out to be enough to express the results of a significant case study in ontology mapping: a mapping between significant subsets of Yahoo and OpenDir was expressed entirely in statements of the above form.

Although RDF(S) does not contain an explicit equality construct, equality of classes from two different ontologies can be expressed by adding the dual subsumption statement:

$$\texttt{subClassOf}(o_2 : c_j \ o_1 : c_i)$$

Strangely enough, there is no way in RDF(S) to state equality between individuals. Thus, given two instances $o_1 : e_i$ and $o_2 : e_j$ that both model the same real-world entity, there is no way of stating this in RDF(S)[7].

Properties

If a property $o_1 : p$ with domain $o_1 : c_i$ is also applicable to elements from another ontology, it would be nice to be able to state

$$\texttt{ObjectProperty}(o_1 : p \ \texttt{domain}(o_2 : c_k))$$

but unfortunately the intersection semantics of **domain** and **range** do not have the right effect here: the domain of p would be restricted to the *intersection* of $o_1 : c_i$ and $o_2 : c_k$, which is unlikely to be what is intended.

---

[7] Some consider this to be the most important deficiency in the design of RDF(S)

An alternative technique is to make no additional **domain** or **range** statements, but instead to relate the domains and ranges of the properties in the different ontologies to each other by subsumption statements:

$$\texttt{ObjectProperty(p domain}(o_1 : c_i)) \qquad\qquad (3.1)$$

$$\texttt{SubClassOf}(o_1 : c_i\ o_2 : c_j) \qquad\qquad (3.2)$$

Note that if we now have some instance $o_2 : e_1$ in the domain of the relation p then the RDF(S) semantics of (3.1) implies

$$\texttt{Individual}(o_2 : e_1\ \texttt{type}(o_1 : c_i))$$

This, together with the RDF(S) semantics of (3.2) implies that

$$\texttt{Individual}(o_2 : e_1\ \texttt{type}(o_2 : c_j))$$

In other words, this behaves just as if p also has $o_2 : c_j$ as its domain, which is exactly what we intended[8]. Of course, a similar construction can be made for the range of a property.

Again as with classes, it is possible to make equality claims between properties with a pair of dual **subPropertyOf** statements.

Transitive properties

Stating transitivity, as in

$$\texttt{ObjectProperty}(o_1 : p_i\ \texttt{Transitive})$$

does not establish any relationship between properties, but it does affect other properties in the context of other mappings. For example, the statement

$$\texttt{ObjectProperty}(o_1 : p_i\ \texttt{super}(o_2 : p_j))$$

makes $o_2 : p_j$ transitive *on the domain of* $o_1 : p_i$. Stating the converse:

$$\texttt{ObjectProperty}(o_2 : p_j\ \texttt{super}(o_1 : p_i))$$

extends the transitivity of $o_1 : p_i$ to the domain of $o_2 : p_j$, but leaves $o_2 : p_j$ itself unchanged. Similar considerations hold for **SymmetricProperty**.

Disjointness

Disjointnes statements allow a strong partitioning of the classes both within the separate ontologies and between classes from either ontology, and this is very helpful in ontology mapping: knowing that $o_1 : c_i$ is disjoint from a large number of classes $o_2 : c_j$ greatly reduces the search space when looking for the o_2 counterparts of instances of $o_1 : c_i$.

---

[8] Also note that for this to work the subsumption relation in (3.2) should not be the other way round

Boolean expressions

More often than not, classes in o_1 do not have exact, named counterparts in o_2: for many $o_1 : c_i$ there is no $o_2 : c_j$ with

$$\texttt{EquivalentClasses}(o_1 : c_i \; o_2 : c_j)$$

or even

$$\texttt{SubClassOf}(o_1 : c_i \; o_2 : c_j)$$

In such cases, it is very useful to replace one or both halves of these statements with a boolean expression. This allows us to state the correspondences between combinations of classes, rather than only between single named classes.

In fact, arbitrary class expressions can be used on either side of subsumption or equivalence axioms. This allows for very strong mappings to be stated, as follows. A class $o_1 : c_i$ is in general defined as some expression over other terms (classes and property restrictions) from o_1. In general, there is no named class in o_2 that corresponds closely to $o_1 : c_i$. However, there might be a class $o_2 : c_j$ that is "close" to $o_1 : c_i$. OWL DL then allows arbitrary complex expressions in o_2 to be applied to $o_2 : c_j$ until the result is equal to $o_1 : c_i$. If necessary, such complex expressions can be applied on either side of the equivalence relation.

However, it is important to realize that we have now arrived at the point where indeed very powerful mapping relations between classes can be expressed, but they are now so powerful that they are very hard to find or, more precisely, useful versions of such mapping relations are very hard to find.

Enumerations

There are cases where it is not possible to define a class in terms of such algebraic expressions. This can be either impossible in principle. In such cases it is sometimes useful to simply enumerate sets of individuals from o_1 that correspond (either closely or exactly) to a given class in o_2:

$$\texttt{EquivalentClasses}(o_2 : c_j \; \texttt{oneOf}(o_1 : e_1 \; ... \; o_1 : e_n))$$

Interestingly enough, this statement does not tell us which instances of $o_2 : c_j$ correspond to which $o_1 : e_i$.

Complements

Sometimes two ontologies divide the universe into similar sections, but decide to give a name to the opposite halves. An example is having a class in o_1 for all national citizens (say $o_1 : e$), and in o_2 a class for all foreigners (say $o_2 : e'$). A simple mapping statement in that case is:

$$\texttt{complementOf}(o_1 : e \; o_2 : e)$$

3.3 Other Web-based ontology languages

Besides the two standards RDF Schema and OWL discussed above, a number of other approaches for encoding ontologies on the World Wide Web have been proposed. A comparison of these languages is reported in [Gomez-Perez and Corcho, 2002]. We will now briefly review the results of this comparison and discuss implications for our work.

Besides RDF Schema and OWL[9], which have been introduced above, the comparison reported in [Gomez-Perez and Corcho, 2002] includes the following languages that have been selected on the basis of their aim of supporting knowledge representation on the Web and their compatibility to the Web standards XML or RDF.

- *XOL (XML-based ontology language).* XOL [Karp et al., 2002] has been proposed as a language for exchanging formal knowledge models in the domain of bio-informatics. The development of XOL has been guided by the representational needs of the domain and by existing frame-based knowledge representation languages.
- *SHOE (simple HTML ontology extension).* SHOE[Luke and Hefflin, 2002] was created as an extension of HTML for the purpose of defining machine-readable semantic knowledge. The aim of SHOE is to enable intelligent Web agents to retrieve and gather knowledge more precisely than it is possible in the presence of plain HTML documents.
- *OML: (ontology markup language).* OML [Kent, 2002] is an ontology language that has initially been developed as an XML serialization of SHOE. Meanwhile, the language consists of different layers with increasing expressiveness. The semantics especially of the higher levels is largely based on the notion of conceptual graphs. In the comparison, however, only a less expressive subset of OML (simple OML) is considered.
- *OIL (ontology inference layer).* OIL [Fensel et al., 2001] is an attempt to develop an ontology language for the Web that has a well defined semantics and sophisticated reasoning support for ontology development and use. The language is constructed in a layered way starting with core-OIL, providing a formal semantics for RDF Schema, standard-OIL, which is equivalent to an expressive description logic with reasoning support, and Instance OIL that adds the possibility of defining instances.

We have to mention that there is a strong relationship between the OIL language and RDF Schema as well as DAML+OIL. OIL extends RDF Schema and has been the main influence in the development if DAML+OIL. The

---

[9] Actually, [Gomez-Perez and Corcho, 2002] discuss DAML+OIL instead of OWL. DAML+OIL [Patel-Schneider et al., 2002a] is the direct precursor of OWL, and all of the conclusions from [Gomez-Perez and Corcho, 2002] about DAML+OIL are also valid for OWL

main difference between OIL and DAML+OIL is an extended expressiveness of DAML+OIL in terms of complex definitions of individuals and data types. DAML+OIL in turn has been the basis for the development of OWL, which carries the stamp of an official W3C recommendation. All observations on DAML+OIL in this comparison also apply to OWL.

Table 3.1. Comparison of web ontology languages with respect to concepts and taxonomies (taken from [Gomez-Perez and Corcho, 2002])

	XOL	SHOE	OML	RDS/S	OIL	DAML+OIL
Partitions	−	−	+	−	+	+
Attributes						
Instance attr.	+	+	+	+	+	+
Class attr.	+	−	+	−	+	+
Local scope	+	+	+	+	+	+
Global scope	+	−	+	+	+	+
Facets						
Default values	+	−	−	−	−	−
Type constr.	+	+	+	+	+	+
Cardinalities	+	−	−	−	+	+
Taxonomies						
Subclass of	+	+	+	+	+	+
Exhaustive comp.	−	−	+	−	+	+
Disjoint comp.	−	−	+	−	+	+
Not subclass of	−	−	−	−	+	+

The comparison of the languages mentioned above was carried out on the basis of the set of elements contained in the language and their ability to encode semantic information about a domain in terms of the following aspects:

- *Concepts and taxonomies.* Ontologies usually group objects of the World that have certain properties in common (e.g. cities or countries). A description of the shared properties is called a concept definition. Concepts can be arranged into a subclass–superclass relation in order to be able to further discriminate objects into subgroups (e.g. capitals or European countries).
- *Relations.* Objects of the same type normally occur in similar situations where they have a certain relation to each other (cities lie in countries, countries have a capital). These typical relations can often be specified in order to establish structures between groups of objects.
- *Instances.* Sometimes single objects (e.g. the continent of Europe) play a prominent role in a domain of interest or the membership to a concept is defined by the relation to a specific object (European countries are those

contained in Europe). For this purpose ontology languages often allow to specify single objects, also called instances.

- *Axioms.* Sometimes a domain follows certain rules that cannot be expressed with the elements discussed above (e.g. the fact that the number of inhabitants of Europe equals the sum of the numbers of inhabitants of European countries). In order to capture these rules some languages allow us to specify axioms in a formal logic.

The comparison revealed significant differences in terms of expressiveness of the different languages. An overview of the results with respect to class definitions and taxonomies is given in Table 3.1. Gomez-Perez and Corcho suggest that before choosing one of the languages, an analysis of the representational needs of a particular application has to be carried out. The result of this analysis should guide the selection of one of the languages considered in the comparison. Assuming that developers of Web-based information follow this suggestion, we will have to be able to handle all of these languages in order to support information sharing.

This observation appears to be quite discouraging. However, the comparison also reveals that DAML+OIL, the predecessor of OWL, is the most expressive language for encoding ontologies on the Web. Therefore we can assume that if we are able to handle OWL models, we should in principle also be able to understand and process models in the other languages, provided that we can establish a formal framework for comparing and relating ontology languages.

3.3.1 Languages for expressing ontology mappings

OWL was of course primarily intended for expressing ontologies themselves, and not for expressing mappings between them. Other mechanisms have been designed specifically for this purpose. The PROMPT ontology-operation tables are a good example [Noy and Musen, 2004], containing such operations as adding, splitting and merging classes in order to transform one given ontology into another. Another example is the proposal for an OWL rule language[10], where the rules can express much more complicated transformations between classes from the different ontologies than is possible in OWL. The standard example is the mapping of the *uncle* relation in one ontology to the composition of the *brother* and *child* relations of another ontology. This can be trivially expressed in the OWL rule language, but cannot be expressed in OWL itself. Another proposal is the proposed C-OWL extension of OWL [Bouquet et al., 2003], where directional bridge rules are used to express relations between different ontologies.

---

[10] http://www.cs.man.ac.uk/~horrocks/DAML/Rules/

It is not surprising that these purpose-designed mapping formalisms are more expressive than (ab)using OWL itself for a goal it was not designed for. Nevertheless, we have seen that OWL can be used to describe a substantial and interesting set of relations between different ontologies.

3.4 Conclusions

We have seen in this chapter that a stack of languages is available for representing ontological information on the Semantic Web: RDF Schema and the various OWL sublanguages. These languages offer an increasing degree of expressiveness. Their development is based on a history of different languages which have all to some degree contributed to the final W3C standards that now form a stable basis for Semantic Web development.

Further reading

Gomez-Perez and Corcho compare different proposals for web-based ontology languages [Gomez-Perez, 2002]. The development of the current language standard is documented in different publications, in particular in [Fensel et al., 2001], [Patel-Schneider et al., 2002a] and [Antoniou and van Harmelen, 2003]. A textbook introduction to Semantic Web languages is [Antoniou and van Harmelen, 2004].

Part II

Creating ontologies and metadata

4

Ontology creation

Summary. In the last chapter we discussed languages for explicating information semantics and argued for the need of an integration at the language level. We now draw attention to the nature and the content of ontologies needed to support information sharing. The goal is to define an architecture combining the advantages of global and local ontologies and to show how this infrastructure can be derived from an information-sharing task.

The acquisition of semantic knowledge has been identified to be a major bottleneck not only in information sharing but also in many other areas going back to expert-system development. A whole scientific discipline called knowledge engineering is devoted to the task of providing tools and methods for supporting the knowledge acquisition and formalization process [Studer et al., 1998]. In connection with the interest in ontologies as a key technology in knowledge and information sharing, the term "ontological engineering" has become popular [Farquhar and Gruninger, 1997] and a number of methodologies for creating ontologies have been proposed [Gomez-Perez and Juristo, 1997, Uschold, 1996]. However, these methods are very general in nature as they aim at providing general guidelines for all kinds of ontologies and purposes. We therefore propose a specialized strategy for the explication of information semantics.

In this chapter, we first review existing work on ontology engineering. We review existing methodologies and focus on approaches that have been proposed in combination with the task of integrating and sharing information. We conclude that existing methodologies do not address the problem of building a representational infrastructure like the one introduced in Chap. 2. We present an iterative approach for building source ontologies and shared vocabularies in a bottom-up fashion. We discuss the general process and useful resources and illustrate the method using a real life integration task.

4.1 Ontological engineering

The previous sections provided information about the use and importance of ontologies. Hence, it is crucial to support the development process of ontologies. In this section, we will describe how the systems provide support for the ontological engineering process.

Recently, several articles about ontological developments have been published. Jones and others [Jones et al., 1998] provide a short overview of existing approaches (e.g. METHONTOLOGY [Gomez-Perez and Juristo, 1997] or TOVE [Fox and Grninger, 1998]). Uschold [Uschold, 1996] and Gomez-Perez and others [Gomez-Perez et al., 1996] propose methods with phases that are independent of the domain of the ontology. These methods are of a good standard and can be used for comparisons. In this section, we focus on the proposed method from Uschold and Gruninger as a "thread" and discuss how the integrated systems evaluated in this chapter are related to this approach.

Uschold defines four main phases:

1. Identifying a purpose and scope: specialization, intended use, scenarios, set of terms including characteristics and granularity
2. Building the ontology:
   (a) Ontology capture: knowledge acquisition, a phase interacting with requirements of phase 1.
   (b) Ontology coding: structuring of the domain knowledge in a conceptual model.
   (c) Integrating existing ontologies: re-use of existing ontologies to speed up the development process of ontologies in the future.
3. Evaluation: verification and validation.
4. Guidelines for each phase.

In the following paragraphs we describe integration systems and their methods for building an ontology. Further, we discuss systems without an explicit method where the user is only provided with information in the direction in question. The second type of systems can be distinguished from others without any information about a methodology. This is due to the fact that they assume that ontologies already exist.

Infosleuth

This system semi-automatically constructs ontologies from textual databases [Hwang, 1999]. The methodology is as follows: first, human experts provide a small number of *seed words* to represent high-level concepts. This can be seen as the identification of purpose and scope (phase 1). The system then processes the incoming documents, extracting phrases that involve seed words, generates corresponding concept terms, and then classifies them into the ontology. This can be seen as ontology capturing and part of coding (phases 2 and 2). During this process the system also collects seed word-candidates for the next round of processing. This iteration can be completed for a predefined number of rounds. A human expert verifies the classification after each round (phase 3). As more documents arrive, the ontology expands and the expert is confronted with the new concepts. This is a significant feature of this system. Hwang calls this "discover-and-alert" and indicates that this is a new feature of his methodology. This method is conceptually simple and allows effective implementation. Prototype implementations have also shown that the method works well. However, problems arise within the classification of concepts and distinguishing between concepts and non-concepts.

Infosleuth requires an expert for the evaluation process. When we consider that experts are rare and their time is costly this procedure is too expert-dependent. Furthermore, the integration of existing ontologies is not mentioned. However, an automatic verification of this model by a reasoner would be worthwhile considering.

KRAFT

This system offers two methods for building ontologies: the building of shared ontologies [Jones et al., 1998] and extracting of source ontologies [Pazzaglia and Embury, 1998].

The steps of the development of shared ontologies are (a) *ontology scoping*, (b) *domain analysis*, (c) *ontology formalization*, (d) *top-level ontology*. The minimal scope is a set of terms that is necessary to support the communication within the KRAFT network. The domain analysis is based on the idea that changes within ontologies are inevitable and the means to handle changes should be provided. The authors pursue a domain-led strategy [Patil et al., 1991], where the shared ontology fully characterizes the area of knowledge in which the problem is situated. Within the ontology formalization phase the fully characterized knowledge is defined formally in classes, relations and functions. The top-level ontology is needed to introduce predefined terms/primitives.

If we compare this to the method of Uschold and Gruninger we can conclude that ontology scoping is weakly linked to phase 1. It appears that ontology scoping is a set of terms fundamental for the communication within the network and therefore can be seen as a vocabulary. On the other hand, the authors say that this is a *minimal* set of terms, which implies that more terms exist. The domain analysis refers to phases 1 and 2, whereas the ontology formalization refers to phase 2. Existing ontologies are not considered.

Pazzaglia and Embury [Pazzaglia and Embury, 1998] introduce a bottom-up approach to extract an ontology from existing shared ontologies. This extraction process consists of two steps. The first step is a syntactic translation from the KRAFT exportable view (in a native language) of the resource into the KRAFT schema. The second step is the ontological upgrade, a semi-automatic translation plus knowledge-based enhancement, where local ontology adds knowledge and further relationships between the entities in the translated schema.

This approach can be compared to phase 2, the integration of existing ontologies. In general, the KRAFT methodology lacks the evaluation of ontologies and the general-purpose scope.

Most Information integration systems, such as PICSEL, OBSERVER, BUSTER and COIN either have no methods or do not discuss them to create ontologies. After reading papers about these various systems it becomes obvious that there is a lack of a "real" methodology for the development of ontologies. We believe that the systematic development of the ontology is extremely important and therefore the tools supporting this process become even more significant.

4.2 Building an ontology infrastructure for Information sharing

The integration process sketched above relies on the existence of a shared ontology suitable to define concepts from all terminologies to be integrated in sufficient detail. This requirement is a challenge with respect to ontology building. In order to support this difficult task, we propose a development strategy that is tailored to the purpose of building shared ontologies. In this section we give an overview of the development process.

The process

The proposed strategy is based on stepwise refinement. It consists of five steps that are executed in an iterative process resulting in a partial specification of the shared ontology. The last step of each run is an evaluation step that triggers one of the previous steps in order to extend and refine the ontology if necessary. Fig. 4.1 illustrates the process model; the individual steps are briefly described below.

1. *Finding common concepts.* The first step is to examine the translation task. Asking the question "what do I want to translate?" leads to a concept that subsumes all classes from the source and destination systems. Because this concept makes a semantic translation from one source into another

possible we call it a bridge concept. By defining its properties and attribute values we achieve the needed shared vocabulary. The most general bridge concept is "top", a concept that subsumes every other possible concept. For an exact classification it is recommended to choose the bridge concept as concretely as possible. If needed, more than one bridge concept can be defined to enable semantic translation.

2. *Definition of properties.* The next step is to define properties that describe the chosen bridge concepts. A car, for instance, can be described through its color, its brand, its price, etc.

3. *Finding property values.* Once we have defined the properties, we search for values which can fill the attributes. These "fillers" are the main part of the shared vocabulary.

4. *Adapt ontology.* The use of existing sources of information will not always be sufficient to describe all concepts of an information source. We sometimes have to handle very specific distinctions made in a system that hardly occur in standard terminologies. In order to capture these subtle differences we have to invent application-specific terms as part of the shared vocabulary.

5. *Refine definitions.* The introduced strategy follows the "evolving" life cycle. It allows the engineer to step back all the time to modify, add and remove ontology definitions, e.g. refining the bridge concept or integrating further taxonomies into the shared vocabulary.

Each of the steps modifies a different aspect of the shared ontology. While step 1 is concerned with the central concept definition, step 2 defines slots, step 3 integrates existing taxonomies and step 4 generates application-specific taxonomies. These facts are useful in order to determine where to go back to if the evaluation step reveals the inability to describe a certain aspect of a terminology to be integrated.

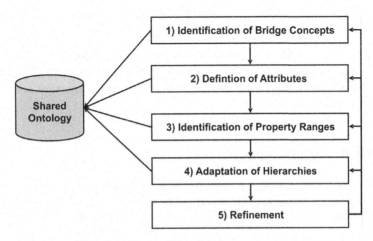

Fig. 4.1. Steps of the development process

Sources of information

The use of the ontology to be built as a common basis for communication between systems makes it necessary to stay as closely as possible to a vocabulary and conceptualization of the domain that is widely accepted as a standard. In order to meet this requirement, we use several sources of information to build upon. These information sources are existing ontologies and thesauri as well as scientific classifications and data catalogues.

- Top-level ontologies are mainly used to find the bridge concept which acts as a template for the definition of all terms to be translated. In most cases, the bridge concept is obvious; however, the use of an upper level ontology provides us with a vocabulary which is partly standardized.
- Scientific classifications are another form of standards describing the conceptualization of a domain. Classifications like taxonomies of animals or plants are common knowledge which can be used to specify concepts from domain-specific ontologies.
- Domain thesauri contain typical terms used in an application domain; therefore, they are a natural source for finding concept names for the shared ontology. Further, many thesauri contain at least free-text definitions of the terms included. These definitions provide guidance for the definition of concepts.
- Linguistic thesauri are used to supplement information taken from domain-specific thesauri. In contrast to the specialized vocabulary defined in domain-specific thesauri, linguistic thesauri can be used to identify correspondences between terms found in different information sources. Especially, we use linguistic thesauri to expand the search for definitions of terms to their synonyms.
- Data catalogues finally contain the definitions of the terminology to be modelled. Therefore, they define the concepts to be modelled and are the basis for evaluating the expressiveness of the shared ontology at a specific point in the modelling process.

In the course of the modelling process, we stick as closely as possible to the information from the sources mentioned above. Therefore, the selection of these sources, though not discussed in this book, is an important step when building a shared ontology.

4.3 Applying the approach

We performed a case study in order to assess the general strategy described above. In the following we will describe the task of this case study and give an impression of how the strategy helps to build the models needed to solve it.

4.3.1 The task to be solved

Geographical information systems normally distinguish different types of spatial objects. Different standards exist specifying these object types. These standards are also called catalogues. Since there is more than one standard, these catalogues compete with each other. To date, no satisfactory solution has been found to integrate these catalogues. In our evaluation we concentrate on different types of areas distinguished by the type of use.

In order to address the semantic translation problem we assume a scenario where the existing land-administration database that is normally based on the ATKIS catalogue, which is the official standard for most administrations, should be updated with new information extracted from satellite images of some area. Satellite images are normally analyzed using image-processing techniques resulting in a segmentation of different areas which are classified according to the CORINE landcover nomenclature, a standard for the segmentation and classification of satellite images. The process of updating the land-administration system with this new data faces two main problems:

1. The boundaries of the objects in the database might differ from the boundaries determined on the satellite image.
2. The class information attached to areas on the satellite image and the type information in the land-administration system do not match.

The first problem is clearly beyond the scope of our investigation, but the second is a perfect example of a semantic translation problem. A successful integration of the two information sources will come with the following benefits for the user of the systems: (a) *integrated views* and (b) *verification*. An integrated view from the user's perspective merges the data between the catalogues. This process can be seen as two layers which lay on top of each other. The second option gives users the opportunity to verify ATKIS-OK-250 data with CORINE landcover data or vice versa.

The basis for our experiment is a small CORINE landcover dataset containing information about the town "Bad Nenndorf" in Lower Saxony. This dataset is available from the German Environmental Agency in different formats and classifications and can therefore be used to compare and evaluate results. In our case study, we want to find out whether land-use classes from the CORINE landcover dataset can be semantically translated into the classification used by the ATKIS catalogue. Such a translation could be the basis for both the generation of an integrated view of the information in both systems and for a validation of ATKIS data with up-to-date satellite images. Fig. 4.3.1 illustrates the integration problem.

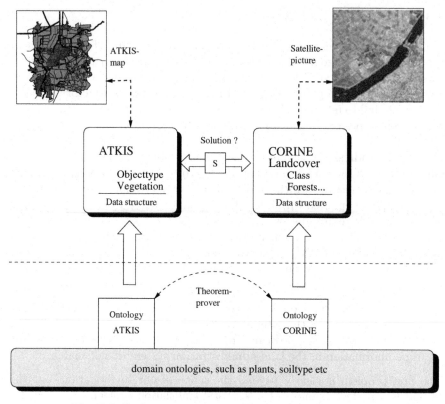

Fig. 4.2. Deductive integration of geographic information

4.3.2 The Information Sources

The ATKIS catalogue [AdV, 1998] is an official information system in Germany. It is a project of the head surveying offices of all the German states. The working group offers digital landscape models with different scales from 1:25000 up to 1:1000000 with a detailed documentation in corresponding object catalogues. We use the large-scale catalogue OK-1000. This catalogue offers several types of objects including definitions of different types of areas. Fig. 4.3 shows the different types of areas defined in the catalogue.

CORINE landcover [European Environmental Agency, 1999a] is a result of the CORINE programme the European Commission carried out from 1985 to 1990. The results are essentially of three types, corresponding to the three aims of the programme: (a) an information system on the state of the environment in the European Community has been created (the CORINE system). It is composed of a series of databases describing the environment in the European Community, as well as of databases with background information. (b) Nomenclatures and methodologies were developed for carrying out the programme, which are now used as the reference at the Community level. (c) A systematic effort was made to coordinate activities with all the bodies involved in the production of environmental information especially at international level. The nomenclature developed in the CORINE programme can be seen as another catalogue, because it also defines a taxonomy of area types (see Fig. 4.4) with a description of characteristic properties of the different land types.

The task of this example is that the data of the CORINE database has to be converted into the ATKIS database. Of course, this transformation can be viewed as a special case of an integration task demonstrating all the problems which can occur. Besides the obvious structural heterogeneity problems, the main problem lies in the reconciliation of the semantic heterogeneity caused by the use of different classification schemes.

The classification schemes of land-use types in Figs. 4.3 and 4.4 illustrate this problem. The set of land types chosen for these catalogues are biased by their intended use: while the ATKIS catalogue is used to administrate human activities and their impact on land use in terms of buildings and other installations, the focus of the CORINE catalogues is on the state of the environment in terms of vegetation forms. Consequently, the ATKIS catalogue contains fine-grained distinctions between different types of areas used for human activities (i.e. different types of areas used for traffic and transportation) while natural areas are only distinguished very roughly. The CORINE taxonomy on the other hand contains many different kinds of natural areas (i.e. different types of cultivated areas) which are not further distinguished in the ATKIS catalogue. On the other hand, areas used for commerce and traffic are summarized in one type.

Despite these differences in the conception of the catalogues the definition of the land-use types can be reduced to some fundamental properties. We identified six properties used to define the classes in the two catalogues. Beside *size* and *general type of use* (e.g. production, transportation or cultivation) the *kinds of structures* built on top of an area, the *shape of the ground* and *natural vegetation* as well as kinds of *cultivated plants* are discriminating characteristics.

4.3.3 Sources of knowledge

For this specific integration task we chose several sources of information to be used for guiding the development process. We briefly describe these sources in the following.

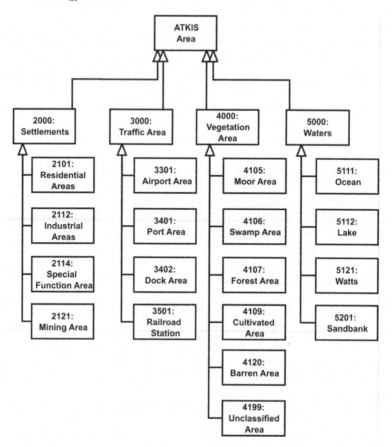

Fig. 4.3. Taxonomy of land-use types in the ATKIS OK-1000 catalogue

UpperCyc ontology

Upper Cyc, developed by the CyCorp corporation [Lenat, 1995] (http://www.cyc.com), is an upper-level ontology that captures approximately 3 000 terms of the most general concepts of human consensus reality. There is also a full Cyc knowledge base (KB) including a vast structure of more specific concepts descending below Upper Cyc, the so-called top-level ontology. It contains millions of logical axioms – rules and other assertions – which specify constraints on the individual objects and classes found in the real world. Therefore the Upper Cyc ontology provides a sufficient common ground for applications. We chose Cyc as a reference for selecting the bridge concept, because it provide a large number of higher level concepts.

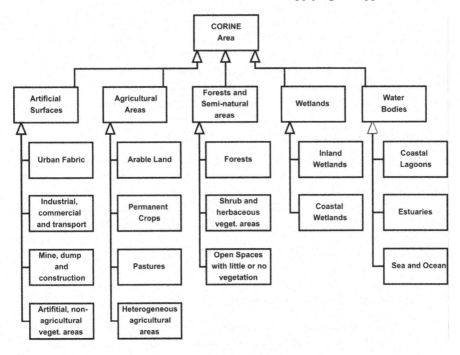

Fig. 4.4. Taxonomy of land-use types in the CORINE landcover nomenclature

GEMET

The general multilingual environmental thesaurus GEMET [European Environmental Agency, 1999b] is a poly-hierarchically structured thesaurus which covers approximately 5 400 terms and their definitions organized by groups, themes and terms. GEMET has been created by merging different national and international thesauri. Analysis and evaluation work of numerous international experts and organizations led to a core terminology of generalized environmental terms and definitions. GEMET ensures validated indexing and cataloguing of environmental information all over Europe. Where available, synonyms or alternate terms can be found likewise. We chose the GEMET thesaurus as a source for definitions of concepts and to supplement the information obtained from Cyc with domain-specific information. These definitions provide for example insight into useful properties of classes.

WordNet

WordNet [Fellbaum, 1998], developed by the Cognitive Science Laboratory at Princeton University, is an on-line lexical reference system whose design is inspired by current psycholinguistic theories of human lexical memory. English nouns, verbs, adjectives and adverbs are organized into synonym sets, each representing one underlying lexical concept. Different relations link the synonym sets. WordNet was mainly used as a source of synonymy information needed to look up concepts across the other knowledge sources (e.g. to find the equivalent of a concept from Cyc to look up the domain-specific defintion).

Standard taxonomies

Scientific taxonomies can be found in many sources, like books or the Internet. For this example we looked at the Google Webdirectory (http://directory.google.com/Top/Science/Biology/Flora_and_Fauna) to obtain a classification of plant life. It is in no circumstances complete, but it satisfies our needs in this case study. We chose the classification of plants to determine possible fillers for the properties of a class as many land types are mostly defined by the vegetation found (e.g. mixed forest).

4.4 An example walkthrough

Based on the information described above we built up a first version of a shared ontology which should be used to solve the integration task mentioned in the last section. In this section we sketch the first development cycle of this ontology using concrete modelling activities to illustrate the different steps of our strategy using modelling example from the CORINE classification. The corresponding definitions of ATKIS concepts that will also be created in the different steps discussed below are not shown.

Step 1: finding bridge concepts

Looking at the given example scenario as described in Sect. 4.2 it is quite obvious to choose a concept like "area" or "region", because all land-use classes are some kind of special "regions" or, in other words, "region" subsumes all land-use classes. We search for the term "region" in the Upper CYC and get the following definition:

> "GeographicalRegion: a collection of spatial regions that include some piece of the surface of PlanetEarth. Each element of GeographicalRegion is a PartiallyTangible entity that may be represented on a map of the Earth. This includes both purely topographical regions like mountains and underwater spaces, and those defined by demographics, e.g. countries and cities [···]".

Fig. 4.5 shows the hierarchical classification of the concept in the Upper Cyc. The definition fits very well, so finally we choose "Geographical Region" as our bridge concept. For further refinement we write it down in the OWL notation.

```
Class(Geographical-Region)
```

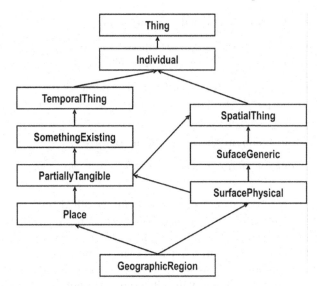

Fig. 4.5. Geographical region in Upper Cyc

Step 2: definition of properties

Now we have to find possible attributes for the bridge concept. We look for "Geographical Region" in GEMET, but the search does not give any results. In that case the decomposition of the search phrase may give better results. For "Geography" and "Region" we get these definitions out of GEMET:

> *"Geography: The study of the natural features of the Earth's surface, comprising topography, climate, soil, vegetation, etc and Man's response to them."*

> *"Region: A designated area or an administrative division of a city, county or larger geographical territory that is formulated according to some biological, political, economic or demographic criteria."*

In the definition of "geography", some attributes are clearly recognizable. For example, climate, soil, vegetation and human activities. We use vegetation to illustrate the next steps in our method. Vegetation is a biological criterion that defines a region, and it is also part of the scientific field "geography". We update the bridge concept by defining a slot "vegetation" and adding it to the bridge concept.

```
Class(Geographical-Region)
ObjectProperty(vegetation domain(Geographical-Region))
```

Step 3: integration of standard taxonomies

To get possible "attribute values" or "fillers" for the slot "vegetation", we take another look at GEMET. Vegetation is defined as:

> "The plants of an area considered in general or as communities [···]; the total plant cover in a particular area or on the Earth as a whole."

We also check the synonym "flora", found in WordNet:

> "The plant life characterizing a specific geographic region or environment."

The attribute "vegetation" or "flora", can be filled with terms out of plant life like "tree" or "rose" for instance. A good top concept is "plants", because many scientific taxonomies of plants exists. The Swedish botanist Carlous Linaeus established in 1753 a classification of plants. His work is considered the foundation of modern botanical nomenclature. In the Google Webdirectory we can access the plant kingdom with more than 10 000 entries on-line. We integrate this taxonomy into our vocabulary, because we need concept from it to distinguish concepts in our information sources through the reference to this hierarchy.

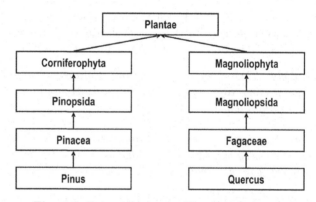

Fig. 4.6. Extract from scientific plant taxonomy

Now it is possible to describe classes from the land-use catalogues. The term "coniferous forest" in the CORINE context is defined as:

> "Vegetation formation composed principally of trees, including shrub and bush understories, where coniferous species predominate."

In our vocabulary we find the term "coniferophyta", comprising the conifers, which are trees or shrubs that bear their seeds in cones, without the protection of a fruit, like angiosperms. This leads to the following OWL class:

```
SubClassOf(Coniferous-Forest interSectionOf(
            Geographical-region
            restriction(vegetation
                allValuesFrom(Coniferophyta))))
```

The division *magnoliophyta* of the plant kingdom consists of those organisms commonly called the flowering plants, or angiosperms. The flowering plants are the source of all agricultural crops, cereal grains and grasses, garden and road-side weeds, familiar broad-leaved shrubs and trees and most ornamentals. So, it is easy to describe the next CORINE class "broad-leaved forest":

```
SubClassOf(Broad-leaved_Forest intersectionOf(
            Geographical-region
            restriction(vegetation
                allValuesFrom(Magnoliophyta))))
```

A "mixed forest" in the CORINE nomenclature consists of conifers and broad-leaved trees.

```
SubClassOf(Mixed_Forest intersectionOf(
            Geographical-region
            restriction(vegetation
                someValuesFrom(Magnoliophyta))
            restriction(vegetation
                someValuesFrom(Coniferophyta))))
```

Step 4: adapt vocabulary

A closer look at the definition of the CORINE forest classes reveals that the classes are defined through the existence of trees and shrubs. Just using the term "magnoliophyta" does not prevent the classification of a region covered with orchids as a broad-leaved forest (orchidaceae is a subclass of magnoliophyta). The mentioned taxonomy classifies plants according to their way of reproduction, therefore distinguishing angiosperm and gymnosperm trees, shrubs and flowers. To handle this problem we need a more general distinction.

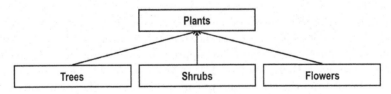

Fig. 4.7. Supplementary plant classification

Fig. 4.7 shows a simple extension of the vocabulary that enables a more robust definition of the CORINE forest classes.

```
SubClassOf(Coniferous-Forest intersectionOf(
            Geographical-region
            restriction(vegetation
                allValuesFrom(Coniferophyta))
            restriction(vegetation
                allValuesFrom(unionOf(trees shrubs)))))

SubClassOf(Broad-leaved_Forest intersectionOf(
            Geographical-region
            restriction(vegetation
                allValuesFrom(Magnoliophyta))
            restriction(vegetation
                allValuesFrom(unionOf(trees shrubs)))))

SubClassOf(Mixed_Forest intersectionOf(
            Geographical-region
            restriction(vegetation
                someValuesFrom(Magnoliophyta))
            restriction(vegetation
                someValuesFrom(Coniferophyta))
            restriction(vegetation
                allValuesFrom(unionOf(trees shrubs)))))
```

The shared vocabulary developed so far allows us to specify many different vegetation areas found in the land-use catalogues:

```
SubClassOf(Pastures intersectionOf(
            Geographical-region
            restriction(vegetation allValuesFrom(Poaceae))))

SubClassOf(vineyards intersectionOf(
            Geographical-region
            restriction(vegetation allValuesFrom(Vitis))))

SubClassOf(Rice_fields intersectionOf(
            Geographical-region
            restriction(vegetation allValuesFrom(Oryza))))
```

This definition might seem to be too restrictive, because it does not allow any other plants other than the dominant species. Our goal here is not, hewever, to provide a complete description of the concepts in terms of all the vegetation that might be found. Such a modelling approach would be much to big an effort to make sense. We rather want to characterize a concept by the properties that distinguishes it from the other concepts in the hierarchy. The definitions above satisfy this requirements. In order to make this more explicit the vegetation property can be read as "dominant vegetation form".

Step 5: evaluation and revision

Not all CORINE landcover classes can be described after this first process cycle. "Mineral extraction sites", for instance, are defined as:

> *"Areas with open-pit extraction of minerals (sandpits, quarries) or other minerals (opencast mines). Includes flooded gravel pits, except for river-bed extraction."*

No vegetation is mentioned, so the bridge concept must be refined. We go back to step 2 "defining properties" and search for another attribute. The definitions of "region" and "geography" show some anthropological aspects, like "Man's response" or economic criteria. So we define a new slot 'anthroposphere' and add it to our bridge concept:

```
Class(Geographical-Region)
ObjectProperty(vegetation
              domain(Geographical-Region))
ObjectProperty(anthroposphere
              domain(Geographical-Region))
```

In the topic area "anthroposphere" of the GEMET thesaurus we find the term "mining district", a district where mineral exploitation is performed. We integrate the partial taxonomy into the vocabulary (Fig. 4.8).

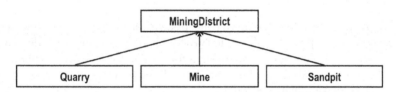

Fig. 4.8. Mining sites from the GEMET thesaurus

This special vocabulary can be used to simulate one-to-one mappings by using equality axioms. The CORINE class "mineral extraction sites" could be described as follows.

```
SubClassOf(Mineral-extraction-sites intersectionOf(
              Geographical-region
              restriction(anthroposphere
                allValuesFrom(mining-district)))))
```

In a similar way, we proceed by iterating the process cycle until all terms from the two catalogue systems can be modelled as a specialization of the bridge concept. A further advantage of this strategy is the fact that the same process will be employed when additional terminologies are to be integrated as well. We cannot guarantee that the shared ontology also covers a new terminology, but our strategy already provides guidance for the adaption of the ontology.

4.5 Conclusions

In real applications the most important question is often not how to arrange ontologies, but how to actually build these ontologies. This problem has been widely recognized and some methodologies have been developed to support the development of ontologies. In most cases, these methodologies are very general and only provide basic guidance for the development of an ontology infrastructure. In our approach the notion of a shared vocabulary is essential and the development of this vocabulary therefore deserves special attention. We had good experiences with a strategy that follows a bottom-up approach that takes the actual integration problem as a starting point and consults general models like top-level ontologies and linguistic resources only if necessary. The resulting vocabularies are general enough to cover at least a certain class of integration problems. We think that this is more valuable than a general top-down approach because it solves real world problems without losing the connection to basic ontological principles.

The examples given above already show that the method leads to better results than an early hands-on approach described in [Stuckenschmidt et al., 2000]. In this early case study, we developed the shared vocabulary solely by relying on textual description of the two catalogues mentioned above. The development strategy proposed here results in a shared model that uses mostly standardized terms and is well integrated with existing higher-level ontologies.

We also managed to describe more concepts with fewer properties. The use of the vegetation property for example turned out to be sufficient for describing about half of all concepts from both information sources. We explain this with the richer vocabularies for describing different vegetation types we got from scientific classifications.

An interesting side effect of the more controlled development is a harmonization of the structure of logical expressions used to define concepts. We explain this by the fact that the strategy forces us not to describe a concept completely without comparing it to other definitions. The strategy rather forces us to define restrictions for a particular property for many concepts in parallel. This direct comparison makes it easier to capture the specific structure of the logical expression required in contrast to the definition of other concepts.

Further reading

Further information about the information sources used for ontology development can be found in the official documentation published, by the German administration [AdV, 1998] and the European environment agency [European Environmental Agency, 1999a]. The Cyc ontology, the WordNet lexical database and the GEMET thesaurus used for identifying and characterizing the bridge concept are described in [Lenat, 1995], [Fellbaum, 1998] and [European Environmental Agency, 1999b], respectively. A detailed documentation of an earlier attempt to model the information sources with the ontology language OIL is described in [Stuckenschmidt et al., 2000].

5

Metadata generation

Summary. In the previous chapter, we defined a general architecture for describing information semantics in terms of ontologies that are derived from shared terminologies of a domain and encoded using terminological languages in order to give them a clean, model-theoretic semantics. We also presented a strategy for building these ontologies. What is still missing at the moment is a strategy of how to actually relate information to its semantics encoded in source ontologies. In this chapter, we will discuss how weakly structured information can be linked to the ontology infrastructure described in the previous chapters using metadata.

Kashyap and Sheth [Kashyap and Sheth, 1997] analyze so-called global information systems where many different and possibly heterogeneous information repositories have to be integrated. In order to achieve interoperability between these repositories they propose to link the information repositories to ontological terms using metadata (compare Fig. 5.1).

We refer to this view of global information systems, because it describes a way of deploying the source ontologies described in the last chapter on the Web. The notion of a source ontology developed in the last chapter directly corresponds to the conceptual context described by Kashyap and Sheth, because source ontologies define the meaning of terms used in an information repository. Following Kashyap and Sheth we have to define a metadata context for information repositories that uses terms from the source ontologies in order to give an abstract description of the information contained in an information repository.

In this chapter, we will develop a strategy for assigning ontological terms to information items and resources using metadata models. We start by recapitulating the role of metadata for information sharing and identify critical

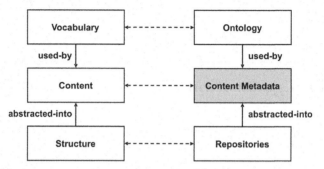

Fig. 5.1. Assigning semantics to information [Kashyap and Sheth, 1997]

problems. We then present an integrated approach for generating and managing metadata that is based on source ontologies.

5.1 The role of metadata

A common approach to the problem of information heterogeneity is to provide so-called metadata, i.e. data about the actual information. As this description is very general and different scientific communities use very different notions of metadata, we first have to define our view of metadata more clearly. For this purpose we use the following distinctions made in [Kashyap and Sheth, 1997]:

- Content-independent metadata is data about information that does not directly relate to the content of the information it describes. It rather describes the context and the environment the information is created and maintained in. Content-independent metadata includes the author of a document or the date of its creation.
- Content-dependent metadata is data about information that is derived from the information, but it does not describe the information content, but rather additional property that directly follow from the content. Examples for content-dependent metadata are the size of a document, the number of words or pages or the language a document is written in.
- Content-based metadata directly reflects the content of an information source, but it adds information or structure that helps to process the original information more efficiently. Examples for content-based metadata are document vectors or full-text indices.
- Content-descriptive metadata finally is data about information that provides an abstract description of the content of an information resource. It helps to summarize the content of an information source and judge whether it is suitable for a particular purpose. Examples of content-descriptive metadata are keyword lists, glossaries or assignments to thematic categories.

The different kinds of metadata cover many aspects of information: technical data about storage facilities and access methods co-exist with content descriptions and information about intended uses, suitability and data quality. Concerning the problem of finding and accessing information, the role of metadata is two-fold: on the side of information providers it serves as a means of organizing, maintaining and cataloguing data; on the side of the information users metadata helps to find, access and interpret information. We briefly discuss this two-fold view in the following paragraphs.

5.1.1 Use of metadata

Organizing large information repositories is a difficult problem. While standard databases provide sophisticated technology for data organization and maintenance, heterogeneous repositories likes data warehouses, federated databases, and especially the World Wide Web suffer from the problem of heterogeneity that demands for sophisticated organization methods. Concerning this problem, metadata can serve different purposes:

- *Structuring.* Metadata can be used to structure heterogeneous information by specifying topic areas, keywords and relations to other information. This kind of meta-information can be used to organize information along different dimension like topic, date, author, etc.
- *Maintenance.* Metadata can help to maintain data by providing information about authors, date of creation and expiry of the information. This information helps to locate outdated information or to find the person who is responsible for changes.
- *Cataloguing.* The bigger an information repository becomes the more important it is to have an overview of the information that is actually present. This can be done by creating information systems based on metadata cataloguing the information available.

Similar problems can be identified in connection with the use of information on the World Wide Web. Standard databases are mostly homogeneous systems with well-defined query languages that can be used to access information available in the database. On the Web, a user first of all has to find the information needed, before it can be used. Then the information may be present in different kinds of data formats and structures. Last but not least, information that seems to fit a user's need can be tailored for a completely different purpose and can therefore be hard to use. Again, metadata can be used to tackle these problems:

- *Search.* By providing topic areas, keywords and content summaries, as well as information about intended use, metadata can be used in order to identify information sources on the Web without having to search every single Web page. Being confronted with the rapidly growing size of the Internet, this ability can be predicted to be very important in the near future.

- *Access.* Metadata related to technical properties of an information source like format, encoding, links to tools or wrappers can significantly reduce the effort required to process available information.
- *Interpretation.* Using information does not only require that information can be accessed; the data also has to be interpreted by the remote system. Information about the terminology used, assumptions made and knowledge required to interpret the content can help both human users and intelligent systems to really understand the content of an information source.

We conclude that the use of metadata is important in order to support the handling and the use of information in heterogeneous environments like the World Wide Web, because metadata helps to organize large information repositories and access these repositories efficiently.

5.1.2 Problems with metadata management

The considerations made above clarify the need for metadata especially for Web-based information systems. Therefore, it is not surprising that various approaches for modelling and using metadata have been developed. Standards evolved that cover different aspects of metadata, especially the syntax for coding, the model structure and the content of a metadata model. Some of these standards are:

- *Syntactic standards.* Features for encoding metadata are already included in common HTML [Ragget et al., 1999]. Meta-tags can be used in order to specify attributes and corresponding values of an HTML document. Recently, RDF [Manola and Miller, 2004] has been proposed as an XML application especially designed for the representation of meta-information about information on the World Wide Web. However, these approaches only define the encoding syntax in order to enable a Web browser to operate on the metadata.
- *Structural standards.* In order to support the development of useful metadata models, a standardization of model structures is an important topic. Structural standards have been defined on top of existing syntactic standards. RDF schema [Brickley and Guha, 2004], for example, defines model structures similar to frame-based knowledge-representation systems. Topic maps [Pepper and Moore, 2001] are another important approach prescribing representation elements to describe information about the contents of information resources.
- *Content standards.* While approaches like RDF Schema or topic maps define structural elements for representing metadata, there is still no guidance with respect to the kind of data to be stored about information in

order to organize and use information efficiently. As a consequence, content standards for metadata have been proposed. One of the most important content standards is the so-called Dublin Core [Weibel, 1999] that defines a set of metadata elements for documents. These elements can be encoded using different syntactic standards, e.g. HTML and RDF.

The standards mentioned above provide good guidance to design and encode metadata for information resources on the World Wide Web. However, there are still some severe problems that are addressed neither by structural nor by content standards. These problems are concerned with the relation between information and metadata about it. Some of the most important are:

- *Completeness.* In order to provide full access to an information source, it has to be ensured that all the information is annotated with the corresponding metadata. Otherwise, important or useful parts of an information source may be missed by metadata driven search methods or cannot be indexed correctly.
- *Consistency.* Metadata about the contents of available information is only useful if it correctly describes these contents. In fact, metadata that is not consistent with the actual information is an even bigger problem than missing metadata, because mechanisms relying on metadata will produce wrong results without warning. Typical cases of inconsistencies we found are cases where a certain keyword is mentioned in the metadata (e.g. surface water) but the content of the page was about a completely different topic (e.g. energy conservation). On the contrary, important keywords were missing (like "energy conservation") in the corresponding pages. This kind of inconsistencies often occur when web pages are created by copying a page and modifying the content without also adapting the metadata. The same situation can often be found with author information in Word documents.
- *Accessability.* In order to be useful, metadata has to be accessible not only by the information provider but especially for users that want to access it. Therefore, an important question is how a comprehensive description of an information source can be provided and accessed by potential users.

As metadata plays an important role in information sharing by enabling remote programs to find, access and interpret information, we have to provide solutions for the problems mentioned in order to be able to support information sharing. When trying to provide partial solutions for these problems we restrict ourselves to content-descriptive metadata, because this type of metadata and especially the use of topic categories provide a very good basis for connecting information with semantic descriptions. We will discuss the process of establishing this connection in the remainder of this chapter.

5.2 The WebMaster approach

In this section, we present an approach for intelligent metadata management that partially solves the problems mentioned above. The starting point for our presentation is BUISY, an existing Web-based information system that serves as an example for the use and problems of metadata on the Web. We will briefly describe this system and the role metadata plays in it. We further present the WebMaster Workbench, a system for the knowledge-based verification of Web sites, and show how it can be applied to the BUISY system solving some of the problems mentioned. The results of this application will be the basis for extensions of the WebMaster approach that will be presented in the next section.

5.2.1 BUISY: A Web based environmental information system

The advent of Web-based information systems came with an attractive solution to the problem of providing integrated access to environmental information according to the duties and needs of modern environmental protection. Many information systems were set up either on the Internet in order to provide access to environmental information for everybody, or in Intranets to support monitoring, assessment and exchange of information within an organization. One of the most recent developments in Germany is BUISY, an environmental information system for the city of Bremen that has been developed by the Center for Computing Technologies of the University of Bremen in cooperation with the public authorities. The development of the system was aimed at providing unified access to the information existing in the different organizational units for internal use as well as for the publication of approved information on the Internet.

Metadata plays an important role in the BUISY system. It controls the access to individual Web pages. Each page in the BUISY system holds a set of metadata annotations reflecting its contents and status [Voegele et al., 2000]. The current version of BUISY supports a set of meta tags annotating information about the data-object's type, author, dates of creation and expiration as well as relevant keywords and the topic area of the page. The "Status" meta-tag indicates whether the data-object is part of the Internet or the Intranet section of BUISY.

```
<meta name="Status" content="Freigegeben"/>
<meta name="Typ" content="Publikation"/>
<meta name="Author" content="TJV"/>
<meta name="Date" content="10-04-1999"/>
<meta name="Expires" content="31-12-2010"/>
<meta name="Keywords" content="Wasser, Gewaesserguete, Algen"/>
<meta name="Bereich" content="Wasser"/>
```

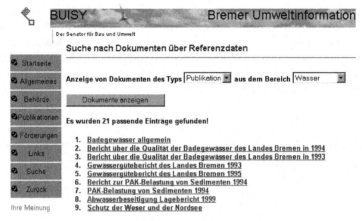

Fig. 5.2. The metadata driven document search facility

At the moment, this metadata is used to provide an intelligent search facility for publications of the administration concerned with environmental protection. The user selects a document type and a topic area. Based on the input, a list of available publications is generated (see Fig. 5.2).

5.2.2 The WebMaster Workbench

We have developed an approach to solve the problems of completeness, consistency and accessibility of metadata identified above. This is done on the basis of rules which must hold for the information found in the Web site, both the actual information and the metadata (and possibly their relationship) [van Harmelen and van der Meer, 1999]. This means that besides providing Web-site contents and metadata, an information provider also defines classification rules (also called integrity constraints) for this information. An inference engine then applies these integrity constraints to identify the places in the Web site which violate these constraints. This approach has been implemented in the WebMaster content-management tool, developed by the Dutch company AIdministrator (www.aidministrator.nl). In this section, we will describe the different steps of using the WebMaster Workbench.

Step 1. Constructing a Web-site ontology

The first step in the approach to content-based verification and visualization of Web pages is to define an ontology of the contents of the Web site. Such an ontology identifies classes of objects on our Web site and defines subclass relationships between these classes. For example, pages can be about water. These can again be subdivided into new subclasses: *Gewaesser* (watercourses), *Weser* (a river in Bremen), *Grundwasser* (groundwater) *Abwasser* (wastewater) and *Anlagen* (technical installations). Further, we included some classes corresponding to types of documents that might appear in the system. We chose *Berichte* (reports) and *Verordnungen* (legislations). This leads to a hierarchy of pages that is based on page contents, such as the example shown in Fig. 5.3.

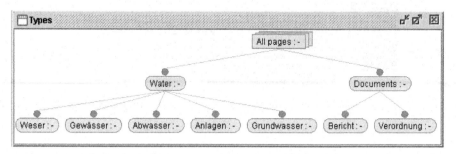

Fig. 5.3. An example classification tree

A subtle point to emphasize is that the objects in this ontology are *objects in the Web site*, and not objects in the real world which are described by the Web site. For example, the elements in the class "river drainage" are not (denotations of) different river-drainage systems in the environment of Bremen, but are *Web pages* (in this case: Web pages talking about river-drainage systems). As a result, any properties we can validate for these objects are properties of the *pages on the Web site*, as desired for our validation purposes.

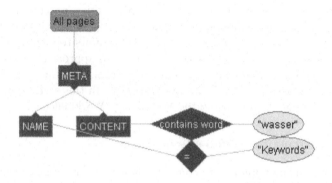

Fig. 5.4. Example of a classification rule using metadata

Step 2. Defining the classification criteria for the ontology

The first step only defines the classes of our ontology, but does not tell us which instances belong to which class. In the second step, the user defines rules determining which Web pages will be members of which class. In this section, we will briefly illustrate these rules by means of three examples. Fig. 5.4 specifies that a Web page belongs to the class "water" if the keyword "Wasser" appears in the meta-information of the page. The rule succeeds for example when the following code appears in the Web page:

```
<meta name="Keywords" content="Wasser">
```

In the typical case, a page belongs to a class if the rule defined for that class succeeds for the page. However, it is also possible to define classes by negation: a page belongs to a class when the corresponding rule fails on that page. This is indicated by a rectangle in the class hierarchy (instead of a rounded box).

Step 3. Classifying individual pages

Whereas the human user of the WebMaster Workbench performs the previous steps, the next step is automatic. The definition of the hierarchy in step 1 and the rules in step 2 allow an inference engine to automatically classify each page in the class hierarchy. Notice that classes may overlap (a single page may belong to multiple classes). The rule format (adopted from [Rousset, 1997]) has been defined in such a way as to provide sufficient expressive power while still making it possible to perform such classification inference on large numbers of pages (many thousands in human-acceptable response time). The rules correspond to positive database updates, the rule format is shown in more detail in equation 5.1. The above figures show graphical representations of this kind of rules. After these three steps, we have a class hierarchy that is populated with all the pages of a given site.

5.2.3 Applying WebMaster to the BUISY system

The ability of the WebMaster Workbench to classify Web pages according to the metadata contained in every page enables us to use the system to perform the tasks we claimed to be necessary for metadata management on the Internet, i.e. the validation, aggregation and visualization of the metadata annotations in the BUISY system. In 2000, the BUISY system contained approximately 1500 pages which are not maintained centrally, but the different topic areas of the systems had been supplemented by different persons after the initial development phase that ended in 1998. Due to this fact, we expected to be faced with incomplete and inconsistent metadata annotations in the different parts of the system. We performed some validation and some aggregation experiments on this metadata which are reported in the next sections.

Validating metadata (consistency)

Checking meta-attributes and values

After extracting the pages that are actually supposed to contain information, we can start to check the completeness of the annotated metadata. In our analysis, we focused on the meta-information assigning a page to a certain topic area. In the BUISY system this information is stored in the meta-attribute named "Bereich". So the first task is to check whether all pages which passed the preselection contain the meta-attribute "Bereich". The result of this test was rather negative. We found that about one hundred of the six hundred and fifty contents pages do not contain the "Bereich" attribute. Another three pages did contain the attribute but without a value. It is very likely that not all pages which were included in the BUISY system are annotated yet. However, using the WebMaster Workbench, we are able to find these pages by creating a corresponding class definition and classifying the web site. For the pages classified into this class we have to decide whether metadata has to be added or not.

Check for missing keywords (completeness)

The validation of the keyword annotations actually existing in the system is the next step of our analysis. In order to judge the quality of the present annotations we defined some keywords covering important aspects of the information found in the system. We chose the keywords according to the classes described in step 1. We used the keywords to compare the keyword annotations with the contents of the page using a full-text search on the whole page.

Fig. 5.5 shows a corresponding class-definition rule. The rule states that if the Web page contains the word "Weser" (the main river in Bremen) then there has to be a meta-tag where the value of the NAME attribute equals "Keywords" and the value of the CONTENT attribute contains the word "Weser".

The validation revealed that most pages containing a keyword in the text did not have this keyword in the metadata annotation. Using the WebMaster Workbench, we were able to identify these pages and present them to the systems administrator who has to decide if the keyword has to be added.

Aggregating metadata (accessability)

The validation of metadata discussed in the previous section is all done on the <META>-tags, which are distributed across the 1500 pages of the BUISY system. At construction time, such a distributed organization of the metadata is rather attractive: each page can be maintained separately,

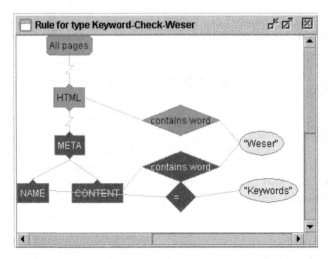

Fig. 5.5. Classification rule for the detection of missing keywords

containing its own metadata. The authors of pages can directly update the metadata annotations when updating a page, and no access to a central metadata repository is needed. However, when we want to use the metadata to create content-based navigation maps (as in the next section), or as the basis for a metadata-based search engine, such a distributed organization of the metadata is no longer attractive. We would prefer having fast access to a central metadata repository instead of having to make remote access to 1500 separate pages when looking for certain metadata.

Using the validation process described in Sect. 4.2 we analyzed the Web site with respect to membership of pages to different topic areas. The result of this step is a classification of pages into a number of classes, based on the application of the classification rules to the <META>-tags in the pages. This yields a populated class hierarchy of pages. Such a populated class hierarchy can be stored in a combined RDF and RDF Schema format. The following statements are taken from the RDF Schema encoding of the WebMaster type hierarchy. The first three show how the types "water", "Gewaesser" and "Weser" and their subtype relationships are encoded in standard RDF Schema.

```
Class(Water)
SubClassOf(Gewaesser Water)
SubClassOf(Weser Water)
  . . .
```

The following is an example of an RDF encoding of instance information: the page at the URL mentioned in the "about" attribute is declared to be a

member of the class "water" (and consequently of all its supertypes, by virtue
of the RDF Schema semantics).

```
Instance(http://www.umwelt.bremen.de/buisy/scripts/buisy.asp?
            doc=Badegewaesserguete+Bremen">
    type(Gewaesser))
```

These automatically generated annotations constitute an aggregated description of a Web site that can be used to get an overview of its contents. The
annotations are machine readable, but they are hard to use by a human Webmaster. This is the reason why we do not only generate an aggregated metadata model, but also provide a condensed visualization on the basis of the
aggregated model.

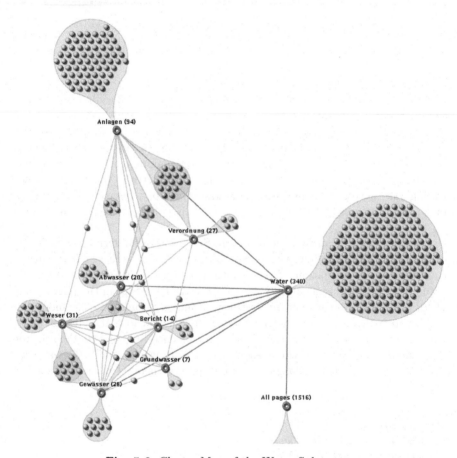

Fig. 5.6. Cluster Map of the Water Subsystem

Given the natural evolution of the content and the metadata of a web site, the aggregation process has to be repeated on a regular basis (e.g. overnight). The required update frequency highly depends on the nature and the use of the information and cannot be determined in general.

Metadata visualization

WebMaster supports the automatic generation of so-called cluster maps about a Web site. A cluster map visualizes an instantiated hierarchy of pages by grouping pages from the same class into a cluster. These clusters may overlap if pages belong to more than one class.

The map generated from the classes described above (Fig. 5.6) shows some interesting features. The first thing that attracts attention is the fact that again most of the pages could not be classified into one of the keyword classes. The better part of the approximately one thousand pages analyzed do not even contain information about the topic area water. This can be explained by the fact that a content map always contains all pages of a Web site. However, there are also many pages which contain relevant contents, but do not belong to one of the keyword classes (page cluster at the right-hand side of the page). The interesting part of the content map is its left-hand side where the pages from the different keyword classes and their membership in these classes are displayed. We can clearly identify pages about technical facilities and waste water as well as pages containing information about legislation concerning one or both of these topics.

Automatically constructed figures such as Fig. 5.6 are compact enough to display many hundreds of pages in a single small image (the map contains 340 pages). This should be compared with the output from traditional search engines, where a set of more than 300 pages is typically presented as 15 pages with 25 URLs each. The format of Fig. 5.6 is much more usable in practice.

5.3 Learning classification rules

We conducted experiments in using the WebMaster Workbench to classify the Web pages in the BUISY system. In the course of this case study eight groups of artificial intelligence students with some experience in knowledge representation and knowledge-based systems independently specified classification rules reflecting the conceptual structure of the system. This corresponds to the second step in the process described above. It turned out that the creation of structural classification rules is still a difficult and error-prone task. We identified the following reasons for the difficulties:

1. People are not familiar with the structure of the pages
2. People are not familiar with the semantics of logical rules

We propose to address these problems directly by:

1. learning classification rules from examples;
2. using a learning approach that is based on logic.

In the following we describe an approach of using inductive logic programming (ILP) in order to learn structural classification rules in the spirit of WebMaster. The reason for using ILP instead of more widely used attribute-based learning approaches is two-fold. First of all, the expressiveness of attribute-based learners is mostly restricted to propositional logic while WebMaster rules are first order. Especially, it is often the case that a rule contains a number of binary predicates connected by common variables. In order to be able to learn a large class of rules, we cannot rely on a propositional learner. Secondly, ILP allows us to incorporate complex background knowledge in the learning process, which is not possible with attribute-based learners. In the current state of the work that is reported in the following sections, we did not make much use of background knowledge; however, we want to keep that option for future work. In the remainder of this section, we give a short introduction to ILP. We relate the general definition to our application and present some interesting results that have been achieved. A more detailed description of the approach can be found in [Hartmann, 2002].

5.3.1 Inductive logic programming

Inductive logic programming (ILP) [Muggleton, 1999] is a technique that combines inductive learning, the generation and validation of hypotheses from observations with logic programming. The latter provides us with the possibility to learn more complex logical formulas and to use complex background knowledge for guiding the search for hypotheses. We will see later that these possibilities are important with respect to learning structural classification rules. The general inductive logic programming problem can be defined as follows [Muggleton and de Raedt, 1994]:

Definition 5.1 (normal semantics of ILP). *Let B, E and H be logical theories where B is given background knowledge and $E = E^+ \wedge E^-$ is given evidence divided into positive and negative evidence. The aim of ILP is to find a hypothesis H, such that the following conditions hold:*

Prior satisfiability: $B \wedge E^- \not\models \bot$
Prior necessity: $B \not\models E^+$
Posterior satisfiability: $B \wedge H \wedge E^- \not\models \bot$
Posterior sufficiency: $B \wedge H \models E^+$

This definition ensures that the learned hypothesis is complete in the sense that it explains all positive evidence (posterior sufficiency) and that it is consistent with negative evidence and background knowledge (posterior satisfiability). Further, the definition excludes trivial results by claiming that the positive examples are not already explained by the background knowledge (prior necessity) and that the background knowledge is consistent with the negative results, because this would enable a logical reasoner to deduce any fact in the theory (prior consistency). Existing approaches implement this general framework in different ways. They can be distinguished by the logical language used to encode evidence, hypotheses and background knowledge and by the learning strategy.

Representation language

Most ILP approaches use logic programs to describe evidence, hypotheses and background knowledge. While background knowledge and hypotheses can be an arbitrary logic program, evidence is normally given in terms of ground facts. ILP systems can be separated between *single-predicate* and *multiple-predicate* learners. All evidence given to a single-predicate learner are instances of a single predicate, in contrast to a multiple-predicate learner whose examples are instances of more than one predicate.

We used the PROGOL system [Muggleton, 1995]. PROGOL is a multi-predicate learner that uses the logical programming language PROLOG for representing knowledge. Any PROLOG program can serve as background knowledge. Evidence can be encoded in terms of two sets of facts (positive and negative evidence). The hypotheses generated by PROGOL are horn clauses defining a single goal predicate.

Learning strategy:

ILP systems can use different strategies to search the hypothesis space. The main operations to generate such a hypothesis are *specialization* and *generalization* which are called *top-down* and *bottom-up* strategy, respectively. Another distinction can be made on how the examples are given to the learner. Given all examples at once, it is called *batch learning*. With *incremental learning* examples are given one by one and the theory covers the actual set of examples. If there is a possible interaction between the teacher and the learner while learning is in progress, it is called an *interactive learner*, otherwise it is a *none-interactive learner*.

PROGOL is a top-down, non-interactive batch learner. It uses inverse entailment to generate only the most specific hypothesis. An A^* like algorithm is used to search through the hypothesis space. To restrict the hypothesis space (*bias*), the teacher defines first-order expressions called *mode declarations*. These models declarations restrict the combination of predicates that are considered in the process of finding hypotheses. We will discuss the use of these declarations in the next section in more detail.

5.3.2 Applying inductive logic programming

In order to apply inductive logic programming to the problem of learning structural classification rules, we have to answer several questions. These include the representation of the problem in the framework of ILP, the generation of this representation from a given dataset and the task of relating the results produced by the induction step to classification rules used in WebMaster. We will discuss these issues in the following sections.

Problem representation

In order to use the PROGOL system for generating hypotheses about classification rules for Web pages, we have to encode knowledge about Web pages and their internal structure in PROLOG. For this purpose, we developed a representation scheme consisting of the following set of predefined predicates:

- `document(object)`: the constant "object" represents a document
- `url(object, ADDRESS)`: the document represented by "object" has the URL "ADDRESS"
- `relation(doc1, doc2)`: there is a directed link between the documents "doc1" and "doc2"
- `structure(object, CLASS)`: the constant "object" represents an element tag of type "CLASS"
- `contains(doc, object)`: the document contains the tag "object" as a top-level element.
- `attribute(parent, object)`: the element tag "parent" contains the attribute "object"
- `contains(parent, object)`: the element "parent" contains the element "object" as a child element
- `value(object, 'VALUE')`: "object" is an element or attribute and it has the value "VALUE"
- `text_value(object, 'TEXT')`: "object" is an element or attribute and it has the value "TEXT"

The distinction between values and text values is necessary, because free-text content of texts is normalized and broken up into single words. A `text_value` predicate is created for every word in a free-text passage.

The predicates form the building blocks for representing background knowledge, hypotheses and evidence. Positive and negative evidence is provided in terms of two sets of `document` predicates, indicating that certain constants represent documents of a certain class or not. The PROLOG representation of the structure of all of these documents is provided as background knowledge. The system then creates hypotheses in terms of rules that have the `document` predicate on the left-hand side and a conjunction of the predicates described above on the right-hand side.

Generating the representation

In order to be able to use an ILP learner for the acquisition of syntactic classification rules, the structures of the documents serving as positive and negative examples have to be translated into the representation described above. We assume that documents are present in XML or XHTML format. Unfortunately, most of the documents came in less standardized form, partly containing syntactic errors. Therefore, all training examples were semi-automatically cleaned and tidied up. We used HTML Tidy[1] and its Java version JTidy[2] for this task. In cases where heavy syntactic errors were found by the software we fixed them manually.

The next step to obtain a usable training set is the *syntactical translation* of the training examples. A Web document like a HTML or an XML document contains predefined tags which describe structure (in particular relations inside a document or between other documents) and layout of documents. The complete translation process is described here in a very abstract way: (i) Every document is parsed into a DOM tree. We used Apache JXERCES 2.0 for this task. (ii) Our written Java program then walks through the DOM tree. Depending on a predefined translation scheme all desired tags are translated into PROLOG clauses. (iii) The positive and negative examples are written into a file which represents the training set. (iv) In order to enable the system to perform a restricted kind of learning on the text of a page, simple normalization techniques are applied that convert the words of a text into lower-case letters, remove special symbols as well as words from a stop list and insert a list of the remaining words in the PROLOG notation.

Relation to WebMaster rules

Rules used in WebMaster have the following general logical form for our rules and constraints, also known as *positive database update constraints* in the database area. A rule for characterizing a class C has the following structure:

$$C \leftarrow \left(\forall \mathbf{x}[\exists \mathbf{y} \bigwedge_i P_i(x_k, y_l)] \implies [\exists \mathbf{z} \bigwedge_j Q_j(x_k, z_m)] \right) \quad (5.1)$$

---

[1] http://www.w3.org/People/Raggett/tidy/
[2] http://lempinen.net/sami/jtidy/

Here $\mathbf{x}$, $\mathbf{y}$ and $\mathbf{z}$ are sets of variables, and each of the P_i and Q_j are binary predicates. Furthermore, the classification rules are always *hierarchical* (i.e. recursion-free) and also free from negation. This class of formulas is less expressive than full first order logic over the predicates P_i and Q_j (because of the limited nesting of the quantifiers), but is more expressive than horn logic (because of the existential quantifier in the right-hand side of the implication).

If we restrict this general rule format, and we drop the existential quantification in the right-hand side, we are left with a very restricted form of logic programs: *hierarchical normal programs over binary predicates*.

This correspondence to logic programs can be used to translate hypotheses generated by PROGOL into the WebMaster rule format. Looking at the general rule format we see that PROLOG clauses are a special case of the rules where all predicates P_i are assumed to be true and omitted. Therefore a Web-Master rule generated by PROGOL has the following format:

$$C \leftarrow \left(\forall \mathbf{x}, [\exists \mathbf{z} \bigwedge_j Q_j(x_k, z_m)] \right) \tag{5.2}$$

In this case the predicates Q_j describe necessary structures for pages of class C. These predicates are taken from the set of predicates described above.

5.3.3 Learning experiments

Our aim is to identify obvious structural regularities within classes of Web pages. The PROGOL system allows us to use background knowledge for focusing the learning process on different kinds of such regularities that are likely to discriminate between classes of Web pages. These regularities have to be specified in terms of goal predicates that can be specified by a horn clause.

In order to assess the quality of our learning approach, we determine the accuracy of the learned rules in terms of the ratio of correctly classified pages. We use the following notation to refer to classification results:

P(A)): correct positive (pages from the class covered by the rule)
$\neg$ P(A): false negative (pages from the class not covered by the rule)
$\neg$ P($\neg$ A): correct negative (pages not from the class that are not covered by the rule)
P($\neg$ A): false positive (pages not from the class that are covered by the rule)

Using these definitions, we use the following definition of accuracy:

$$Accuracy = \frac{P(A) + \neg P(\neg A)}{P(A) + \neg P(A) + \neg P(\neg A) + P(\neg A)} * 100. \tag{5.3}$$

The accuracy is determined by splitting the set of all Web pages into a training set and a test set, where 70% of all pages belong to the training and 30% to the test set. Further, we used a ratio of 1:2 between positive and negatives examples (for each positive example there are two negative ones) Below, we give accuracy measures for our experiments based on this ratio.

Tested criteria

As mentioned above, the PROGOL system allows us to focus the search for hypotheses on parts of the overall knowledge available. This possibility, implemented in so-called *mode declarations*, can be used to define classification criteria to be used in generated classification rules. In our case, we can use mode declarations to prescribe what kinds of Web-page structures should be tested by the system. For this purpose, we first invent the new predicate *descendant* as a transitive closure of the *contains* predicate mentioned above.

$$descendant(A, B) \leftarrow contains(A, B)$$
$$descendant(A, C) \leftarrow contains(A, B) \wedge descendant(B, C)$$

A mode declaration is a definition of a new predicate that should be used on the right-hand side of classification rules. In order to enable the learner to generate hypotheses containing this new predicate it has to be related to the knowledge provided by the reasoner. We do this by defining new predicates in terms of the basic set of predicates used to describe page structures. In the following, we briefly present the mode declarations we used for the generation of structural classification rules.

Document titles:

Document titles often contain information about the type of the page. A personal home page for example will in most cases contain the phrase "home page" in its title. We therefore use the predicate *doctitle* that relates a page words occurring in its title as a first criterion. The corresponding predicate is defined as follows:

$$doctitle(D, T_i) \leftarrow descendant(D, Q) \wedge structure(Q, \text{'}title\text{'}) \wedge$$
$$contains(Q, W) \wedge text\_value(W, T_i)$$

In the following we refer to this mode declaration as H1.

Metadata

Existing metadata annotations on a Web page are an obvious choice for defining classification criteria. We use HTML meta-tags as a search criterion. As different Web sites may use different metadata attributes, we do not further restrict the search to specific metadata such as keywords or authors. The corresponding predicate that locates HTML metadata on a Web page in a general way is the following:

$$metatag(I, N, C) \leftarrow descendant(D, I) \land structure(I, meta) \land$$
$$attribute(I, Q) \land attribute(I, W) \land$$
$$structure(Q, x) \land value(Q, N) \land$$
$$structure(W, y) \land value(W, C)$$

In the following we refer to this mode declaration as H2.

E-mail addresses

More complex Web sites often contain links to a special contact e-mail. Assuming that different persons are responsible for different topic areas according to their field of expertise, we can exploit the occurrence of a certain mail address on a page for defining classification criteria. The corresponding predicate is defined as follows:

$$mail(D, Q, W) \leftarrow descendant(D, S) \land structure(S,' a') \land attribute(S, R) \land$$
$$structure(R,' href') \land value(R,' mailto :' +Q +' @' + W).$$

In the following we refer to this mode declaration as H3.

Links

Web sites are often organized in a hierarchical way. Different topic areas are often accessed via a top-level page containing a table of content or an introductory page. In order to exploit these common access points for classification, we use links to other pages as another classification criterion. These links are identified by an anchor tag with an *href* attribute. The corresponding predicate is the following:

$$relation(D_1, D_2) \leftarrow descendant(D_1, Q) \land structure(Q, a) \land attribute(Q, W) \land$$
$$structure(W, href) \land value(W, Z) \land url(D_2, Z).$$

In the following we refer to this mode declaration as H4.

An example of using mode declarations

We illustrate the impact of the search guidance using results we achieved on classifying the Web site of the University of Bremen. The goal was to learn classification rules that uniquely identify pages of the research group on theoretical computer science. For this purpose we used about 150 pages of that group as positive and about 300 other pages from the University Web site as negative examples. Table 5.1 shows generated rules for the different mode declarations and the accuracy of the rules.

Table 5.1. An Example of the criteria

Experiment A1-0		TrainingSet0
	TZI – Theorie	
Mode Dec.	Hypotheses	Acc.
H 1	document(A) :- doctitle(A,research).	100
H 2	document(A) :- metatag(A,keywords, theoretical).	100
H 3	document(A) :- relation(A,B), relation(B,C), mail(C,helga,'informatik.uni-bremen.de').	86.82
H 4	document(A) :- relation(A,B), url(B,'[URL]/cs/ref.num.html'). document(A) :- relation(A,B), relation(A,C), url(B,'[URL]/projects.html'). document(A) :- relation(A,B), relation(A,C), url(B,'[URL]/cs/ref.num.html').	86.82
URL: `http://www.tzi.de/theorie`		

The results show the different kinds of classification rules we get when using different mode declarations for guiding the search process. Using the page title as a criterion, we find that the pages of the theoretical computer science group are exactly those that contain the word "research" in their title. An analysis of metadata shows that the keyword "theoretical" uniquely identifies the pages we are interested in. We get more surprising results that still have an accuracy of more than 85% when analyzing e-mail addresses and links to other pages. For the case of e-mail addresses we find out that most pages are linked over steps with a page that contains the mail address of the secretary of the group. If we only consider links, we see that most pages are linked to pages containing references and to a page listing projects of the group.

The real benefit of the learning approach, however, is its ability to find classification criteria that are not obvious. In order to discover such unexpected patterns as well, we defined a learning strategy on top of the PROGOL system. Once a valid hypothesis is found, it is stored in a separate solution file. Then all occurrences of the defining structures are deleted from the training data and the learner is run on the data again. This process is repeated until no more valid hypotheses are found. As a result of this strategy we get alternative definitions of the different classes.

Summary of results

We conducted an experiment in learning classification rules by assigning the Web pages of the Web-based environmental information systems of the following cities or federal states, respectively:

- Bremen: `www.umwelt.bremen.de`
- Vienna: `www.ubavie.gv.at`
- Bavaria: `www.umweltministerium.bayern.de`

We applied our learning approach in order to sort pages in these systems into the topic areas waste, soil, air, nature and water. In the following, we present the results we achieved for the BUISY system (see Sect. 5.2.1). The complete experiment including the two other systems is reported in [Hartmann and Stuckenschmidt, 2002].

Table 5.2. Summary of the learning results for the BUISY systems

BUISY summary					
Class	*P(A)*	*¬P(A)*	*¬P(¬A)*	*P(¬A)*	*Acc.*
Abfall	13	0	26	0	100
Boden	11	0	22	0	100
Luft	28	0	56	0	100
Natur	20	1	42	0	98.41
Wasser	58	0	116	0	100

Table 5.2 shows that we achieved an accuracy of almost 100%. The reason for this is the existence of metadata annotations on almost all pages that directly link the pages to the topic areas. Some of the more interesting results are discussed in the next section.

5.3.4 Extracted classification rules

Beside the rather trivial results we achieved in classifying metadata based on pre-existing classifications encoded in meta-tags, we were also able to extract some more surprising classification rules. This section gives an overview of the rules with more than 50% accuracy that have been found by the learner.

Class "Abfall"

The first class of Web pages is concerned with waste management. We used a sample of 45 positive and 90 negative examples. The resulting rules for the different mode declarations are shown in Table 5.3.

Table 5.3. Experiment B1-0: BUISY – Abfall

Experiment B1-0		TrainingSet0
	BUISY – Abfall	
Mode Dec.	*Hypotheses*	*Acc.*
H 1	document(A) :- doctitle(A,abf).	74,36
H 2	document(A) :- metatag(A,bereich,abfall).	100
H 3	–	–
H 4	–	–
H 1-4	document(A) :- metatag(A,bereich,abfall).	100

We can see that the main classification criterion was the predefined classification encoded in the "Bereich" attribute. Besides this, about 75% of all pages of this class had the acronym "abf" in their title.

Class "Boden"

The second class of pages is concerned with soil protection. For the generation of classification rules for this class we used a sample of 37 positive and 74 negative examples. Table 5.4 shows the results of the learning process.

Table 5.4. Experiment B2-0: BUISY – Boden

Experiment B2-0		TrainingSet0
	BUISY – Boden	
MD	*Hypotheses*	*Acc.*
H 1	document(A) :- doctitle(A,bodenschutz).	
	document(A) :- doctitle(A, boden).	90.91
	document(A) :- doctitle(A, bo).	
H 2	document(A) :- metatag(A,keywords,bodenschutz).	100
	document(A) :- metatag(A,keywords,boden).	
H 3	–	–
H 4	–	–
H 1-4	document(A) :- metatag(A,keywords,bodenschutz).	
	document(A) :- metatag(A,keywords,boden).	100

The results for this class are similar to the one before. Beside the pre-defined classification, only the analysis of the page title produced results. This time, the learner found more than one words frequently occurring page titles. The combination of these word leads to a higher classification accuracy of about 90%.

Class "Luft"

The third class considered contains pages about air pollution. We used a sample of 94 positive and 184 negative examples to learn classification rules for this class of Web pages. The results are shown in Table 5.5.

Table 5.5. Experiment B3-0: BUISY – Luft

Experiment B3-0		TrainingSet0
	BUISY – Luft	
MD	*Hypotheses*	*Acc.*
H 1	document(A) :- doctitle(A,karte).	
	document(A) :- doctitle(A,blues).	
	document(A) :- doctitle(A,ost).	
	document(A) :- doctitle(A,so2diagramm).	
	document(A) :- doctitle(A,lu).	
	document(A) :- doctitle(A,stickstoffoxiddiagramm).	95.24
	document(A) :- doctitle(A,aktuelle).	
	document(A) :- doctitle(A,verkehr).	
	document(A) :- doctitle(A,ozondiagramm).	
	document(A) :- doctitle(A,staubdiagramm).	
	document(A) :- doctitle(A,stickstoffoxid).	
H 2	document(A) :- metatag(A,expires,thu).	
	document(A) :- metatag(A,bereich,luft).	100
H 3	–	–
H 4	document(A) :- relation(A,B),	
	url(B,'[URL]/p_strassensuche').	69,05
H 1-4	document(A) :- metatag(A,expires,thu).	
	document(A) :- metatag(A,bereich,luft).	100
URL: http://www.bremen.de/Web/owa		

For this class of Web pages we did not only get results on metadata and page titles, but also for relations between documents. It turned out that about 70% of all pages of this class are linked to a special search page, where users can access air pollution information for their particular area. Another interesting point is the fact that the rules learned for page titles associate the page s with words that are not obvious but rather refer to specialized terms from the area.

Class "Natur"

The fourth class consists of pages about the protection of plants and animals. The sample for this class consisted of 71 positive and 142 negative examples. We were able to generate rules based on titles and metadata of the pages. The corresponding rules are shown in Table 5.6.

Experiment B4-0		TrainingSet0
	BUISY – Natur	
MD		*Hypotheses Acc.*
H 1	document(A) :- doctitle(A,naturschutzgebiete).	
	document(A) :- doctitle(A,nsg).	
	document(A) :- doctitle(A,richtlinie).	
	document(A) :- doctitle(A,vogelschutzgehoelz).	92.06
	document(A) :- doctitle(A,naturschutzgebiet).	
	document(A) :- doctitle(A,vogelschutzgebiet).	
H 2	document(A) :- metatag(A,author,'zdl30-13').	
	document(A) :- metatag(A,author,brendel).	98.41
	document(A) :- metatag(A,bereich,naturschutz).	
H 3		– –
H 4		– –
H 1-4	document(A) :- doctitle(A,richtlinie).	
	document(A) :- metatag(A,author,'zdl30-13').	98.41
	document(A) :- metatag(A,bereich,naturschutz).	

Table 5.6. Experiment B4-0: BUISY – Natur

Beside the page title that again contained some rather specialized terms like "vogelschutzgebiet", we found rules that linked the pages to a specific author. In this case "zdl30-13" identifies a special position in the organization of the environmental administration. We can conclude that this position includes the obligation to create and maintain the information on this specific topic area.

Class "Wasser"

The last class considered in our case study is concerned with water pollution. This part is the largest topic area of the BUISY system. We were able to use a sample consisting of 194 positive and 388 negative examples. The results for the class of water protection pages are summarized in table 5.7.

The results for this class also contained some surprises. First of all, most characteristic words in the document titles have no connection at all with the topic of water protection. The combined use of all mode declaration also produced

MD	Experiment B5-0 TrainingSet0,1
	BUISY – Wasser

MD	Hypotheses Acc.
H 1	document(A) :- doctitle(A,wa).
	document(A) :- doctitle(A,landes). 94.25
	document(A) :- doctitle(A,von).
H 2	document(A) :- metatag(A,bereich,wasser). 100
H 3	– –
H 4	– –
H 1-4	document(A) :- metatag(A,bereich,wasser).
	document(A) :- doctitle(A,fuer), 100
	metatag(A,generator,microsoft).

Table 5.7. Experiment B5-0: BUISY - Wasser

a rule that identifies the pages of this class in terms of the tool used for their creation. In this case, the meta-tag "generator" that is automatically added to Web pages by the tool Microsoft "Frontpage" is found to be characteristic for the class of pages.

Conclusions

The experiments showed that our learning approach can be successfully applied to the problem of checking the completeness and consistency of the metadata of existing information systems on the web. In particular we were able to identify topic areas with correct and complete meta-data and such topic where the metadata has top be improved (compare [Hartmann and Stuckenschmidt, 2002]).

The system produced very good results on the identification of existing meta-data, which already helps to classify unknown systems. In the absence of metadata, the approach is able to find various other classification criteria like words occurring in page titles or links to other Web pages. In this case the average accuracy is significantly lower, but still we managed to achieve results that are comparable to other work reported in the literature. A good example is the dataset used in the WebKB project [Craven et al., 2000]. We reached an accuracy of about 65% by just applying our approach without customizing it to the task.

5.4 Ontology deployment

In the last section, we described a mostly automated approach for assigning Web pages to classes in a hierarchy. We used the WebMaster Workbench to

classify pages based on structural classification rules and showed that these
rules can be learned from examples. If we compare this approach to the ontology infrastructure proposed in Chap. 4, we face the problem, that the
notion of ontology used by WebMaster differs from our view on source ontologies. WebMaster operates on a very simple form of ontology consisting only
of a hierarchy of classes while source ontologies as defined in Chap. 4 consist of complex logical definitions. In this section, we show that despite the
difference between the notions on ontologies used, we can use the metadata-
generation approach in order to deploy source ontologies by assigning Web
pages to classes in the ontology in a mostly automatic way.

5.4.1 Generating ontology-based metadata

Our approach for connecting information resources with ontologies relies on
the definition of a source ontology to consist of a plain class hierarchy that
is connected to logical definitions by a corresponding mapping (compare
Definition 2.3). This definition enables us to use the class hierarchy independently from the logical definition of the classes in the hierarchy and use it
in the WebMaster Workbench. Further, we can use the mapping to logical
definitions to perform reasoning on class hierarchy and instances.

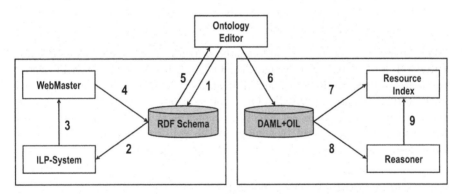

Fig. 5.7. Deployment strategy for source ontologies

Fig. 5.7 illustrates the process of generating metadata in terms of Web-page
categorization from pre-existing source ontologies having been built in the
way described in Chap. 4. Assuming that a complete source ontology exists,
the steps of this process are the following:

1. In the first step, we export the class hierarchy of the source ontology as
   an RDF schema definition as input for the rule-learning and Web page
   categorization process.

2. The exported classification is used for determining goal classes for the ILP system. Based on the class hierarchy, the user determines examples for the learning process.

3. After the generated classification rules have been validated by the user, they are transformed into the WebMaster format and imported into the Workbench.

4. Using the generated classification rules, the WebMaster Workbench assigns the pages of the Web site to classes from the hierarchy and exports the assignment by extending the RDF Schema model of the hierarchy.

5. In the ontology editor, the RDF Schema model that has been extended by instance information is linked to the complete definition of the ontology that includes logical definitions of classes.

6. The complete ontology that now includes instance information in terms of classified individuals representing Web pages is exported as a DAML+OIL model for further processing.

7. On the basis of the class names defined in the ontology a Web-site index is created in terms of a dynamic data structure that can be queried by other systems.

8. The complete DAML+OIL model is shipped to a description logic reasoner. The reasoner is used to verify the ontology and the instance information. Further implicit subclass and membership relations are derived.

9. The membership relations that have been found by the reasoner (including those already created by WebMaster) are used to insert the information about Web pages in the index structure.

This process can mostly be implemented with existing technologies. Besides PROGOL and WebMaster, we used the OILed Editor [Bechhofer et al., 2001] to create source ontologies. The editor supports the export of ontologies in both RDF Schema and DAML+OIL. The editor is directly integrated with the description-logic reasoner FaCT [Bechofer et al., 1999] that can be used for perform terminological reasoning on the exported ontology. The use of these reasoning services is described in the next section.

5.4.2 Using ontology-based metadata

One of the major benefits of basing metadata on source ontologies is the already mentioned reasoning support for a limited number of tasks concerned with ontology management.

- *Consistency checking.* The reasoner is able to check the satisfiability of the logical model of the ontology. In particular, inconsistent concept definitions are detected. If we, for example, defined animals to have four legs and we try to include an instance of the class animal with five legs, the reasoner will find the contradiction.

- *Computation of subclass relations.* an ontology normally contains two different kinds of subclass relations: explicitly defined relations from the class hierarchy and implicit subclass relations implied by the logical definitions of concepts. The latter can be detected using a reasoner for terminological languages and included in the ontology thus completing it.
- *Deriving class membership.* A special case of the computation of subclass relation is the automatic classification of individuals. Terminological languages normally allow us to describe an individual by its relation to other individuals without naming all classes it belongs to. The reasoner will find the classes we omitted in the definition. An example would be if we had defined our dummy page to be about the "Sodenmattsee" without assigning it to a special topic area. However, we stated that the domain of the "about" relation is the class topic area and we defined water-pollution-control to be concerned with watercourses. This information and the fact that the "Sodenmattsee" is a lake and therefore a watercourse enable the reasoner to decide that our dummy page should be classified as belonging to the topic area "water pollution control".

Making use of these reasoning services, we can check the result of the metadata generation for consistency. This is necessary because the criteria used to describe classes in the systems only refer to syntactic structures of the page contents. Especially, the WebMaster Workbench has no possibility to check whether the classification of a page makes sense from a logical point of view. For example, we can include a description of the administrative units in our ontology and classify pages according to the unit which is concerned with the specific topic of the page. We will define the units to be mutually disjoint because the competency is strictly separated. If we now classify one page to belong to both units we get a clash in the logical model. In this case, we have to check the page and assign the right administrative unit by hand. Thus the logical model helps us to find shortcomings of the generated model.

The second benefit of the logical grounding of the metadata model is the possibility to derive hidden membership relations. This is important because the RDF metadata schema makes some assumptions about implicit knowledge. Examples of these assumptions can be found in [Champin, 2000]. We use the following axiom as an example:

$$\frac{\mathcal{T}(r, \text{rdf} : \text{type}, c_1) \wedge \mathcal{T}(c_1, \text{rdfs} : \text{subClassOf}, c_2)}{\mathcal{T}(r, \text{rdf} : \text{type}, c_2)}.$$

The equation states that every resource r (i.e. Web page) that is member a of class c_1 (indicated by the triple $\mathcal{T}(r, \text{rdf} : \text{type}, c_1)$) is also a member of class c_2 ($\mathcal{T}(r, \text{rdf} : \text{type}, c_2)$) if c_1 is a subclass of c_2 ($\mathcal{T}(c_1, \text{rdfs} : \text{subClassOf}, c_2)$). This correlation can easily be computed using the FaCT reasoner by querying all super-concepts of a given concept. The result of this query can be used to supplement the description of a page. The description of the page referred to above, for example, will be extended with the following statement:

```
type(watercourse)
```

Using this mechanism, we are able to build a site index that provides efficient access to Web pages by the topic class they belong to.

5.5 Conclusions

Metadata plays a central role in information sharing and in information processing in general. It establishes the connection between information sources and ontologies that explicate the meaning of their content. In weakly structured environments this is harder than in structured ones. XML documents, for example, can be directly linked to an ontology on the basis of the tags used in the documents by relating the tags to classes or relations in the ontology. In the absence of a real data structure the connection either has to be loose or we have to spend much more effort on the task of establishing the connection.

We claim that the assignment of individual Web pages to classes in an ontology provides a good tradeoff between the strength of the connection and the effort of establishing it. We show that Web-page classification can be done using classification rules that refer to the structure of HTML documents. The resulting classification can be used for content-based navigation and search. We also demonstrated that structural classification rules can be generated in a mostly automatic way using techniques from machine learning. Though using a very limited learning approach we achieved classification results with an accuracy of ninety percent and more. Our results show that the approach is successful though there is still potential for improving the learning method.

In principle, Web-page classification can be done without relating to an ontology, but using a source ontology as a starting point for the classification enables us to benefit from its formal semantics. Especially, we can use terminological reasoning to support the metadata-creation process by verifying classification results against the definitions of the classes involved and by deriving implicit classifications that are implied by the semantics of the ontology.

Further reading

The metadata model of the BUISY system is presented in [Voegele et al., 2000]. The idea and some other applications of the Web-Master system are described in [van Harmelen and van der Meer, 1999], the use of cluster maps for visualizing ontologies and their instances in [Fluit et al., 2003]. The theory and applications of inductive logic programming can be found in [Muggleton, 1999]. A similar approach using inductive logic programming for learning from Web structures is reported in [Craven et al., 2000].

Part III

Retrieval, integration and querying

6

Retrieval and Integration

Summary. In the last part, we discussed how information sources can be semi-automatically enriched by semantic information. In this chapter, we show how information can be retrieved and transformed between different systems based on their semantic descriptions. We show that translations between different ontologies can be approximated using a minimal shared terminology. We further describe how this transformation can be exploited for content-based information filtering across different systems.

In order to benefit from having access to different information systems, we have to provide sophisticated methods to separate relevant from irrelevant information. This problem is also referred to as *information filtering*, which is characterized as the task of removing irrelevant information from an incoming stream of unstructured textual information according to user preferences [Belkin and Croft, 1992]. A different perspective on the same problem is that of information retrieval [Salton and McGill, 1983]. In information retrieval, a collection of information represented by surrogates in terms of content descriptions is searched on the basis of a user query, and those documents whose descriptions match the query are returned to the user. Many systems support the *Boolean query model* [Frakes and Baeza-Yates, 1992] that allows us to state queries as Boolean expressions over keywords.

The use of background knowledge has been discussed in classical information retrieval [Yarowsky, 1992, Gaizauskas and Humphreys, 1997] in order to increase the precision and recall of free-text queries. Corresponding knowledge models often define relationships between words, such as the synonym relation. Using the infrastructure described in Chap. 2, we cannot only use such relationships that are encoded in the shared terminology (Definition 2.1). Our infrastructure transfers these relations into a logical framework, the shared ontology (Definition 2.2) that can be used to define specialized terms in different information systems (source ontology, see Definition 2.3). This background information is linked to information items by the assignment of Web pages to classes in the source ontology. The assignment to a certain ontological class provides us with a unique interpretation of the meaning of a resource. Using the concepts of a specific ontology, we can state Boolean queries over concept names with maximal precision and recall with respect to the semantics of their definition if all relevant information resources have been assigned to the right ontological categories.

In this chapter, we provide a detailed discussion of methods for retrieving and integrating information from different sources within the general framework presented in Chap. 2. We start with a didactic example that illustrates our approach before providing a formal definition of approximate re-classification which is the basis for our approach. We discuss the use of the method for retrieving information items based on their type and extend this simple ting to the problem of retrieving information using conjunctive queries. We conclude with a discussion of a small case study of applying these methods in the tourism domain.

6.1 Semantic integration

In this section we adopt the notion of translatability introduced by Ciocoiu and Nau for the problem of handling multiple classification systems. Analyzing the requirements for performing translations, we will see that the approach for explicating information semantics described in section 2.4.2 largely fulfills these requirements. The sentences to be translated are class names in the different classifications, the logical rendering is achieved through the use of a terminological language and the interpretation is given by the definition $d(C_i)$ of a class name C_i. The shared ontology corresponds to Ω. These analogies imply that we can use logical deduction in order to perform translations.

In the following, we first define the translation task with respect to information systems and classifications. We then show how reasoning in a terminological language can be used in order to perform partial translations from one system into the other. Based on these transformations, we introduce an approach for information filtering that is based on re-writing Boolean queries across heterogeneous classifications.

6.1.1 Ontology heterogeneity

Ontologies can differ in many ways [Visser et al., 1997]. We will not try to discuss them in general. We will rather give an example of ontologies that even though they describe the same domain of interest represent very different conceptualizations of that domain. We start with a simple ontology that discriminates animals into domestic, foreign and production animals and contains some kinds of animals that fall under one or more of these categories (compare Fig. 6.1).

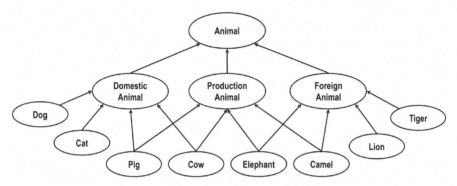

Fig. 6.1. An ontology of animals

Now consider an ontology that describes classes of animals in the way a child would possibly categorize them (compare Fig. 6.2). The main distinctions made in this ontology are pets, farm animals and zoo animals. These distinction are based on the experience of a child that some animals are kept at home, at farms or in zoos.

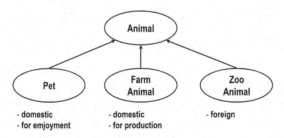

Fig. 6.2. A "childish" ontology of animals

While both ontologies do not share any class except for the general class animal, it should be possible to establish a relation between the two. Using common World knowledge and the informal descriptions of the classes in Fig. 6.2 we can conclude that "Pet" should be a subclass of "Domestic Animal" and include "Cat" and "Dog". "Farm Animal" should be a subclass of "Domestic Anima" and include "Cow" and "Pig". Finally, "Zoo Animal" should be subsumed by "Foreign Animal" and contain all the subclasses of "Foreign Animal" shown in Fig. 6.1.

In this example, we only show the hierarchy of the ontologies, because the methods described in this section can be explained solely using the notion of subsumption of concepts. The connection to the use of a shared vocabulary as described before lies in the fact, that we need the shared vocabulary in order to compute subsumption relations between concepts from different hierarchies. So actually the concepts in the example ontologies would be specified by their characteristic properties (e.g. habitat, use, etc.) which are defined using terms from a shared vocabulary that has been constructed beforehand.

6.1.2 Multiple systems and translatability

In order to get a clearer notion of the problem to be solved, we give an abstract definition of an information source in terms of a set of information items that are classified according to a source ontology. This general notion of an information source covers Web-based information system like the one discussed in the last chapter. An information item corresponds to a single Web page that has been classified according to a source ontology. In the case of a conventional database, we can think of single rows in a database table as an information item. The connection to a source ontology can be given by a corresponding reference in the data dictionary that may also contain the ontology itself.

Definition 6.1 (information source). *An information source is a tuple $\langle O, I, M \rangle$, where $O = \langle S, C, d \rangle$ is a source ontology with shared ontology S, a set of class names C and a mapping d that assigns a class definition over terms from S to every class name from C, I is a set of information items and $M : I \times C$ is a membership relation that relates information items to classes of the source ontology.*

Building on this abstract view of an information source, we can define the problem of integrating the classifications employed in two different systems. Roughly speaking the task is to extend the membership relation M_1 of an information source IS_1 by an additional relation M' that relates the information items of a second information source IS_2 according to the source ontology of IS_1. In order to be able to reason about instances of classes as well, we extend the semantics of a terminological language in a straightforward way, by assuming that the assignment mapping $\mathcal{A}$ does not only apply to class names but also to instances. We define that:

$$x^{\mathcal{I}} \in W \text{ for every } x \in I \qquad (6.1)$$

The notion of an interpretation of individuals allows us to reason about the membership of instances to classes, denoted as $x : C$. We define membership as follows:

$$x : C \iff x^{\Im} \in C^{\Im} \tag{6.2}$$

Using this definition of the semantics of individuals with respect to an ontology, we can define the translation problem. we have to solve as follows:

Definition 6.2 (integration problem). *Let $IS_1 = \langle\langle S_1, C_1, d_1\rangle, I_1, M_1\rangle$ and $IS_2 = \langle\langle S_2, C_2, d_2\rangle, I_2, M_2\rangle$ be information sources; then a bilateral integration problem is equivalent to finding a membership relation $M : I_1 \cup I_2 \times C_1$ such that for all $x \in I_2 \cup I_2$ and $c_i \in C_1$:*

$$(x, c_i) \in M \text{ iff } x : d_1(c_i)$$

In order to generate this new relation M' we have to rely on the semantics of both information sources that are given by their source ontologies. In general, we cannot assume that both information sources use the same source ontology. We cannot even assume that the source ontologies of both information sources are comparable at all. If we want to make assertions about the relation of the ontologies of two information sources, we have to ensure that we can perform terminological reasoning across these ontologies. This in turn is given, if both ontologies share the interpretation $\Im$ of concept terms. We can ensure this if both source ontologies are based on the same shared ontology.

6.1.3 Approximate re-classification

The comparability criterion given above allows us to reason across source ontologies; however, the definitions included in the different ontologies will often be similar but not equivalent. This might lead to a situation where we are not able to decide whether an instance really belongs to a certain class in a different system or not. However, we can identify cases where we are able to decide whether an instance from a remote information source definitely belongs to a certain class or definitely does not belong to a certain class.

Consider the situation where we want to classify an information item from an information source IS_2 into the local ontology of IS_1 by computing M. The only information we have about x is its classification M_2 with respect to the source ontology of IS_2. In order to make use of this information, we have to determine the relation between possible classifications of x in IS_1 and the source ontology of IS_2. In this context, we can use subsumption testing in order to determine hypotheses for M with respect to IS_2 by computing the class hierarchy for $C_1 \cup C_2$ using the definitions of individual classes (provided that the encoding languages belong to the same family of languages).

As the classes in the hierarchy form a partial order, we will always have a set of direct superclasses and a set of direct subclasses of c_1. We can use these classes as upper and lower approximations for c_1 in IS_2:

Definition 6.3 (upper approximation). *Let* $IS_1 = \langle\langle S_1, C_1, d_1\rangle, I_1, M_1\rangle$ *and* $IS_2 = \langle\langle S_2, C_2, d_2\rangle, I_2, M_2\rangle$ *be information sources and* $c \in C_1$ *a class from* IS_1*; then a class* $c_{lub} \in C_2$ *is called a least upper bound of* c *in* IS_2*, if the following assertions hold:*

- $d_1(c) \sqsubseteq d_2(c_{lub})$
- $(\exists c' \in C_2 \text{ such that } d_1(c) \sqsubseteq d_2(c')) \implies (d_2(c_{lub}) \sqsubseteq d_2(c'))$

The upper approximation $lub_{IS_2}(c)$ *is the set of all least upper bounds of* c *in* IS_2*.*

Definition 6.4 (Lower Approximation). *Let* $IS_1 = \langle\langle S_1, C_1, d_1\rangle, I_1, M_1\rangle$ *and* $IS_2 = \langle\langle S_2, C_2, d_2\rangle, I_2, M_2\rangle$ *be information sources and* $c \in C_1$ *a class from* IS_1*; then a class* $c_{glb} \in C_2$ *is called a greatest lower bound of* c *in* IS_2*, if the following assertions hold:*

- $d_2(c_{glb}) \sqsubseteq d_1(c)$
- $(\exists c' \in C_2 \text{ such that } d_2(c') \sqsubseteq d_1(c)) \implies (d_2(c') \sqsubseteq d_2(c_{glb}))$

The lower approximation $glb_{IS_2}(c)$ *denotes the set of all greatest lower bounds of* c *in* IS_2*.*

The rationale of using these approximations is that we can decide whether x is a member of the classes involved based on the relation M_2. This decision in turn provides us with an approximate result on deciding whether x is a member of c_1, based on the following observations:

- If x is a member of a lower bound of c_1 then it is also in c_1
- If x is not a member of all upper bounds of c_1 then it is not in c_1

In [Selman and Kautz, 1996] Selman and Kautz propose to use this observation about upper and lower boundaries for theory approximation. We adapt the proposal for defining an approximate classifier $M' : I_2 \times C_1 \to \{0, 1, ?\}$ in the following way:

Definition 6.5 (approximate re-classification). *Let* $IS_1 = \langle\langle S, C_1, d_1\rangle, I_1, M_1\rangle$ *and* $IS_2 = \langle\langle S, C_2, d_2\rangle, I_2, M_2\rangle$ *be information sources and* $x \in I_2$*; then for every* $c_1 \in C_1$ *we define* M' *such that:*

- $M'(x, c_1) = 1$ *if* $x : \left(\bigvee\limits_{c \in glb_{IS_2}(c_1)} d_2(c) \right)$

- $M'(x, c_1) = 0$ *if* $x : \neg \left(\bigwedge\limits_{c \in lub_{IS_2}(c_1)} d_2(c) \right)$

- $M'(x, c_1) = ?$*, otherwise*

where the semantics of disjunction and conjunction is defined in the obvious way using set union and intersection.

Based on the observation about the upper and lower bounds, we can make the following assertion about the correctness of the proposed approximate classification:

Theorem 6.6 (correctness of the approximation). *The approximation from Definition 6.5 is correct in the sense that:*

- *If $M'(x, c_1) = 1$ then $x^\Im \in d_1(c_1)^\Im$*
- *If $M'(x, c_1) = 0$ then $x^\Im \notin d_1(c_1)^\Im$*

Using the definition of upper and lower bounds the correctness of the classification can be proven in a straightforward way (see Appendix).

This result provides us with the possibility to include many of the information items from remote systems into an information source in such a way that we get a semantic description of the item we can use for information management. Another interesting application of this approach, namely information filtering, is described in the next section.

6.2 Concept-based filtering

The translation approach described in the last section allows us to include arbitrary information items into our own system, provided that we are able to re-classify them using the approximate method we introduced. However, in most cases we are not interested in the whole information of a remote system, but only in information about a specific topic. The approach of first trying to translate the whole information source in most cases leads to a significant overhead, especially when we consider the amount of information available on the World Wide Web. We therefore strive for methods that allow us to preselect relevant information from remote systems by posing specific queries to these systems.

As the major structuring method we use in this work is the classification of information entities according to the source ontology, we want to use the semantics defined in the ontology also as a basis for selecting information from remote systems. For this purpose we propose to use Boolean queries over concept names from the classification hierarchy. However, if we want to use the vocabulary provided by the ontology of our information source, we again face the problem of heterogeneity with respect to the ontologies used in other systems. We show how we can use approximate re-classification in order to translate the queries we want to post to remote systems in such a way that we can guarantee that all returned information items indeed satisfy the query expression.

Due to the approximate nature of the re-classification, we will not be able to guarantee that all interesting information items are actually returned on a query, because we just do not have an appropriate vocabulary for stating queries in such a way that they cover all information items from the remote system. So our approach, while not being able to provide maximal recall, it guarantees maximal precision with respect to the semantics of the query.

6.2.1 The idea of query-rewriting

Assume that we want to post a query formulated using the ontology from Fig. 6.2 to an information source that has been classified according to the ontology in Fig. 6.1. In order to answer this query, we have to resolve the heterogeneity discussed above. The use of a shared ontology in combination with a definition of the classes in both ontologies enables us to do this. As an example we take the following query (Animal ∧ ¬(Farm Animal)). This query cannot be directly answered, because the term "Farm Animal" is not understood, but we know what are the characteristic properties of "Zoo Animal" and can compare them with the definitions of classes in the other ontology.

As described in the introduction, the idea of our approach is to re-write this query in such a way that it covers the same set of answers using terms from the other ontology. In general, an exact re-writing is not possible because the concepts of our ontology do not have corresponding concepts. In this case, we have to look for re-writings that approximate the query as closely as possible. Re-writings that are an upper approximation of the original query are know from the database area as *minimal subsuming mappings* [Chang and Garcia-Molina, 2001]. Whereas in the area of databases upper approximations are often used in combination with an additional filter that removes irrelevant results, our approach aims for correctness rather than for completeness and therefore uses a lower approximation.

The idea of the re-writing is the following. Based on the formal definitions of the classes in both ontologies, we can find those concepts in the ontology of Fig. 6.1 that are most closely related to a query concept. Taking a concepts from our query, we can for example decide that "Domestic Animal" and "Production Animal" are upper approximations for "Farm Animal" while "Cow" and "Pig" are lower approximations. Using these concepts, we can define lower boundaries for "Farm Animal" (Cow ∨ Pig) and use this expression instead of the original concept still getting correct results. In our example, however, the concept occurred in a negated form. In order to return a correct result, we therefore cannot use the lower bound because not all irrelevant resources might be excluded. Based on the considerations made above we can replace the concept "Farm Animal" within the scope of the negation by its upper bound (Domestic Animal ∧ Production Animal). Using this rewriting, we get the following query that can be shown to return only correct results: (Animal∧¬(Domestic Animal∧Production Animal).

The situation becomes slightly more complicated if complex expressions occur in the scope of a negation. An example is the following query: ¬(Pet ∨ Farm Animal). In this case we first have to convert the query into negation normal form where negation only applies to atomic concepts. In negation normal form the above query will be of the form (¬Pet ∧ ¬Farm Animal). Using upper and lower bounds this query translates to ¬Domestic Animal ∧ ¬(Domestic-Animal ∧ Production Animal). This query normalizes to (¬Domestic Animal ∧ ¬Production Animal), which in our example only includes the classes "Lion" and "Tiger".

6.2.2 Boolean concept expressions

In order to apply the idea of approximate re-classification to information filtering, we first have to define the type of filtering expressions we want to use. As mentioned in the introduction, we use the Boolean query model widely used in information retrieval and filtering. In information retrieval, Boolean queries consist of keywords that are combined by Boolean operators. The assignment of information items to concepts of an ontology as proposed in the last chapter enables us to use concept names instead of keywords. The resulting notion of a Boolean concept query is defined as follows:

Definition 6.7 (Boolean concept query). *Let $IS = \langle\langle S, C, D\rangle, I, M\rangle$ be an information source; then a Boolean query is formed by a legal query expression that is defined in the following way:*

- *every $c \in C$ is a legal query expression,*
- *if e is a legal query expression then $\neg e$ is also a legal query expression,*
- *if e_1 and e_2 are legal query expressions, then $e_1 \wedge e_2$ and $e_1 \vee e_2$ are also legal query expressions.*

The advantage of using concept names instead of keywords is the possibility of defining a clear semantics of a query that makes it possible to reason about the query result in the framework of terminological languages. By defining the semantics of a Boolean concept query on the basis of the semantics of the concept contained therein, we get a direct connection between queries and the underlying ontology. This is of particular interest for the case where queries are not posed by human users, but by computer programs, because the semantics of the queries enables the system to precisely interpret the returned result.

Definition 6.8 (query semantics). *Let $IS = \langle O, I, M \rangle$ be an information source. The semantics $Q^{\mathcal{I}}$ of a query Q is defined by an interpretation mapping $\mathcal{I}$ into the abstract description model of O in the following way:*

- $c^{\mathcal{I}} = d(c)^{\Im}$
- $(\neg e)^{\mathcal{I}} = W - e^{\mathcal{I}}$
- $(e_1 \wedge e_2)^{\mathcal{I}} = e_1^{\mathcal{I}} \cap e_2^{\mathcal{I}}$
- $(e_1 \vee e_2)^{\mathcal{I}} = e_1^{\mathcal{I}} \cup e_2^{\mathcal{I}}$

The reason for relating queries to ontologies on a semantic level is the possibility to use terminological reasoning for determining the query result. We can treat the query as a concept expression in the ontology and classify it with respect to the other concepts therein. Especially, we can determine those concepts in the ontology that are subsumed by the query:

Definition 6.9 (subsumed concepts). *A concept C is said to be subsumed by a query q if $d(C)^{\Im} \subseteq Q^{\mathcal{I}}$. We denote this fact by $C \sqsubseteq Q$.*

On the other hand, what we are interested in are those information items that are members of the concept expression that is equivalent to the query. These items that we refer to as the *query result* are formally defined as follows:

Definition 6.10 (query result). *Let $IS = \langle \langle S, C, D \rangle, I, M \rangle$ be an information source and Q be a Boolean query over IS then the result of Q is given by:*

$$\{ x \in I \mid x^{\Im} \in Q^{\mathcal{I}} \}$$

We denote the fact that an instance x belongs to the result of a query Q by $x : Q$.

Subsumed concepts directly provide us with the result to a terminological query, because the union of their members is exactly the query result we are looking for. As information items are explicitly assigned to concepts in the ontology, the task of computing the query results reduces to looking up the members of the subsumed classes.

Theorem 6.11. *An information item x is in the result of a query Q if*

$$M_2(x, C) \wedge d(C) \sqsubseteq Q$$

This theorem directly follows from the definitions of subsumption and membership. Though being trivial, we include it for the sake of completeness. These considerations justify the use of description logic reasoners for answering Boolean concept queries.

6.2.3 Query re-writing

In the last section we described how information filtering with Boolean queries can be implemented using terminological reasoning. We showed that in our framework the problem of filtering relevant information can be reduced to subsumption reasoning. However, the approach assumed that the concept names used in the Boolean query are taken from the ontology of the information source that is queried, because the definitions of those concepts have to be known in order to determine subsumption relations. At this point, the re-classification results given in the last section come into play. The idea is to approximate the meaning of concepts in a query by its re-classification, i.e. by the upper and lower bounds in the other system (compare Sect. 6.1.3).

The adaption of a query to remote systems can be done in a three step process:

1. **Normalization:** the original query is transformed into negation normal form (see Definition 6.12).
2. **Re-writing:** the concept names in the query are replaced by their approximations in the remote source (this is done for each remote source individually).
3. **Classification:** the re-written query is classified into the ontology of the remote source and instances of subsumed concepts are returned as the result.

The transformation to negation normal form is necessary in order to decide whether a concept name has to be replaced by its lower or its upper bound. As argued in the first section of this chapter, negated concepts have to be replaced by their upper bound and non-negated ones by their lower bound in order to ensure the correctness of the query result. The negation normal form supports this process by revealing which concept names are negated and which not.

Definition 6.12 (negation normal form). *A query is said to be in negation normal form if negations only apply to concept names $c \in C$ and not to compound expressions.*

Every Boolean query can easily be transformed into negation normal form using the following equalities:

$$\neg(e_1 \wedge e_2) \equiv \neg e_1 \vee \neg e_2 \tag{6.3}$$
$$\neg(e_1 \vee e_2) \equiv \neg e_1 \wedge \neg e_2 \tag{6.4}$$

Once we have transformed the query, re-writing can be done locally on the concept names using the least upper and greatest lower bounds that have already been discussed in the last section:

Definition 6.13 (query re-writing). *The re-writing of a query Q in nega-tion normal form over concepts c_i from an information source IS_1 to a query Q' over concepts from another information source IS_2 is carried out as fol-lows:*

- *replace every negated concept name c by:* $\bigwedge\limits_{c' \in lub_{IS_2}(c)} c'$

- *replace every non negated concept name c by:* $\bigvee\limits_{c' \in glb_{IS_2}(c)} c'$

The re-writing and execution of a query can easily be implemented using exist-ing description logic reasoners. We have implemented the basic approximate-reclassification algorithm using RACER [Haarslev and Moeller, 2001]. The implementation is used in the BUSTER system (compare section 9.3). We can compute the re-writing using Algorithm 1 below. The input for the algorithm is the query to be re-written, the class names in C_2 and a terminological knowledge base including the definitions of the concepts in C_1 and C_2 as well as the shared ontology.

Algorithm 1 rewrite-query

Require: A Boolean query in negation normal form: Q
Require: A list of class names: N
Require: A terminological knowledge base T
　racer.in-tbox(T)
　for all t is an atomic term in Q **do**
　　if t is negated **then**
　　　$B[t] :=$ racer.directSupers(t)
　　　$B'[t] := B[t] \cap N$
　　　$Q(t) := (c_1 \wedge \cdots \wedge c_n)$ for $c_i \in B'[t]$
　　else
　　　$B[t] :=$ racer.directSubs(t)
　　　$B'[t] := B[t] \cap N$
　　　$Q(t) := (c_1 \vee \cdots \vee c_n)$ for $c_i \in B'[t]$
　　end if
　　$r(Q) :=$ **proc**　Replace t in Q by $Q(t)$
　end for
　return $r(Q)$

As the re-writing builds upon the approximations discussed in the last section we can guarantee that the result of the query is correct. Moreover, we can use subsumption reasoning in order to determine this result. To be more specific, a resource x is indeed a member of the query concept if membership can be proved for the re-written query.

Theorem 6.14 (correctness of re-writing). *The notion of query re-writing defined above is correct in the sense that:*

$$x : Q' \implies x^{\Im} \in Q^{\mathcal{I}}$$

The results proven in this section provide us with a tool to filter information items according to Boolean expressions across heterogeneous information sources provided that they use the architecture described in the second part of this book. We consider this a great advantages because the search for interesting information no longer has to be based on plain keywords, whose meaning is not precisely defined leading to problems concerning precision and recall.

Unfortunately, proving the correctness of the approximation says nothing about the quality of the approximation. In the worst case, the upper and lower boundaries of concepts in the other hierarchy are always $\top$ and $\bot$, respectively. In this case the translated query always returns the empty set as result. We were not able to investigate the quality of approximations on a theoretical level; however, we can provide some rules of thumb that can be used to predict the quality of an approximation:

- *Depths of hierarchies.* The first rule of thumb we can state is that deeper class hierarchies lead to better approximations. For hierarchies of depth one it is easy to see that we will not be able to find good upper and lower bounds. We can also assume that deeper hierarchies provide finer-grained distinctions between concepts that in turn often produce closer approximations.
- *Degree of overlap.* our approach assumes a shared vocabulary for building class definitions; however, we cannot guarantee that different systems indeed use the same parts of this shared vocabulary. Therefore, the actual overlap of terms used in the existing definitions that are compared is important for predicting the quality of approximations. In general, we can assume that a high degree of overlap leads to better approximations.

Both criteria used in the rules of thumb above strongly depend on the application and on the creator of the corresponding models. At least for the degree of overlap, we can assume that hierarchies that are concerned with the same domain of interest will share a significant part of the vocabulary, thus enabling us to compute reasonable approximations.

6.3 Processing complex queries

The results of the last section provide us with the possibility to compute a set of objects that are definitely members of a concept expression and a set of objects that are possibly members of a concept. This approach can directly be used to answer Boolean queries. This corresponds to an expressiveness similar to the capabilities of existing search engines. One of the main advantages of using semantic technology, however, is the ability to make use of semantic relations between objects. Using such relations in queries provides an expressiveness that clearly goes beyond the abilities of free-text querying. In this section, we show how the approach for approximate information filtering can be applied to more complex queries that also use relations between query variables. In particular, we consider conjunctive queries over ontologies.

6.3.1 Queries as concepts

In order to compute (approximate) answers for ontology-based conjunctive queries, however, we also have to deal with unary and binary predicates in the query expression that correspond to classes and relations from the ontology. Using the general notion of terminological knowledge provided in Sect. 3.1 we define complex queries in the following way.

Definition 6.15 (terminological queries). *Let V be a set of variables disjoint from $\mathcal{IN}$; then a terminological query Q over a knowledge base $\mathcal{T}$ is an expression of the form*

$$q_{1_i} \wedge \cdots \wedge q_{m_i}$$

where q_i are query terms of the form $x : c$ or $(x, y) : r$ such that $x, y \in V \cup \mathcal{IN}$, $C \in \mathcal{CN}$ and $R \in \mathcal{RN}$.

The following query is an example from the case study reported later in this chapter. The query asks for an accommodation of type hotel that lies in city in Mecklenburg (a part of Germany). Further it has to be located in a castle and have less than 25 rooms:

$$
\begin{aligned}
Q(X) \leftarrow{} & Hotel(X) \wedge liegt - in - Ort(X, V) \wedge liegt - in - land(X, W) \text{(6.5)} \\
& hat - Zimmer(X, Y) \wedge liegt - in - schloss(X, Z) \wedge \\
& W = meckelnburg \wedge Y \leq 25 \wedge Z = ja
\end{aligned}
$$

In order to cope with terminological queries as defined above, we use a method for translating conjunctive queries into concept expressions that has been proposed by Horrocks and Tessaris [Horrocks and Tessaris, 2000]. The idea of the approach of Horrocks and Tessaris is to translate the query into an equivalent concept expression, classify this new concept and use standard inference methods to check whether an object is an instance of the query expression. This approach makes use of the fact that binary relations in a conjunctive query can be translated into an existential restriction in such a way that logical consequence is preserved after a minor modification of the A-box. Details are given in the following theorem.

Theorem 6.16 (Role Roll-Up (Horrocks and Tessaris 2000)). *Let* $\langle C], \mathcal{R}, \mathcal{A} \rangle$ *be a description-logic knowledge base with concept definitions* C, *relation definitions* $\mathcal{R}$ *and assertions* A. *Let further* R *be a role,* C_I *concept names in* T *and* a, b *individual names in* A. *Given a new concept name* P_b *not appearing in* T, *then*

$$\langle C, \mathcal{R}, \mathcal{A} \rangle \models (a, b) : R \wedge b : C_1 \wedge \cdots \wedge b : C_k$$

if and only if

$$\langle C, \mathcal{R}, \mathcal{A} \cup \{b : P_b\} \rangle \models a : \exists R(P_b \sqcap C_1 \sqcap \cdots \sqcap C_k)$$

The transformation of a complete query is more difficult due to the dependencies between the variables that occur in the query expression. In order to keep track of these dependencies during the transformation Horrocks and Tessaris introduce the notion of a query graph.

Definition 6.17 (query graph (Horrocks and Tessaris 2000)). *The graph induced by a query is a directed graph with a node for every variable and individual name in the query and a directed edge from node* x *to node* y *for every role term* $(x, y) : R$ *in the query.*

The correct transformation of a query into a concept expression depends on the kinds of dependencies between the variables in the query, which is reflected in the structure of the query graph. While the approach of Horrocks and Tessaris is more general, we restrict ourselves to queries where the query graph is a (directed) tree and its root node corresponds to the variable we are interested in. Especially, this requires that none of the roles used in the query is declared to be functional and that each constant only appears once in a query. While using this simplification, we would like to emphasize that the translation can be done for unions of conjunctive queries with an arbitrary number of result variables and a very expressive logical language for defining class expressions. Our simplifying assumptions lead to a simple method for transforming a query graph into a concept expression.

Definition 6.18 (query roll-up (Horrocks and Tessaris 2000)). *The roll-up of a query* Q *with query tree* G *is a concept expression derived from* Q *by successively applying the following rule:*

- *If* G *contains a leaf node* y *then the role term* $(x,y):R$ *is rolled up according to definition 6.16. The edge* (x,y) *is removed from* G.

The result of applying this translation technique to an example query could be the following expression asking for hotels in Mecklenburg-Vorpommern that are located in a castle and have less than 25 rooms:

$$(Hotel \sqcap (\exists\, liegt - in - Ort.(\exists\, liegt - in - Land.\{mecklenburg\}))) \sqcap$$
$$(\exists\, hat - Zimmer.(\leq 25)) \sqcap$$
$$(\exists\, ist - in - Schloss.\{ja\})) \tag{6.6}$$

As this expression defines a new concept in the overall ontology we can now apply the approximation techniques described in the last section in order to compute the sets of possible and the set of definite answers to the query.

6.3.2 Query relaxation

In the presence of sparse mappings, we face a situation where the descriptions of different peers referring to the same real-world object can be significantly different. In most cases, the descriptions are different in the sense that different relations are used to relate the same object to other objects in the domain. These relations may refer to the same properties of the object that cannot be matched due to a missing mapping or the set of properties itself used might be different. As a consequence, real-world objects that are meant to be an answer to a query are not returned because their description does not match the query that is formulated using terms from a different ontology. We address this problem by relaxing the query, i.e. by weakening those constraints from the query expression that are responsible for the failure. In order to be useful, this weakening process has to fulfill certain formal properties. Especially, we want to make sure that we do not lose any answers when modifying the query. We can guarantee this using the notion of query subsumption as described by Halevy:

Definition 6.19 (query containment and equivalence (Halevy 2001)).
Let $\mathcal{T} = \langle \mathcal{C}, \mathcal{R}, \mathcal{O} \rangle$ and let Q_1, Q_2 be conjunctive queries over $\mathcal{T}$. Q_1 is said to be contained in another query Q_2, denoted by $Q_1 \sqsubseteq Q_2$, if for all possible sets of object definitions of a terminological knowledge base the answer for Q_1 is a subset of the answer for Q_2 : $(\forall \mathcal{O} : res(Q_1) \subseteq res(Q_2))$. The two queries are said to be equivalent, denoted as $Q_1 \equiv Q_2$, iff $Q_1 \sqsubseteq Q_2$ and $Q_2 \sqsubseteq Q_1$.

Based on these notions we compute a sequence of queries $Q_0, ..., Q_n$ such that the following properties hold:

1. $Q_0 \equiv Q$
2. $i < j \Longrightarrow Q_i \sqsubseteq Q_j$

The intuition behind this approach is to start with the original query and generate queries where each is more general than the one before, i.e. each query following in the sequence returns all results of the previous one, but might return more results. Our hope is that these new results contain the description of some real-world objects that should be answers, but were not found due to their description.

There are many different ways of making a query more general in order to increase the chance of matching a potential answer. In the following we discuss relaxation heuristics we consider useful for the purpose of query processing in a peer-to-peer setting.

Variable elimination

The first heuristic is based on the fact that each variable in a conjunctive query might fail to match a specific object if the object does not satisfy the constraints. Therefore, a way of increasing the chance of matching the target object in the head of the query is to successively eliminate non-answer variables from the query. In the example query in Equation 6.6 for example, we have the variables V, W, X, Y and Z, where X is the answer variable. Therefore we can weaken query by eliminating the variables V, W, Y and Z. This can be done by removing all conjuncts containing a specific variable from the query expression. It is easy to see that successively removing conjuncts from the query leads to a sequence of queries with the desired properties.

The main question that arises when adopting the variable-elimination approach is the order in which the variables should be removed from the query. This order is partially constrained by the dependencies between the different variables. Removing the wrong variable first can break these dependencies and make the remaining conjuncts useless. Looking at the example query this would happen if we first removed the variable Y. In this case the conjunct $V = mecklenburg$ would be isolated, because the variable V only occurred in the removed conjuncts that connected it to the answer variable. In order to avoid breaking dependencies when removing conjuncts, we can use the query graph of the query to be relaxed (compare Definition 6.17) as it explicates existing dependencies. In the query graph dependencies between variables are represented by arcs between nodes. Therefore, we have to ensure that the query graphs remains connected when removing the node that represents the variable we want to eliminate. Obviously, this is only the case if we eliminate variables that correspond to leaf nodes in the graph. Fig. 6.3 illustrates the successive elimination of the variables V, Y, Z and W from the example query, showing the corresponding sequence of query graphs.

Guided elimination

The major drawback of the variable-elimination heuristic as explained so far is the high number of arbitrary choices that still exist in the order of elimination. More specifically, whenever the query tree has more than one leaf node, we have no strategy yet to decide which one to eliminate. In general, there are many possibilities for defining ordering heuristics, based on:

1. The nature of the domain.

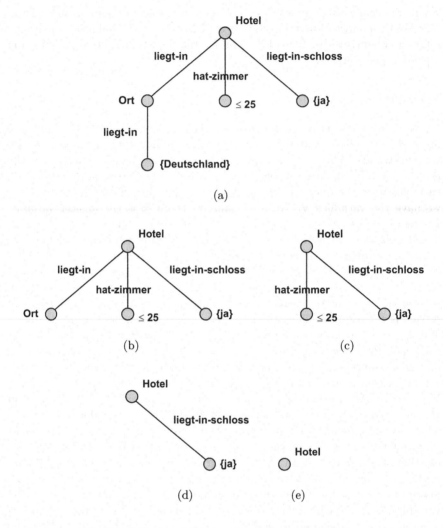

Fig. 6.3. A possible sequence of query graphs

2. The preferences of the user.
3. The task to be solved.

As our approach does not aim at a specific domain, user or task, we will have to rely on rather general heuristics being aware that they will never be optimal. In our case, the only information we can use to decide on an elimination order is the existence of local mappings that relate the query vocabulary to the shared one that is actually used to compute the answer. The general idea is that we would rather drop conjuncts that represent concepts or relations without a suitable mapping into the shared ontology, because they can never be satisfied by any object classified according to that ontology. We have seen that for the case of concepts, we can often find a suitable approximation even if there is no direct counterpart in the shared ontology. Therefore, we focus on conjuncts representing relations and eliminate such variables first that are constrained by a relational conjunct that has no direct mapping to the shared ontology. The effect of this strategy is illustrated in the next section where we describe some experiments with approximating concepts and relaxing queries in a case study.

6.4 Examples from a case study

We performed a case study in order to validate the methods described above. The case study is based on three different ontologies in the domain of tourism. The ontologies are available in the DAML ontology library (`www.daml.org`) and have been created by independent groups of students at the University of Karlsruhe. All ontologies aim at describing the conceptualization of an Internet site that is advertising tourism in north-east Germany. All ontologies contain information about accommodation, tourist attractions and transportation facilities. While sharing these general topics, the different ontologies describe them in a very different way focusing on different parts of the overall domain. We chose these ontologies, because they very closely resemble the situation we expect in a peer-to-peer network, where peers model information about the same domain in different ways.

In the course of our case study, we imported the ontologies, each containing about 300 concepts and 50 to 70 relations, into an ontology editor using some syntactic transformations. We then analyzed the ontologies and created about 150 obvious mappings using simple string matching. In this way we created mappings mostly between concepts that have exactly the same name and between concepts where one name is the plural form of the other. Based on these mappings we computed two overlapping concept hierarchies consisting of about 600 concepts each. These hierarchies served as the basis for evaluating our concept approximation and query relaxation techniques. In the following, we describe examples of concept-approximation and of query-relaxation with respect to this hierarchy.

6.4.1 Concept approximations

As an example of concept approximation we use the concept "Ferien-Wohnung" (a flat used as accommodation during holidays). The relevant part of the overall hierarchy can be seen in Fig. 6.4. We can see that concepts from private and shared ontologies occur in this part of the hierarchy (The private concepts are shaded).

The approximations we are interested in are the direct sub- and superclasses of tourism example concept that are not from the same ontology. We can see in the figure that these are: "Bungalow" and "Appartment". If we look at the view of Peer B on the World we see also that the concept "Ferienhaus" (house used during holiday) would fall under this category. While this result is not completely true, because houses are not flats, it still serves the purpose very well, because all of the concepts describe accommodations that are reasonable replacements in the case that no flat is available.

If we determine the upper approximation of the example concept, we get the general concept "Unterkunft" (accommodation). Our method now determines all instances of this general concept to be potential members of the example concept. Besides the members of the already mentioned concepts, this also includes objects that are members of the concepts "Hotel" and "Campingplatz" (camp site) in the view of the answering peer B. We see, that these results are still closely related to the example concept, because they are all accommodations mainly used during holidays; however, hotels and camp sites are not really the kind of answer the user would assume to get when asking for a flat. Still, returning hotels and camp sites as answers to a query for a flat is still better than not returning any result, because the user might want to change her choice in favor of other preferences (e.g. the location).

6.4.2 Query relaxation

As an example for query relaxation, we take the example query. If we transform this query into a concept expression (Equation 6.6) and classify it into the overall concept hierarchy of the case study, it end up as a subconcept of "Schlosshotel" (castle acting as a hotel). Computing the answer to the query we get an empty set, because there are no instances of "Schlosshotel" satisfying all properties of the query concept. Using the upper bound, however, we already get the members of the concept "Schlosshotel". If we do not want to rely on this result, we have to analyze the reason for the failure of returning definite answers. Looking at the ontologies in the case study, we see that none of the ontologies except for the one the query is based on contains information about the number of rooms of a hotel, which makes it impossible to prove that a specific hotel is an answer to the query. As a response to this observation, we relax the query by removing the restriction on the number of rooms. This leads to a situation where we already get some definite results, namely those members of the concept "Schlosshotel" that satisfy the requirement of being in the federal state of Mecklenburg. Note that this provides us with a better result than the use of the upper bound, because we already have a preselection of results according to the geographic criterion.

The ability to retrieve relevant information using this second query relied on the fact that the ontology describing the information defines the concept

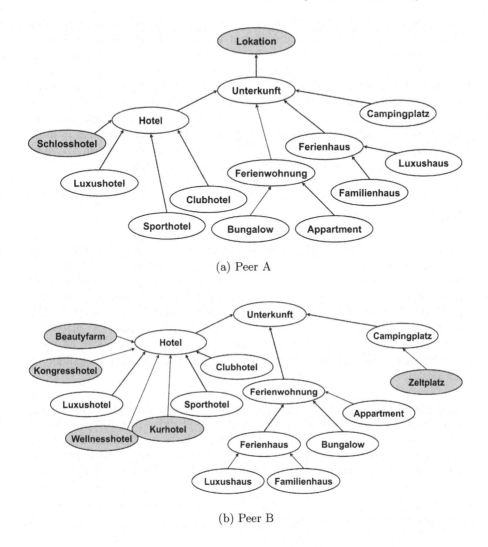

(a) Peer A

(b) Peer B

Fig. 6.4. The views of two different peers of the same domain

"Schlosshotel" as the set of all hotels for which the property "liegt-in-Schloss" (is located in a castle) is true. We were able to use this implicit information about the specific relation in order to retrieve information without having an explicit assertion stating that a hotel has this specific property. In a case where the ontology does not contain the necessary information, we would still get no results for the relaxed query, because the property "liegt-in-Schloss" is not satisfied by any information item. In this case we can again use the upper bound for answering the query, which would now be the concept "Hotel".

Consequently, we would get all hotels as potential answers. Again, this result is too general, as we want to preserve at least the geographic constraint. A solution is to further relax the query by removing the "liegt-in-Schloss" property from the query. The resulting query will match all hotels in the federal estate of Mecklenburg. Admittedly, this result is not a very good one; however, it resembles the functionality of many current Web-based information systems, where lists of hotels can be accessed by selecting a specific area. We would like to stress that our approach leads to more precise answers in most cases, especially if the queries are not too complicated, and we only have to fall back on very imprecise results if all other attempts fail.

6.5 Conclusions

While the idea of maximizing precision and recall by using concept expressions in Boolean queries is appealing, the practical application in information sharing suffers from the fact that there will not be "the one" ontology that is used to classify information. We will rather face a situation, where a multitude of classification hierarchies organize different or even the same information according to different discrimination principles. A successful information-filtering approach will have to make use of as many of these ontologies as possible. This claim raises the problem of comparing different ontologies.

While description logics allow us to reason about the relation between concepts a problem that still persists is the fact that different source ontologies will almost never contain concepts with exactly the same meaning. Therefore, we cannot exactly map concepts from two information sources on each other. However, following the idea of theory approximation we can use upper and lower bounds to get mapping results that can be proven to be correct in the sense that they provide maximal precision, but not completeness (i.e. the recall cannot be guaranteed to be maximal).

This approximate mapping approach can also be used to contribute to the problem of finding relevant information in different information sources. We can answer Boolean queries over concept names by replacing unknown concept names by their lower bound in the corresponding source ontology. The resulting query can be processed in the context of the remote information source, delivering a query result that can be proven to be a correct approximation of the intended result.

We conclude that approximation techniques for processing queries and for logical reasoning in general are important in weakly structured and heterogeneous environments such as the World Wide Web, because they can be used to partly overcome semantic heterogeneity that is omnipresent.

Further reading

Visser and others [Visser et al., 1998] discuss the problem of ontology heterogeneity and classify different kinds of mismatch. Beeri and others [Beeri et al., 1997] show that the problem of re-writing queries over terminological knowledge is undecidable in the general case. The idea of using upper and lower approximations for logical theories is presented in [Selman and Kautz, 1996]. Horrocks and Tessaris [Horrocks and Tessaris, 2000] describe a method for reducing query answering to concept classification. An approach similar to the one presented here is reported in [Mena et al., 2000b].

7

Sharing statistical information

Summary. In the last chapter, we introduced a number of basic techniques for retrieving and integrating heterogeneous information sources. In this chapter, we report an application of some of these techniques in a project on the integration of European fishery statistics. We identify the special characteristics of statistical information and focus on the use of the Web Ontology Language for representing statistical information and for retrieving information based on a semantic description.

Statistics are indispensable for political decision making. Economic, demographic and environmental statistics are used for monitoring social and physical processes and for measuring policy effectiveness. National governments usually have organized statistical services in order to fulfill their demand for decision support. At supranational level, and even at national level, homogeneous statistics are often not available. So, for supranational economic research and policy evaluation, heterogeneous statistics from a variety of independent sources must be integrated. In integration of statistics, all general problems known from other areas of information integration occur, such as ontological and notational differences and differences in units of measurement and typology. In addition there are some specific problems in the integration of statistics. The first class of problems specific for statistics are differences in the population, e.g. differences in the threshold for inclusion of objects. For example, does a boat with engine power less than 20 hp count as a fishing vessel? A second class of problems are differences in reported statistics, e.g. sum vs. average. Further, there are classification differences, e.g. age classes bounded by 20, 35, 50 and 65 years vs. 15, 35 and 55 year; length vs. gross register tonnage as vessel size indicator; differences in nomenclature. In order to overcome these heterogeneities, we often need background information like the correlation between the membership in different classes. In order to find and compare such statistics with needed information, we need to be able to formally describe the domain ontology underlying a statistic and the statistical information itself. For these purposes we need an ontology of statistical terms and a framework for describing, comparing and translating the domain ontologies of heterogeneous statistical tables. Fig. 7.1 shows an example of a statistical table that will be used in the remainder of this chapter.

Table 7.1. Summary of the German fleet's catch in 2000

Zone	Grosse Hoch-seefischerei	Ab 20m	10 bis 19,99m	Bis 9,99m	Gesamte kleine Hochsee und Kuestenfischerei	Gesamte Kutter und Hochseefischerei
EG	93.932,0	53.258,2	30.222,0	6.268,3	89.748,5	183.680,5
A	7.966,5	0,2	0,8	0,0	1,0	7.967,5
FAR	0,0	213,4	0,0	0,0	213,4	213,4
NF	2.995,3	0,0	0,0	0,0	0,0	2995,3
NFGD	1.924,5	0,0	0,0	0,0	0,0	1.924,5
GD	5.005,6	0,0	0,0	0,0	0,0	5.005,6
IS	0,0	659,6	0,0	0,0	659,6	659,5
EST				0,0	0,0	
LET				0,0	0,0	
LIT				0,0	0,0	
NN	2.564,1	0,0	0,0	0,0	0,0	2.564,1
NSP	2.206,0	0,0	0,0	0,0	0,0	2.206,0
MAU	0,0	0,0	0,0	0,0	0,0	0,0
Gesamt:	116.594,0	54.131,4	30.222,8	6.268,3	90.622,5	207.216,5

In this chapter, we first discuss the special nature of statistical information that has to be taken into account when trying to integrate and share it and present a core ontology os statistical information. We then introduce a framework for modelling statistical information using OWL for capturing the ontology of statistics and combining it with domain concepts as well as data items to be shared. We explain the different features of the representation using the example of European fishery statistics and show the benefits of this representation with respect to the retrieval of information using conjunctive queries.

7.1 The nature of statistical information

Before we can define a representation for statistical data, we first have to get a better understanding of the nature of the information we have to capture. For this purpose we adopt the abstract model of statistical data described in [Sundgren, 1995]. Following this model, we first have to distinguish statistical microdata and macrodata. The former refers to the actual observations that have been made about single objects in the World (statistical units) and their properties at a certain point in time (e.g. the salary of a person in a certain month). It can be modelled as a list of quadruples: object, property, value, time point or interval. Each of these quadruples forms an elementary message. A number of messages form a statistical register of observations about some phenomenon of interest. A register is the basis for generating aggregated information about a population of objects, also called macrodata. Note that a register is intended to represent a population, but that it is not identical: the register may be a sample or some other incomplete selection. The generated macrodata are estimates of the actual values of population properties. At large the process of statistics involves the following activities: (1) identify the objects to be included in the register; (2) observe the objects and enter observed values into the register and (3) process register data to obtain estimates for the population or cross classifications. The first two activities result in the production of microdata. The third activity results in macrodata. Models for describing statistical information systems are given by [Catarci et al., 1998] and [De Giacomo and Naggar, 1996].

7.1.1 Statistical metadata

When we talk about statistical tables, we always refer to aggregated information. Therefore, a general model of macrodata is needed as a foundation for modelling these statistics. Because microdata are in most cases not available for end users, from the user's perspective the model should abstractly describe the table contents, in stead of the statistical information system that produced them. Such a general model has four components that will be discussed in the following.

The reference population

Macrodata always refers to the characteristics of a set of objects. This set of objects, called a population, is important in order to draw conclusions about the relevance for a specific question. Statistics are often used in order to compare two different populations without having to compare single objects. Further, correlation between the values of two properties can only be established if the statistics refer to the same population. The population of statistical macro-data is described by a set of criteria that hold for all objects in the population. These criteria include the type of objects under consideration (e.g. employed persons). Often the type criterion is combined with other criteria, in particular geographic constraints (employed persons in central Europe) or combinations of different type constraints (e.g. employed females).

Aggregation criteria

(Cross-classifications) In most cases statistics do not consider a population as a whole, but define additional aggregation criteria that split the underlying population into a number of disjoint, exhaustive subgroups. The values for each of the subgroups are determined independently and can be compared in order to make assertions about the specific group. Aggregation criteria again can be very different, the only restriction is that they cross-classify the population. We find aggregation criteria related to the type of objects (male vs. female employees, age groups), the geographic location (inhabitants of different federal states) or time (months of a year). The aggregation criteria are especially important when the statistic is intended to be used to answer a particular question (e.g. are female employees discriminated with respect to their salary ?).

Aggregation operator

The next important aspect is the method used in order to aggregate the values of the observed property in the different subgroups. Its function is to abstract from the properties of individual objects. It serves as a means for normalizing and abstracting the observations contained in the microdata. This method can range from a simple count of the objects in a subgroup to complex aggregation functions. The concrete function depends on the nature of the observed property. Often, the values of a considered property is a numerical value. In this case the aggregation function can be defined by any mathematical formulas mapping a set of numbers onto a single one. Typical examples of aggregation functions beside the count are the sum, the average and the median of a set of values.

The time frame

Properties of objects often change over time. Therefore, it is important to consider the time frame in which the microdata a statistic is based on has been acquired. It is also relevant for comparing the properties of different populations on the basis of the same time frame or the same population in different periods of time. There are two different aspects in the definition of the time frame. The first is the beginning and the end of the observation period and the second is the frequency and the time points for which data has been acquired (once, monthly, yearly,...). Both aspects are relevant when trying to compare two statistics. In the case of different frequencies, the results of the statistic that is based on more frequent observations can still be aggregated to match the other given that the other aspects are the same.

7.1.2 A basic ontology of statistics

The general data model of statistical data is the data matrix, the rows representing objects of interest, the columns representing attributes (properties) of the objects. For microdata, the rows represent statistical units and the columns represent observed variables. For macrodata, the rows represent classes of statistical units and the columns represent estimators of population properties. Statistical methods are generic. They map data matrices to data matrices. The semantics of the data matrices is in the meaning we give to the rows and the columns, and in the definition of the represented population. For reasoning about statistics, we need an ontology of statistical terms – referring to the generic properties of data matrices and statistical operators – and an ontology of the domain described by the statistics. The statistical ontology should provide the framework for relating statistical knowledge to the domain ontology by giving definitions of reference populations, their properties and cross-classifications (compare [Grossmann, 2002]). Statistical metadata literature emphasizes three main properties that describe statistical tables: the population represented by the table, the population characteristics represented by the data content and the variables used to cross-classify the population. Some models have an explicit notion of time ([Sundgren, 1995], [Grossmann, 2002]), while others ([Catarci et al., 1998]) rely on explicit modelling of time as a cross-classifying variable. Where temporal awareness is included in the model, it has two roles: (1) as a validity label of metadata definitions and (2) as a time-coverage label for the data. In some models there is a more or less formal definition of the classes used for cross-classifying the data, but the population is taken as primitive in most models: there is a slot for specifying a textual definition, but no formal definition of population constraints. For integration purposes a formal specification is necessary because we need to reason about populations and differences between them, in contrast with the statistical production process where the population is given. Denk and Froeschl [Denk and Froeschl, 2000] treat temporal as well as geographic coverage as a special variable category. They define a request template for a table to be mediated from heterogeneous macrodata sources, with clauses for specification of: the mediated source table, the estimator to report, geographical constraint, temporal constraint, cross classification, and additional constraints. The template does not explicitly specify the population or the type of statistical units. The definition of the population to report about is hidden in the constraints part of the request specification and is implicitly bounded by the available sources.

While the general aspects are assumed to be the same for any source of statistical information, the domain-specific aspects may be different. This corresponds to the basic distinction between ontology (a shared conceptualization of a specific subject matter) and context (a subjective view of a domain). In this section, we concentrate on those aspects of statistical information that are the same across different domains and define a basic ontology of statistical information. This ontology will provide the backbone for modelling statistical information in different contexts.

Statistical Units and Attributes

The basis of statistical information is the notion of a "statistical unit" which refers to an individual object in the domain of discourse. These objects have certain "attributes" that provide input to the generation of aggregated information. The value of a specific attribute of a statistical unit is referred to as an "observation". Observations are further defined by the unit and the scale they are measured in. Both, unit and scale are defined in the particular context the statistic has to be interpreted in.

We can further distinguish between different types of attributes that demand a different treatment due to their conceptual nature. A basic distinction is between qualitative and quantitative attributes. Quantitative attributes often contain the information that is presented in an aggregated way by the statistics. Qualitative attributes are often used as a grouping criterion for statistical units. Specific types of qualitative attributes are classifications and spatial attributes further defined in the context of the statistics.

Classes and estimates

A fundamental property of statistics is that they do not provide information about individual objects, but abstracted information about groups of objects sharing some common property. In our basic ontology of statistics, such groups of objects are referred to as "classes". We distinguish interval classes and nominal classes. Mutually exclusive lists of classes, used for discriminating and grouping of statistical units, are called "classifications".

Classes can have a special role in statistical datasets, namely as a "reference population", the set of all statistical units that are described by the statistics. In a register a population is normally represented by a subset of statistical units – e.g. a random sample – whose attribute values have actually been observed. A register may contain special attributes for identification of the statistical units, that will never be included in statistical tables.

The actual numbers contained in a statistical table represent the result of applying a certain statistical "operator" to the values of one or more particular attribute of all members of the population. The particular attribute that is observed for a complete population or subclass of it is called a statistical indicator. The result of aggregating the observations is called an estimate. The connection between an estimate and a particular context is established via the definition of the classes involved and via the statistical indicator that is based on attributes of objects in the domain.

The ontology

Based on the terminology used in the statistical domain explained above, we formalized a basic ontology of statistics that is shown in Fig. 7.1. We start from the basic idea of a data source as a data matrix. Correspondingly, we describe information sources by the three elements of a data matrix: the statistical attributes it describes (the columns), the classification used to aggregate information (the rows) and the observation it contains (the actual entries of the matrix). The corresponding classes of the ontology are connected to the classes of information sources using the relations *contains* for the observations, *based-on* for the classification and *describes* for the statistical attribute. Further, each information source refers to a class of objects that act as a population.

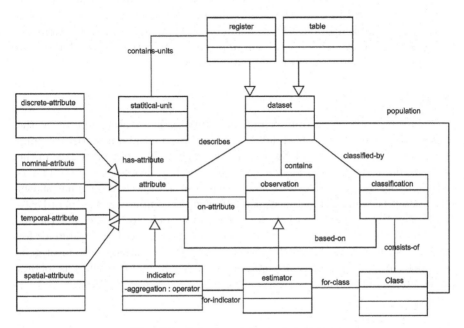

Fig. 7.1. A basic ontology of statistics

We distinguish registers and tables as special types of data sources. While registers contain information about individual objects (the classification consists of one class per object), tables contain aggregated information for classes of objects. Entries containing this aggregated information are special observations called estimators. They refer to a class of objects and describe a statistical indicator rather than a statistical attribute. Indicators are special kinds of attributes that include the notion of an aggregation operator (e.g. total income or average age).

This ontology is not meant to provide a complete conceptual model of all phenomena in statistics. It is rather a core model with the specific purpose to support the process of sharing statistical information. In the following section, we will show how the ontology can be used to provide a general structure for modelling and finding statistical data.

7.2 Modelling Statistics

The basic statistics ontology described above provides us with a domain-independent vocabulary for describing information in statistical tables. In particular, the different elements of a table correspond to the terms introduced. The columns of a table correspond to statistical indicators, the rows to classes and the actual numbers in the table are estimators of a certain indicator with respect to a class of statistical units. The union of all classes in a table is assumed to cover the underlying population. Further, the classes in the rows of a table are defined by a common observation of a certain attribute. A question that remains open is an appropriate structure to combine these elements into a description of a statistical table.

7.2.1 Statistics as views

A promising approach is to interpret the estimator in a statistical table as the answer to a query to a virtual database of observations about statistical units (compare [De Giacomo and Naggar, 1996]). The main problem we face in the integration of these query answers is that we do not have access to the underlying virtual database. Nevertheless, research in database systems has shown that under certain circumstances it is sufficient to compare queries in order to make assertions about the relation of two result sets [Calvanese et al., 1998a]. The ontology described in the last section provides us with a vocabulary for defining such queries. Using the terms defined in the ontology the most general description of an entry in a statistical table can be formulated as follows using an SQL-like syntax:

```
SELECT
    indicator
FROM
    population
WHERE
    class = ...
```

An example of how this pattern describes different values would be: select the total catch of the German fishing fleet in 2000 where the size class is 20 to 50 meters and the fishing are is the Irish Sea. In this example, total catch is the indicator that is estimated. The population consists of all fishing vessels of German nationality that had been registered in the year 2000. The size class and the fishing area define classes that have been used to aggregate objects and estimate the value for the indicator.

We can immediately see that the initial format for describing estimators needs to be refined. In particular, the description of the population and the classes can be refined as they are defined using restrictions on the observation of a certain statistical attribute such as the nationality. The actual description would therefore rather look as follows:

```
SELECT total-catch
FROM
    nationality = German
    year = 2000
WHERE
    size-class = [10m, 20m]
    fishing-area = is
```

Another thing we notice is that the SELECT and the FROM part of the view are the same for an information source in most cases. In the unlikely case that a table contains more than one indicator, we can easily see it as being two information sources with the same population and cross-classification. In order to reduce the modelling effort necessary to describe a set of information sources, we also model the complete data source and explicitly connect the description of single estimators to the description of the table they are contained in. We further include information about the classification in the description of the source. A corresponding description has the following format:

```
Source1:
    SELECT indicator
    FROM
        population
    GROUP-BY
        class_1, class_2, ...

Estimator1:
    SELECT *
    FROM
        Source1
    Where
        class = class_n
```

This way of modelling assumes a number of constraints that must hold amongst the descriptions of information sources and their content. The classes named in the descriptions of the information sources are assumed to completely cross-classify the population; therefore, all classes must describe strict subsets of the population. Further, the estimator is indirectly typed by the select statement of the source description. Finally, the classes mentioned in the description of the estimators have to correspond with the classes mentioned in the grouping, and their descriptions have to be consistent with the cross-classification constraint mentioned above. We will come back to these constraints when describing how to formalize and reason about descriptions in the next section.

7.2.2 Connection with the domain

As mentioned above, a complete description of statistical information has to combine statistical and domain-specific terminology and background knowledge. As the statistical part of the terminology has already been covered, we now turn our attention to domain-modelling aspects and their combination with the notions introduced above.

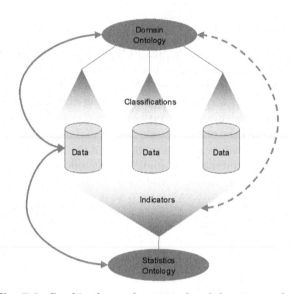

Fig. 7.2. Combined use of statistical and domain ontology

The general strategy for connecting the statistics ontology with the domain is by means of the view definitions above. In particular, the statistics ontology provides the general schema for describing data; the domain ontology is used to describe the concrete definitions of the population and classifications. Another point of connection is the definition of indicators as they mix domain vocabulary (e.g. catch) with general statistical terms (e.g. average or total) thereby connecting the ontologies. Fig. 7.2 sketches the combined use of statistical and domain ontologies in modelling statistics.

As indicated in Fig. 7.2, the domain ontology mainly provides the definitions of classes used in the different tables. Here we assume that a general domain ontology provides a shared vocabulary and the different classifications use terms from this general domain ontology. This enables us to use the techniques described in Chap. 6 to translate between different classification thus guaranteeing interoperability of data sources. Elements in the different data sources are linked to the domain specific classifications. At the same time they are linked to the general ontology of statistics (bold arrows). The link to the domain is mainly established through the notion of a statistical attribute which normally refers to a property of domain objects specified in the domain ontology. In our model this connection is made by the definition of a hierarchy of indicators linking domain relations to concepts in the statistical model. In order to clarify the connection between the models we use the ontology of the fishery displayed in Fig. 7.3.

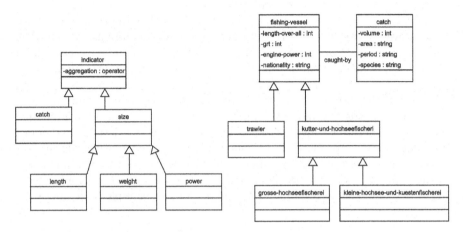

Fig. 7.3. Domain ontology of the fishery domain

In the ontology we see that the two central concepts we are concerned with in the fishery domain are fishing vessels and catch. The two concepts are connected by the *caught-by* relation. Further, each of the concepts has a number of attributes that describe the individual objects of the domain. In principle, each of these attributes can also act as a statistical variable and can therefore be the basis for defining classes and for indicators and corresponding estimates. In the example used to introduce the modelling notation for estimates, for example, the attribute length is used to define a class of vessels while the attribute volume is the basis for the statistical variable total catch.

In order to link domain relations to statistical indicators, we introduce a hierarchy of indicators rooted at the statistical concept *has-indicator*. Certain objects in the domain can be linked to certain indicators using the has-indicator relation. In the fishery domain, fishing vessels are the domain objects that are linked to indicators. As vessels are often aggregated based on size classes, size indicators are of central interest here. We can also define special size indicators such as length, power and weight. These specific indicators can now directly be linked to domain relations. We do this using mapping rules from domain relations to indicators. For our example, these mappings look as follows:

$$has - indicator(x, length) \leftarrow length - over - all(x, y)$$
$$has - indicator(x, power) \leftarrow engine - power(x, y)$$
$$has - indicator(x, weight) \leftarrow grt(x, y)$$

In order to be able to make use of these mapping rules, we have to design the description of data sources in such a way that we actually derive the existence of indicators in a source. In particular, this means that the rule bodies have to be derivable from the descriptions of tables and observations. At the same time, we have to make sure that the descriptions are expressive enough to capture the domain semantics implicitly contained in the information.

It turns out that for describing the data sources from a domain point of view, we can stay inside the metaphor of statistics as views by using conjunctive queries for describing object classes. More specifically, we describe the population of a data source as well as the classes used for aggregating information in terms of a query over the domain ontology that would return all members of the population or the class if we had access to a database with all objects in the domain. The corresponding definitions for the example table above are the following:

$$population(source1, X) \leftarrow nationality(X, german),$$
$$caught - by(Y, X), period(Y, 2000)$$
$$for - class(estimator1, X) \leftarrow length - over - all(X, Y), Y > 10, Y < 20,$$
$$caught - by(Z, X), area(Z, ire)$$

This way of describing has several advantages. First of all conjunctive queries are a natural formalism for defining queries, as it is the underlying model for languages like SQL. Therefore, it fits naturally in our modelling syntax. The corresponding description of our example would look as follows:

```
Source1:
    SELECT total-catch of X
    FROM
        nationality(X,german),
        caught-by(Y,X), period(Y,2000)

Estimator1:
    SELECT X
    FROM
        Source1
    Where
        length-over-all,
        Y > 10, Y < 20,
        caught-by(Z,X),
        area(Z,is)
```

By restricting the predicates allowed in the queries to a domain ontology, we can provide guidance for modelling populations and classes. The corresponding ontology can also provide additional background knowledge about the intended meaning of classes and hidden dependencies like the one between domain relations and indicators described above. Finally, as we have seen in Sect. 6.3.1, we can translate conjunctive queries over ontologies into concept expressions and use existing description-logic reasoners to retrieve answers. In the following section we will describe how the description of complete tables can be translated into OWL. Based on this translation we can provide a number of reasoning services for information integration and retrieval that will be described afterwards.

7.3 Translation to Semantic Web languages

There are at least two reasons for translating the semantic descriptions of statistical data sources into Semantic Web languages. The first reason is the ability to publish these semantic descriptions on the Web. This enables other people to locate them and decide whether the information contained in a source is relevant for them. This does not only save the overhead of downloading and checking large amounts of data, it also supports the commercial exploitation of statistical data. Companies whose business is to sell statistical data can make all relevant information available without actually publishing data they want to sell. Potential customers of such companies get the possibility to better check whether an information source meets their information needs without having to buy it. The second reason is the availability of reasoning services for Semantic Web languages that we can use for retrieving and integrating statistical information based on their semantic description.

While an actual online version of the semantic description would be in the RDF-based version of the OWL syntax, we use the abstract syntax defined in [Patel-Schneider et al., 2002b] to illustrate the way our modelling framework can be encoded in OWL. This encoding basically consists of two parts. The first is the representation of the underlying ontologies. It can be done in a straightforward way as OWL is intended to capture this kind of knowledge. The second part is the representation of the statistical information itself. Here we use complex typing axioms that are rather untypical for Web ontologies in order to capture the underlying domain constructs. Both parts of the description will be explained in the following.

7.3.1 Ontologies

As mentioned before, the ontological knowledge used to model statistical information consists of two parts. The first one is the generic ontology of statistics described in Sect. 7.1.2. The other part is an ontology of the domain that is used to give the information contained in a table a domain-related semantics.

Statistical ontology

The core notions of the statistical ontology can be described by a set of concepts representing datasets and their content (compare Fig. 7.1). We model these concepts as OWL classes:

```
Class(DataSet)
Class(Observation}
Class(StatisticalAttribute)
Class(Classification)
Class(Class)
```

The basic relations between these classes that link for example a dataset to its population are modelled as properties that link dataset objects to population objects. The latter fact is captured by restrictions on the range and domain of the properties. Further, we capture the fact that the population of a dataset is unique by declaring the corresponding property to be functional.

```
ObjectProperty(population
               domain(DataSet)
               range(Class)
               Functional)
```

The same is done for the other basic relation in Fig. 7.1. The fact that there are special cases of the general notion of datasources, observations and statistical attributes can be captured by the SubClassOf relation. The corresponding subclass relations shown in Fig. 7.1 are represented as follows.

```
SubClassOf(Table DataSet) SubClassOf(Register DataSet)
SubClassOf(DiscreteAttribute StatisticalAttribute)
SubClassOf(NominalAttribute StatisticalAttribute)
SubClassOf(StatisticalIndicator StatisticalAttribute)
SubClassOf(Estimator Observation)
```

In the concrete modelling of statistics, we are often interested in these subclasses as they represent the concrete cases we find in the data. The same holds for relations defined between the more concrete classes. In particular, the following two relations are used because they establish a connection to the domain ontology by relating estimators to indicators and classes of objects.

```
ObjectProperty(forIndicator
               domain(Estimator)
               range(StatisticalIndicator)
               Functional)

ObjectProperty(forClass
```

```
domain(Estimator)
range(Class)
Functional)
```

Before showing how the connection is made, we first introduce the representation of the fishery domain ontology used in our example.

The fishery domain

The basic objects we talk about in the fishery domain are fishing vessels and their properties. In order to be able to do so we introduce the class of fishing vessels and datatype properties for capturing relevant properties of vessels such as length, engine power and gross registry tonnage, etc.

```
Class(FishingVessel)

ObjectProperty(nationality
                domain(FishingVessel)
                range(Country))

DatatypeProperty(lengthOverAll
                domain(FishingVessel))

DatatypeProperty(enginePower
                domain(FishingVessel))

DatatypeProperty(grt domain(FishingVessel))
```

The second central part is the information about the amount of fish caught by fishing vessels. This information cannot be represented in a single number (it depends for example on a period of time and the fishing area). We therefore introduce catch as a class which enables us to talk about catch object related to vessels and having certain properties, the volume of catch being amongst them.

```
ObjectProperty(caughtIn
                domain(Catch)
                range(fishingArea))

ObjectProperty(caughtBy
                domain(Catch)
                range(fishingVessel)
                InverseOf(caught))

DatatypeProperty(volume
                domain(Catch))
```

Vessel classes

While classes are atomic objects from the point of view of the statistical ontology, they actually have a deeper meaning in terms of domain objects and their properties. The use of OWL enables us to make this meaning explicit in terms of class definitions. These definitions can also be used for semantic integration and filtering as described in Sects. 6.1.3 and 6.2.

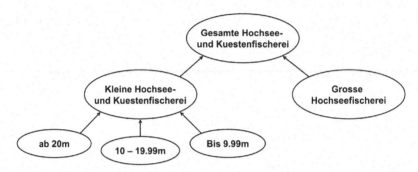

Fig. 7.4. Classification hierarchy of German fishing vessels

The German fishery statistics is a good example for the existence of domain-related semantics of object classes. German vessels are organized in a hierarchy of classes shown in Fig. 7.4. The names of the classes at the bottom of the hierarchy already indicate that the classification of vessels is based on the length. Using the *lengthOverAll* property of vessels defined in the domain we can formally express the intended meaning of the classes using property restrictions on the length property:

```
Datatype(<10)
Datatype(10-20)
Datatype(20-50)
Datatype(>50)

EquivalentClasses(grosseHochseeFischerei
                  restriction(lengthOverAll
                              someValuesFrom(>50)))

SubClassOf(restriction(lengthOverAll
                       someValuesFrom(20-50))
           kleineHochseeUndKuestenfischerei)

SubClassOf(restriction(lengthOverAll
                       someValuesFrom(10-20))
           kleineHochseeUndKuestenfischerei)
```

```
SubClassOf(restriction(lengthOverAll
                       someValuesFrom(<10))
            kleineHochseeUndKuestenfischerei)
```

Together with a straightforward encoding of the hierarchy from Fig. 7.4 in terms of subclass statements, we get a formal model of the classification of German fishing vessels.

Indicator classes

As described in the last section, domain relations such as the length of vessels are also used to link domain objects to statistical indicators. For this purpose, we encode the hierarchy of indicators shown in Fig. 7.3 in OWL and some concrete indicators as instances of the indicator classes in the hierarchy. Total catch for example would be an instance of the indicator class catch. Further, we can encode the mapping rules from domain properties to indicators using subclass axioms between general class expressions in OWL. The mapping rules mentioned above can be encoded as follows:

```
SubClassOf(restriction(grt someValuesFrom(integer))
            restriction(hasIndicator someValuesFrom Weight))
SubClassOf(restriction(lengthOverAll someValuesFrom(integer))
            restriction(hasIndicator someValuesFrom Length))
SubClassOf(restriction(enginePower someValuesFrom(integer))
            restriction(hasIndicator someValuesFrom Power))
```

Here, each property restriction represents a predicate in the mappings. The implication is simulated by the subclass statement itself. In the case of more complex rules, the OWL operators intersectionOf, unionOf and disjointFrom can be used to model conjunction, disjunction and negation in the rules.

7.3.2 Description of information

The descriptions introduced so far represent background knowledge that helps to interpret statistical information. An OWL-based representation of the actual description of statistical data sources in terms of views as introduced in the last section will be discussed in this section. In short, we model a statistical data source as a set of objects that belong to classes in the statistical as well as the domain ontology. The distinction between these two ontologies is necessary due to the dual nature of classes as atomic objects and as complex definitions. In the following, we first describe how data sources and their content are translated into objects. Afterwards, we discuss how these objects are linked to definitions in the ontologies.

Instance information

The most straightforward way of giving a semantic description of statistical information is in terms of instances of the statistics ontology presented above. We can derive the type of an object with respect to the statistical ontology from its position in the view definition that describes a table or an observation. The FROM clause of a view definition contains information about population objects. We directly encode them as instances of the Class concept, which is the range of the population property. We define three example classes representing fishing vessels of the German fleet in 1998 and 2000 as well as of the Danish fleet in 2000.

```
Instance(germanFleet2000 type(Class))
Instance(germanFleet1998 type(Class))
Instance(danishFleet2000 type(Class))
```

In the same way, we introduce instances for the other parts of the description of an information source and represent concrete sources as an instance that is related to these objects by the corresponding relations. In particular, we look for definitions of observations contained in a table, introduce objects for each observation found and link them to the names of the class of objects they describe. The following definition corresponds to the example view definition given on page 150.

```
Instance(germanCatch2000 type(Table)
        value(population germanFleet2000)
        value(describes TotalCatch)
        value(contains sumG1))

Instance(sumG1 value(for-class '10-20m')
              value(for-class 'is'))
```

This basic way of encoding view definitions in OWL already helps to share statistical information, because the reference to the statistical ontology provides a common vocabulary for heterogeneous information. This shared vocabulary can be used to query certain kinds of information across information sources. We could for example ask for the populations of all registers available.

Typing information

We have argued above that an important part of the semantics of information is encoded in the definition of the population and the classification of a source. We chose to capture these definitions by conjunctive queries over the domain ontology. One of the rationales for choosing this kind of representation was that they can be translated into OWL class definitions [Horrocks and Tessaris, 2000]. When translating view definitions to OWL, the corresponding class objects are modelled as instances of the resulting class expression. This, however, is not done directly but by means of declaring the corresponding data-source objects to be members of the class of things that have a population of a certain type, where this type is defined by the translation of the conjunctive query defining it. The following definition corresponds to the refined view definition shown on page 154.

```
Instance(germanCatch2000 type(
      intersectionOf(
      restriction(population allValuesFrom(
            restriction(nationality
                value(Germany))))
      restriction(caught allValuesFrom(
            restriction(period
                value(2000))))))))
```

The indirect description allows us to explicitly state that the observation is about objects in the intersection of the two classes:

```
Instance(sumG1 type(
      intersectionOf(
      restriction(for-class allValuesFrom(
            restriction(lengthOverAll
                someValuesFrom(10-20))))
      restriction(for-class allValuesFrom(
            restriction(caught allValuesFrom(
            restriction(area
                value('is'
                )))))))))
```

The best argument for an indirect description of classes is the possibility to generalize from the description of individual observations in the table. This is necessary for very large data sources. Typical examples in the fishery domain are fleet registers that contain thousands of entries each containing the same information about different objects in the domain. Instead of introducing an observation object for each of these entries, we can use the indirect description of the population represented by the register to provide information about the aspects represented in the data. A corresponding description of the register containing data about the German fleet in the year 2000 is shown below:

```
Instance(germanRegister1998 type(
      intersectionOf(
      restriction(population allValuesFrom(
          restriction(nationality value(Germany))))
      restriction(contains someValuesFrom(
          restriction(for-class someValuesFrom(
              intersectionOf(
                  restriction(lengthOverAll
                          someValuesFrom(integer))
                  restriction(enginePower
                          someValuesFrom(integer))
```

```
restriction(grt
              someValuesFrom(integer))
))))))))
```

The definition states that the corresponding data-source object belongs to the class of objects that have a population of a certain type (the same as in the example above) and that it contains some information about the length, the power, and the weight of the objects it represents. Note the compactness of the representation as compared to an explicit modelling of thousands of register entries. Depending on the requirements on the retrieval of information, this kind of indirect description of the content of an information source can be used for all data sources if there is no need to retrieve individual entries in a table.

7.4 Retrieving statistical information

The logical interpretation of view definitions allows us to reason about available information on a conceptual level. In particular, we can use the logical model to check whether a piece of information matches our information needs and to retrieve all available information that matches our requirements. In principle, the encoding above allows us to answer any conjunctive query that uses the vocabulary defined by the statistical and the domain ontologies. In the following we discuss some typical kinds of queries users often want to ask about information.

Classes of objects

When asking about statistical information, the user always has a class of objects in mind that is described by the information. In the fishery domain, these are almost always classes of fishing vessels that fulfill certain requirements that act as the population of an information source. As we encoded populations explicitly as instances of the statistical ontology, we can retrieve populations present in the information by asking for vessels with certain properties. We could for example ask for object classes that describe German vessels using the following query:

$$Q(X) \leftarrow FishingVessel(X), nationality(X, Germany) \qquad (7.1)$$

This query will return a set of objects representing different populations that underly information sources known to the system. The result will be a list of populations that consist of German fishing vessels in different years. We assume that the user is interested in information from the year 2000. As the names of objects returned do not necessarily provide some information about the year, we explicitly have to ask for classes of vessels that are relevant to the catch in the year 2000. This can be done by the following query:

$$Q(X) \leftarrow FishingVessel(X), caught(X, Y), period(Y, 2000) \qquad (7.2)$$

For this query, the result will be classes of fishing vessels from different countries that are related to the catch in the year 2000. If we combine these two queries, we get the German fleet in the year 2000 as an example.

Data sources

Once we have retrieved a class of objects, we can use the name of this class in queries in order to find out more about information related to that class of objects. We can for example ask for registers that contain information about the members of this class using the following query:

$$Q(X) \leftarrow register(X), population(X, german - fleet - 2000) \qquad (7.3)$$

Normally, a user is not interested in any kind of information about a population, but in a specific aspect of that population in terms of a statistical indicator. This requirement can easily be formulated by asking for data sources that contain observations for a specific indicator using the query below:

$$Q(X) \leftarrow contains(X, Y), for - indicator(Y, total - catch) \qquad (7.4)$$

Directly referring to a specific indicator like the total catch might sometimes be too restrictive, because we can also derive that information from the average catch if we know the number of vessels. Using the indicator hierarchy, we can ask for data sources that contain information about certain types of indicators. We might for example be interested in some indicator for the capacity of vessels. Specific instances of this general aspect are length, engine power or gross registry tons. The following query will return all those data sources that contain information on one of these aspects:

$$Q(X) \leftarrow contains(X, Y), for - unit(Y, Z),$$
$$has - indicator(Y, Z), capacity - indicator(Z) \qquad (7.5)$$

The possibility to ask for a wider range of aspects leaves space for an interaction with a human expert knowing about ways to combine and process information in order to get the required result.

Observations

Depending on the level of detail we chose in modelling the information, we can even ask more specific questions concerning individual values in tables.

Retrieving specific entries in a table can be done based on explicit relations of entries to other objects in the semantic model or based on the class of objects it describes. An example for retrieving information based on explicit relations is the following:

$$Q(X, Y) \leftarrow contains(german - catch - 2000, X), for - class(X, Y) \quad (7.6)$$

The query returns pairs containing observations found in the table german-catch-2000 and the vessel class the observation is assigned to. In this way, we can get more detailed information about the content of a data source. The real benefit of the semantic description, however, only becomes clear when asking for specific information about a certain class of objects based on an abstract description of that class. The following query is an example of a simple case of looking for statistics based on a description of a set of objects.

$$Q(X) \leftarrow for - class(X, Y), kleineHochseeUndKuestenFischerei(Y) \quad (7.7)$$

The query asks for all observations made about the vessel class "kleine Hochsee- und Kuestenfischerei" (compare Fig. 7.4). The answer to this query will not only contain the observations that are directly made about this class, but also observations about subclasses of this class, in our example all vessels with a length of less than 50 meters, independent of the name of the class they are explicitly assigned to.

7.5 Conclusions

Literature study reveals that the results of intelligent information integration do not cover the specific problems of statistical information integration. An exception is [Klinkert et al., 2000], in which an overall model was proposed that is dedicated to the statistical integration process used to support the European Common Fisheries Policy. That model does not use either a generic ontology of statistics or generic models of statistical methods. Furthermore, the problem of possible classification differences was solved in an ad hoc manner for specific data sources.

Statistical techniques that are an obvious source of inspiration are not generally applicable. This is caused by the inaccessibility of data and by lack of domain specific statistical models. Formalization of human expert knowledge did not solve these problems. However, the acquired heuristic knowledge did enable the formalization and implementation of a model that can be used to explicitly represent the domain-related semantics of statistical information.

The model supports selection of datasets based on an abstract description of their expected content and has been found useful for selecting primary sources, weight matrices and registers. The structure of the model is set up in such a way that it allows easy extension with other methods such as the following that are not supported in the current system:

- An explicit model of space: we have to able to define the geographic region in which the population and the classes of objects used for aggregation are located. Further, we need to be able to analyze and reason about the relation between the locations of objects in two different statistics.
- An explicit model of time: we have to able to define the time frame in which information about a population has been acquired. We need to be able to analyze and reason about the relation between the time frames of two data sources.
- An explicit model of statistical operators: we need the possibility to describe a variety of statistical operators that might occur in a statistical table. We need the possibility to identify and define possible transformations between values that are the result of these operators and the background information needed for the transformation.

While the last point is currently mainly unexplored, work on extending semantic descriptions of information with explicit notions of space and time exist. We address spatial aspects of information sharing in the following chapter.

Further reading

Sundgren [Sundgren, 1995] proposed a unifying model for modelling statistical metadata that is based on the different components considered here. The use of description logics for formalizing descriptions of statistical information is described in [Catarci et al., 1998] and [De Giacomo and Naggar, 1996], who also introduce the use of views for modelling statistics. Earlier work on a knowledge-based approach to integrating fishery statistics is reported in [Klinkert et al., 2000] and [Jonker and Verwaart, 2003].

8

Spatially-related information

Summary. In the last chapters we described techniques for retrieving information based on a semantic description of the content. As the application described in the last chapter illustrates, the relevance of information often not only depends on their content but also on their spatial context. In this chapter, we discuss the problem of representing the spatial context of information and of using it to determine relevance with respect to a certain request.

Many real-life applications such of information sharing as the one described in the last chapter have to deal with some notion of geographic space. In the field of environmental science, for example, most documents and other data sources have some sort of spatial connotation. Obviously all geospatial data, i.e. data which are typically handled by GISs (geographic information systems), refer to a specific geographic area. But also for non-spatial data sources, such as reports, documents and databases, references to geographic locations are typically important attributes. For example, a report about the installation of new groundwater-monitoring wells very likely refers to a specific (geographic) investigation area. Consequently, spatial attributes are important for both information retrieval and the description and management of data sources with the help of metadata catalogues. However, most online systems, like metadata catalogues and other browser-based information-retrieval systems, offer only very little to represent and query the complex relations of data sources and their respective locations in space.

In this chapter, we first give a brief summary of different paradigms for representing and reasoning about spatial information and discuss they benefits and drawbacks. We then discuss limitations of languages like OWL when used to reason about spatia information providing some examples of the possible use as well as by reviewing theoretical work on the combination of terminological and spatial reasoning that clearly states the limits of this combination.

We conclude by sketching an alternative approach for spatial information retrieval that treads terminological and spatial aspects independently and uses a graph-based representation to abstract from spatial information and supports efficient reasoning about spatial relevance.

8.1 Spatial representation and reasoning

The representation and reasoning of spatial knowledge is an important aspect of commonsense reasoning. This special attention is justified by the importance of space in human cognition and the special properties that have to be taken into account in order to draw expected conclusions. A number of approaches for spatial reasoning have been been proposed that differ with respect to the level of formalization and the conceptualization of space. In this section, we give an overview of different aspects of spatial representations and different formalizations used. This overview provides the basis for a discussion of representations suitable for supporting the exchange of spatially-related information.

8.1.1 Levels of spatial abstraction

Techniques for representing spatial information have been studied thoroughly by AI research on qualitative spatial reasoning (see [Cohn, 1997] for an overview). A basic insight from this line of research is that efficient spatial problem solving relies on abstracting from spatial detail. Three levels of spatial abstraction can be distinguished according to the degree by which the spatial position is determined: topological, ordinal and metrical information.

Topological information

Spatial properties that stay invariant under the most general group of spatial transformations, namely homomorphisms (intuitively: rubber-sheet distortions), convey topological information. A connected region, for instance, remains connected under these transformations. In other words: connectedness constitutes a topological property of regions. Among the different systems of spatial relations proposed for encoding topological information, the most widely used in GIS applications is a system of eight relations which was described in [Egenhofer, 1991] and given a logical formalization by Randell et al. [Randell et al., 1992]. It is known as the region-connection calculus RCC-8 and can express facts such as "region A touches region B" or "region A lies within region B".

Ordinal information

The fact that a region is convex constitutes a piece of ordinal information about the region's shape. Convexity is neither preserved under topological transformations nor does it imply any metrical properties. In other words, ordinal information provides an intermediate level of abstraction between topological and metrical information. Systems of ordinal relations describe the locations of points with respect to reference systems consisting of directed lines. A typical example is the system of cardinal directions north, west, south and east which locates a point with respect to another point by means of an absolute reference system [Frank, 1992]. Often, a relative reference system is needed which yields descriptions of spatial positions that are rotation invariant. Examples of such systems are the line-segment relations [Schlieder et al., 2001] or the panorama representation [De Rougemont and Schlieder, 1997].

Metrical information

Distances or angles are metrical invariants. Generally, metrical invariants are measures, i.e. they can be expressed by real numbers that obey certain mathematical criteria. Nevertheless, it is often necessary to abstract qualitatively even from metrical information. In natural language, adverbs such as "close" or "far" are frequently used to express distance information. Several systems of qualitative distance relations have been proposed which can be used to represent the semantics of linguistic expressions (e.g. [Clementini et al., 1997]).

8.1.2 Reasoning about spatial relations

A crucial design decision for any spatial information system is the choice of an adequate reasoning mechanism. There exist several alternative approaches to spatial inference which all show a trade-off between genericity and efficiency. In other words, the generic approaches are less efficient and the efficient ones are less generic. We briefly describe the four major classes of approaches to spatial reasoning in order of increasing specificity.

Geometric theorem proving

[Kapur and Mundy, 1988] First-order logic can be used to express spatial problems which are then solved by applying a theorem prover. Several specialized proof techniques for geometrical reasoning have been proposed. From the user's point of view, a theorem-proving approach is very convenient. It allows him to simply state the problem not having to worry about how to solve it. Unfortunately, due to the computational complexity of the proof procedures, only small problem instances can be approached this way.

Constraint-based spatial reasoning

[Marriott and Stuckey, 1998] Most problems studied in the field of qualitative spatial reasoning are solved with constraint solvers. Inferences consist in determining some relational terms, i.e. spatial relations holding between objects, given some other relational terms. If, for example, it is known that regions A, B, C, and D are arranged in such a way that "A inside B", "B inside C", and "C disjoint from D", we can infer that "A disjoint from D" and "B disjoint from D". Such an inference problem can be mapped onto the problem of finding an instantiation for a constraint satisfaction system. Although this type of instantiation problem cannot be solved efficiently, instantiations can be computed by means of efficient approximative algorithms. Typically, polynomial constraint propagation methods (e.g. path consistency) are used for that purpose. For GIS-related problems, the trade-off that is realized by the constraint-based approaches has turned out to be most effective.

Computational geometry

[de Berg et al., 2000] For specific geometric problems (e.g. intersection of polygons) asymptotically optimal algorithmic solutions are known. Almost all efficient algorithms rely on some explicit problem representation in a dynamic data structure. Although the approaches from computational geometry are the most efficient, they are very specific. Variants of a problem may require the use of entirely different data structures, used to avoid inconsistency problems. The locations of all other spatial objects in the spatial model are represented using relations that ultimately refer to a set of landmarks. This principle of relative locations also allows an easy integration of new spatial objects. It suffices to describe the new object by spatial relations to already existing points, i.e. landmarks.

Diagrammatic reasoning

[Glasgow et al., 1995] Classical theorem provers and constraint solvers do not use an explicit spatial problem representation. The advantage of such a representation consists in providing information for guiding the flow of control to make spatial inference more efficient. Diagrammatic reasoning uses map-like representations in analogy to mental images that play a prominent role in human spatial problem solving.

8.2 Ontologies and spatial relevance

If we want to include spatial criteria in the process of retrieving relevant information, we have to include explicit representations of space as well as notions of spatial relevance in the semantic descriptions of the information. In this section, we explore the use of OWL ontologies for encoding spatial relevance. As we will see, we can indeed represent geographic regions as instances of some concepts and describe their relations using special properties. Further, we can define notions of spatial relevance based on these relations and use these notions in combined spatial and terminological queries. As we will discuss at the end of the section, however, a proper treatment of geographic space in terms of being able to reason about complex spatial arrangements quickly encounters serious limitations.

8.2.1 Defining Spatial Relevance

We use the spatial configuration depicted in Fig. 8.1 to illustrate the determination of spatial relevance on the basis of topological relations. In our example, we are concerned with different project areas in a city. The project areas are spatially associated with specific districts using topological relations.

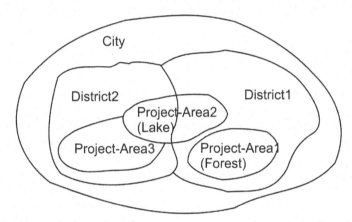

Fig. 8.1. An example arrangement of spatial regions

The first relation we use to refer to project areas is spatial containment. Project Area 1, for example, is contained in District 1, while Project Area 3 is contained in District 2. We further declare that every area which is contained in another area is automatically spatially relevant with respect to the including area. This can be achieved by defining a relation contained-in as a special case of a relation definitely-spatially-relevant. Using the OWL language, we can define contained-in as well as its mathematical properties (i.e. transitivity) in the following way:

```
ObjectProperty(contained-in
    supers = definitely-spatially-relevant
    InverseOf(contains)
    Transitive)
```

We can now use the relevance relation to retrieve areas which are spatially relevant to District 1. Using the FaCT reasoner interface, we can formulate a query Q_1 for areas spatially relevant to District 1 in the following way:

$$Q_1(X) \leftarrow area(X) \wedge$$
$$definitely - spatially - relevant(X, district1) \qquad (8.1)$$

Not surprisingly, the result of this query is Project Area 1, because it is contained in District 1. However, Project Area 2 may also be of interest when querying areas related to District 1, because it is at least partially contained in District 1. We cover this kind of relevance by using another topological relation, namely partial overlap. As we are not absolutely sure that Project Area 2 is really relevant, we use a relation probably-spatially-relevant to describe a weaker level of relevance. Again, we define relevance in terms of topological relations by stating that partial overlap is a special kind of spatial relevance. The OWL definition of the relation partially-overlapping is the following:

```
ObjectProperty(partially-overlapping
    supers = probably-spatially-relevant
    SymmetricProperty)
```

We further define that, because of its weaker character, our previous notion of relevance also falls under this new relation. The result of a query searching for areas probably-spatially-relevant to District 1 consists of Project Area 1 and Project Area 2, because the latter overlaps with District 1.

As mentioned above, areas in the neighborhood may also be of interest. We therefore include a further level of spatial relevance based on neighborhood defined by the relation connected-to. We assume that this third level of spatial relevance is even weaker than the ones introduced above, because our notion of connectedness implies that there is no overlap.

```
ObjectProperty(connected-to
 supers = might-be-spatially-relevant
 SymmetricProperty)
```

Using this notion of spatial relevance, we still find Project Areas 1 and 2. Additionally, we get District 2 as an area spatially relevant to District 1. However, using OWL it is not possible to derive the spatial relevance of Project Area 2, which is contained in the relevant area District 2, in a straightforward way because we cannot chain relations in order to determine spatial relevance.

8.2.2 Combined spatial and terminological matching

Type information about information items to be retrieved can be organized using structured concept hierarchies like thesauri and ontologies. Above, we argued that description logics are very well suited for the formalization of such concept hierarchies as well as for concepts of spatial relevance. Therefore, using description logics to encode both spatial relations and type

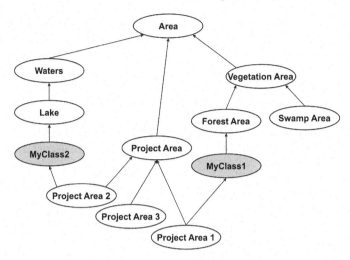

Fig. 8.2. Results of Matching Process

information allows for the specification and fine tuning of integrated queries.

In order to include terminological information in queries, we further describe the project areas using class definitions and defining the areas to be instances of these classes. We might for example know that Project Area 1 has solid ground and its vegetation consists of oaks. Using OWL we can capture this knowledge in the following class definition.

```
Equivalent(MyClass1 intersectionOf(
          Area
          restriction(ground allValuesFrom(land))
          restriction(vegetation someValuesFrom(oak))))
```

Using the FaCT reasoner, we can automatically determine the super-class of this definition and therefore the terminological category that Project Area 1 belongs to. In our case we derive that Project Area 1 is a forest because its class definition constitutes a special case of the following general definition of a "forest area":

```
Equivalent(forest-area intersectionOf(
          vegetation-area
          restriction(ground allValuesFrom(land))
          restriction(vegetation someValuesFrom(
            unionOf(trees shrubs)))))
```

In the same way, we model the class of Project Area 2 in such a way that it can be derived to belong to the category "lake" (see Fig. 8.2 for a complete class hierarchy of the example). We can use this terminological information to find answers to more sophisticated queries. The first possibility is to restrict the type of areas we are interested in. For example, we can ask for "forest areas" that might be spatially relevant to District 1:

$$Q(X) \leftarrow forest - area(X) \wedge$$
$$might - be - spatially - relevant(X, district1)) \quad (8.2)$$

Using this additional type restricting, the result of the query is reduced to Project Area 1, because the other areas also relevant to District 1 are not of type forest area.

Another application of terminological information is not to seek areas that are relevant to a specific area, but rather to a specific class of areas. For example, we can ask for areas that are spatially relevant to "lakes" in general. The corresponding query is the following:

$$Q(X) \leftarrow area(X) \wedge lake(Y) \wedge$$
$$might - be - spatially - relevant(X, Y) \quad (8.3)$$

Because the logic reasoner is able to infer that Project Area 2 is a "lake", we retrieve all areas that are spatially related to Project Area 2. In our case these are Districts 1 and 2 because they overlap with Project Area 2 and, because of its connectedness to Project Area 2, also Project Area 3.

8.2.3 Limitations

The examples above illustrate the naive use of ontology representation languages such as OWL for representing relations between spatial objects. A closer look reveals that the possibilities of this approach are rather limited. In particular, the ability to draw inferences related to spatial relations such as "if region A is a tangential part of B and B is part of C then A is connected to C" are not supported. Inference capabilities are restricted to the use of built-in features of OWL relations such as defining relations to be transitive (part-of) or symmetric (connected). Further, we can use property hierarchies to capture some of the semantics of the relations (compare Fig. 8.3).

In order to benefit from more complete reasoning about topological relations, terminological models have to be connected to specialized reasoning services for spatial knowledge. In early approaches this was done using functional extensions of concept languages such as LOOM (compare [Haarslev et al., 1994]). A tighter integration of terminological and spatial reasoning can be achieved by defining spatial regions as special datatypes with a special set of predicates that correspond to relations between spatial regions. Using special data-type properties, class definitions can be linked to spatial

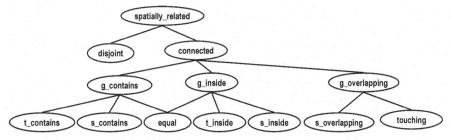

Fig. 8.3. Hierarchy of spatial relations (from [Haarslev and Moeller, 1997])

regions defined by applying a predicate on a set of region names. While this
approach allows us to define and reason about spatial properties of instances
of a class, a tighter integration of spatial relations into the concept language
requires an extension of the formal semantics that turns out to be undecidable
even for much simpler languages than OWL [Haarslev et al., 1998].

The complexity problems that arise from a tight connection of terminological and spatial representations make combined representations unsuitable for
large scale information sharing. We conclude that we need to treat spatial aspects separately from terminological ones. This means that queries will contain
conceptual and spatial criteria that are evaluated separately. In the following,
we sketch an approach that separates the evaluation of spatial criteria from
conceptual ones and uses diagrammatic techniques for efficient determination
of spatial relevance.

8.3 Graph-based reasoning about spatial relevance

In order to build truly expressive spatial queries as well as to annotate data
sources in an intuitive way, we need constructs to describe

- partonomic relations,
- topological relations,
- relations of direction,
- relations of distance

between spatial objects as well as Boolean combinations over these relations.
In the following we introduce an approach to reasoning about these concepts.
We evaluate our approach using the following example query in an imaginary
query language that could be stated in connection with the planning of a
holiday trip:

```
(and capital historic-place)
@
(and (part-of western-europe)
```

```
(or (connected-to mediterranean-sea)
    (connected-to north-sea))
(not (north-of belgium))
(next-to germany))
```

Intuitively, we search for information about historically interesting places that are capitals of a country. We further claim that these places have to be in a location (i.e. a country) that is part of western Europe either connected to the Atlantic Ocean or the North Sea. Further, the location should not be north of Belgium. Of all these objects, we want to have the one that is next to Germany.

The conceptual part of the query can already be handled by the BUSTER system. Using a small ontology of cities and their attractions, we retrieve the following five cities: Amsterdam, Madrid, Paris, Rome and Lisbon. We have different options for implementing the retrieval process for the spatial part. A straightforward approach would be to encode spatial relations in the ontology and use a reasoner for the spatial part. However, the language supported by this reasoner is not expressive enough to cover even the axioms of a rather theory of space such as RCC-8 [Egenhofer, 1991]. In particular, it can only reason about general subset-relations without a notion of connectedness. The use of a more expressive logic, on the other hand, will lead to a reasoning complexity that is not acceptable for the retrieval process. Constraint-based approaches that are prominent in spatial reasoning also have problems with respect to this specific application. We argued [Schlieder et al., 2001] that RCC-8 fails to capture relevant two-dimensional inferences, because the formalism does not encode spatial dimensions. We concluded that a diagrammatic reasoning approach [Glasgow et al., 1995] is the most suitable for this kind of reasoning task. We therefore use a graph-based representation of space that can be derived from actual polygon data using computational geometry and apply graph algorithms for selecting interesting locations. In the following we present representation for the relations mentioned above and describe the reasoning process. Thereby we follow and extend the ideas described in [Schlieder et al., 2001].

8.3.1 Partonomies

In order to find a type of abstraction for describing partonomies, we take a look at different geometrical arrangements of polygons. In the following, polygons are closed sets of points, i.e. edges and vertices belong to the polygon.

We consider polygons $P_1, \ldots, P_n$ that are contained in a part of the plane bounded by a polygon P. Some special types of arrangements of the polygons within the containing polygon P can be distinguished:

- In a *polygonal covering* $P_1 \cup \ldots \cup P_n = P$. The polygons cover the containing polygon. In general, they will overlap.

- In a *polygonal patchwork* for all $i \neq j$ from $\{1, \ldots, n\}$ $interior(P_i \cap P_j) = \emptyset$. The polygons are either disjoint or intersect only in edges and/or vertices.
- A *polygonal tessellation* is a polygonal covering which also forms a polygonal patchwork.

Polygonal tessellations occur frequently: in a map of Germany, for instance, the federal states constitute a tessellation. Because of their importance, we will pay more attention to tessellations than to any other arrangement of spatial parts.

Partonomies are the result of recursively applying the standard part-of relation to describe parts of parts. Similarly, the polygons of a covering, patchwork or tessellation can contain other polygons. In analogy to partonomies we introduce decompositions, which are defined recursively as hierarchical data structures for encoding the spatial part-of relation together with the type of arrangement of the parts.

By abstraction from the type of spatial arrangement one obtains the partonomy that underlies a decomposition. This partonomy is encoded by the *decomposition tree*, which has the same nodes as the decomposition and whose edges denote the binary part-of relation between polygons (compare Fig. 8.4).

In order to process the first part of the spatial expression, we have to check which of the cities that match the concept expressions lies in countries that belong to western Europe. We decide this by consulting the decomposition graph which represents the tessellation. Fig. 8.4 shows such a decomposition tree that shows the distinction between countries assumed to belong to western Europe: Portugal (P), Spain (E), France (F), Luxembourg (L), Belgium (B) and the Netherlands (N). The other countries on the map belong to central Europe: Germany (G), Switzerland (S), Austria (A), Denmark (D) and Italy (I).

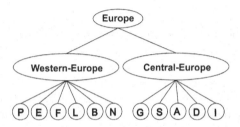

Fig. 8.4. A decomposition tree for the tessellation

By simply following the arcs in the tree downwards starting at the node representing western Europe, we find all countries that fulfill the requirements. As Rome lies in Italy that is defined to belong to central Europe, we can exclude this city from the collection of possible solutions.

8.3.2 Topology

A common way of representing the topology of a collection of polygons in a tessellation is a neighborhood graph. The neighborhood graph of a homogeneous decomposition by tessellation is a graph $\mathcal{N} = (V, E)$ with the set of un-decomposed polygons as nodes V and all pairs of neighboring polygons as edges E. If only the neighborhood graph is used, then the two arrangements of polygons shown below cannot be distinguished (Fig. 8.5). Both have the same neighboring graph but they differ fundamentally with respect to neighborhood: neighbors of P_1 and P_3 can never be neighbors of P_2 if the polygons are arranged as in (a) while they can be in the arrangement (b). The problem is linked to multiple neighborhoods, that is, the fact that in (a) P_1 and P_3 have two disconnected edges in common. Therefore, the qualitative representation of the decomposition should be able to encode multiple neighborhood relations between two polygons.

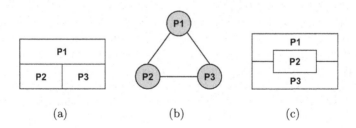

Fig. 8.5. Multiple neighborhood relations

As a solution to the problem of finding an adequate abstraction for a decomposition we propose to represent it by a connection graph. Fig. 8.6 shows the connection graph $\mathcal{C}$ of a homogeneous decomposition by a tessellation . Each polygon from the tessellation is represented by a vertex from $\mathcal{C}$. In addition there is the node 1 representing the external polygonal region. The edges from $\mathcal{C}$ which are incident with a vertex are easily obtained together with their circular ordering by scanning the contour of the corresponding polygon. As the example shows, the connection graph is a multi-graph in which several edges can join the same pair of vertices, i.e. Spain has two connections with the Atlantic Ocean.

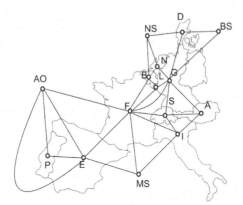

Fig. 8.6. Connection-graph representation of a decomposition by tessellation

The connection graph can be used to process the second part of the spatial expression stating that the polygons we are looking for have either to be connected with the Mediterranean or to the North Sea. Again, this can easily be decided by following all edges in the connection graph starting at the nodes that represent the Mediterranean and the North Sea, respectively.

Looking at the connection graph in Fig. 8.6, we can see that this criterion is met by the cities Madrid, Paris and Amsterdam, because the countries they lie in, i.e. Spain, France and the Netherlands, are connected to one of these seas. Lisbon is excluded from the collection of possible solutions, because Portugal does not have this connection.

8.3.3 Directions

We argued that the representation of a tessellation in terms of a connection graph preserves the topological relations. The problem with this representation concerning directional information is the fact that topological information is rotation invariant by nature. Therefore it is not possible to encode directions in the connection graph. In order to include directions, we assign special direction labels to edges in the graph. These labels are described by the following function:

$$DIR : E \rightarrow 2^{\{N,NO,O,SO,S,SW,W,NW\}}$$

The function assigns a set of qualitative directions according to points of the compass. We use the qualitative description N to refer to directions between 315 and 45, NW for 0 to 90, W for 45 to 115 degree and so on. An edge is labelled with a set of these descriptions because connected polygons often fall into more than one of these angle sections due to their spatial extension. Fig. 8.7 shows the connection graph of the example together with the labelling for the edges between France and its neighbors.

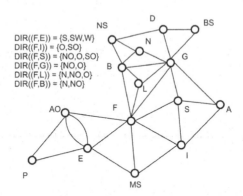

Fig. 8.7. Direction labels used to describe direction of France's neighbors

This kind of labelling allows us to reason directly about directional information of connected polygons. Reasoning about directions of polygons which are not directly connected, however, is more complicated. In this case, we have to extract labels of the transitive closure of the connection graph. The advantage of this approach is the ability to refer to complete directional information in the course of the reasoning process. However, a larger representation that contains redundant information is needed in this case because we know that directional relations are transitive. Another approach is to use an additional calculus on direction labels. This approach preserves the minimality of the representation, but we cannot assume that such a calculus will be correct and complete.

In the example query, we restricted interesting locations to those that are not north of Belgium. This means that the labels NW, N and NO must not be contained in the label of the edge between Belgium and the location we seek. Applying this criterion to the locations of the remaining cities (Amsterdam, Paris and Madrid) we can decide that the Netherlands do not meet this criterion because they are directly connected to Belgium and the edge contains all three forbidden labels. France (directly) and Spain (by transitivity) can be proven to meet the criterion. Therefore, Amsterdam is excluded from the set of possible solutions.

8.3.4 Distances

Concerning distance information, we find a situation similar to the one we observed concerning directions. The connection graph only implies a very weak notion of distance. It allows to compute the shortest path between two nodes (i.e. the graph-theoretic distance) but it does not capture the real distances between polygons. Fig. 8.8 shows an example that illustrates the problems that occur if only the connection graph is used. We consider the distance between Luxembourg and the Netherlands on one hand, and Luxembourg and Spain on the other hand. While the graph-theoretic distance is the same, Fig. 8.8 clearly shows that Spain is much further away from Luxembourg than the Netherlands.

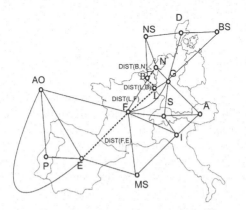

Fig. 8.8. Using distance information

In order to overcome this problem we use additional distance labels for edges. Again we have to decide whether to choose a local or a global assignment of distances. In order to avoid redundant information, we prefer a local assignment. There are many options for defining these labels. First of all, we have to decide whether to use a qualitative or a quantitative notion of distance. A quantitative approach again requires a suitable calculus while a quantitative measure allows the application of standard algebra. The next problem is how to derive distance information from the actual data. Again there are various options. The mean distance between connected polygons should be a good approximation. A possibility of computing this distance is to determine the centroids of two polygons and use the Eucledian distance between them.

Regardless of the kind of distance measure we choose, we get a result for our example query, because France lies on the shortest path from Germany to Spain. This implies that Madrid which lies in Spain is definitely further away from Germany than Paris which lies in France. As a consequence, this last criterion restricts the set of solutions for our query to exactly one city, namely Paris. Looking at the actual situation, we see that the result meets the intuitive expectations. In the general case it might happen, that the result is not completely correct as a result of the level of spatial abstraction chosen. In cases of oddly shaped areas, the abstraction might lead to errors, e.g. when an area is completely surrounded by another one (an example would be Italy and the vatican). In most relevant cases, however, we can assume that the abstraction produce relevant results.

Reasoning methods that use these kinds of representations for determining spatial relevance have been developed and integrated into the BUSTER system (compare section 9.3). Details about the corresponding methods can be found in [Voegele et al., 2003] and [Voegele, 2004].

8.4 Conclusions

Spatial relevance is an important issue with respect to information sharing in many areas. Spatially related information can be found in many application areas such as environmental information, in the geosciences and in political decision making. In order to address the needs of these areas, we have to represent and reason about the spatial relevance of information items. There is a variety of different approaches to the problem of spatial representation and reasoning that differ in the level of spatial abstraction and the way space and spatial relations are represented. We argued that spatial information sharing benefits from the ability to enhance queries by spatial criteria on different levels of abstraction that have to be combined with terminological parts of a query. Theoretical work has shown that a tight integration of terminological and spatial reasoning suffers from serious problems. In order to be decidable, the expressiveness of either the terminological or the spatial part of a query has to be reduced significantly. Even in the case of representations supporting decidable reasoning the complexity of combined reasoning puts strong restrictions on the scalability. In order to include spatial aspects in query processing for information sharing, we therefore have to treat terminological and spatial parts of a query separately. We sketched a graph-based approach that covers different levels of spatial abstraction when determining spatial relevance. A limited form of this approach has been implemented in the BUSTER system described in Sect. 9.3 showing the practical benefit of the approach. Unfortunately, the separation on the computational level suffers from the lack of a unifying theory of spatio-terminological reasoning. A promising area for providing such a formal foundation is the area of hybrid logics that investigate integrated reasoning with different logical systems. Recently, Lutz et al. [Kutz et al., 2002] proposed a formal model based on so-called $\mathcal{E}$-connections for combining terminological and spatial logics without losing decidability of the overall framework. Using this notion to provide a formal foundation for spatial information retrieval is an interesting topic for further investigations.

Further reading

Cohn [Cohn, 1997] provides an overview of the field of qualitative spatial reasoning. Techniques of diagrammatical reasoning that are the motivation for our approach are described in [Glasgow et al., 1995]. The integration of spatial and terminological reasoning in a specialized description logic is discussed in [Haarslev et al., 1998], who also show that the logic is undecidable for expressive class definitions. More sophisticated methods for modelling and reasoning about spatial relevance can be found in [Schlieder et al., 2001] and [Voegele et al., 2003].

9

Integration and retrieval systems

Summary. The goal of this chapter is to give evidence for the practical applicability of the models and methods presented. After having proposed a logical framework and an architecture for representing information semantics as well as the possibility to generate metadata based on this framework and methods to reason about information contents, we now present existing systems that implement some of the methods discussed. We focus on these methods and explain the specific implementation using a common example.

In this section we will discuss some existing systems for retrieving and integrating information on the Web. Rather than giving an overview of the variety of systems available, we select three systems that address the issues discussed in the last chapters. We start our discussion with the OntoBroker system, which implements the basic functionality of a single ontology information integration and retrieval system. Further OntoBroker provides support for rule-based context transformation. As a second system, we look at OBSERVER, a multiple-ontology system. We will focus on the use of more than one ontology in the system and describe how ontologies are integrated in OBSERVER. Further, OBSERVER uses a query re-writing technique to translate between different ontologies that is based on the same ideas as the approach discussed in Chap. 6. Finally, we turn our attention to the BUSTER system, which uses the hybrid approach. Here we focus on the use of the shared terminology in query formulation and processing. Further, the BUSTER system implements functionality for querying spatially related information similar to the ideas described in Sect. 8.3. We describe these techniques and their use in information retrieval.

In order to give a better impression of the systems, their differences and similarities, we use a simple example from the travel domain and describe how the systems solve this specific integration problem. The task of the example is to retrieve hotels with a room rate that is under a certain threshold from different information sources with accommodations. Table 9.1 shows the part of the available information we will focus on.

Table 9.1. Data from the example problem

Name	Location	Category	Price
Radisson	Copenhagen	Congress Hotel	580
Mercure	Hamburg	Four star	190
Ritz	London	First Class	130
...	...	...	...

This small set of information already contains a number of very relevant integration problems that arise in many practical applications. First of all, we have to decide, whether all of information items are actually representing hotels. This is a problem in particular if the categories mentioned in the table are defined in different ontologies. As the hotels are in different countries, the room rates are given in different currencies that have to be normalized and finally the questions of spatial relevance with respect to the users needs arises. In the following we will see that the different systems differ in the way they focus on a specific problem.

In the following, we first discuss the use of the Ontobroker system that uses a global ontology and flexible transformation functions for comparing hotel types and prices. In the following session, the use of multiple ontologies in the OBSERVER system is presented. We show how OBSERVER uses semantic relationships between classes from different ontologies to compare data in the different sources and to select an optimal translation. Finally, we discuss the BUSTER system and explain the use of a shared vocabulary for describing features of accommodations as well as the determination of spatial relevance as a part of the information sharing process.

9.1 OntoBroker

The OntoBroker system [Decker et al., 1999] has been developed for supporting the access to distributed sources of digital information such as document repositories or Web sites. OntoBroker mediates between the different formats and structures that might be present in these sources by encoding the available information in a pivot format and relating it to a domain ontology that is shared across all sources. Consequently, the domain ontology is the central part of the OntoBroker architecture. As a successful use of OntoBroker relies on the existence of the shared ontology, OntoBroker comes with an editor that supports the creation of domain-specific ontologies [Sure et al., 2002]. In order to link information to the ontology, available information items have to be modelled as instances of the ontology. In the case of well-structured information sources such as databases and spreadsheets, this step is done using specialized wrappers that extract information from the sources and assign it to classes and relations in the ontology. For less structured information like text documents and web pages, OntoBroker relies on an annotation tool that supports the user in adding special markup to the available information, thereby explicitly linking it to the ontology [Staab et al., 2001].

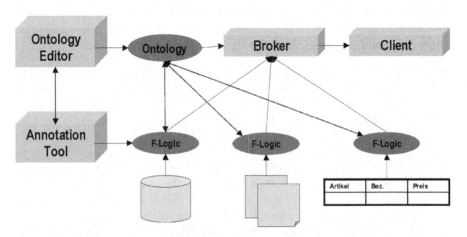

Fig. 9.1. The general architecture of the OntoBroker system

The ontology together with the instance information extracted from the different information sources behave like a deductive database. The actual broker system provides the corresponding reasoning facilities in terms of providing answers to complex queries concerning information items, their properties and relations. The broker makes this query-answering functionality available to client applications which may be rather generic query interfaces for arbitrary information or specialized applications relying on a specific domain ontology and a fixed set of information sources. Fig. 9.1 gives an overview of the OntoBroker architecture and its different components. In the following, we will have a closer look at the way OntoBroker represents information and ontologies and the use of rules for implementing functional context transformation.

9.1.1 F-Logic and its relation to OWL

The representation formalism for ontologies and information used in OntoBroker is F-Logic. Unlike the Web Ontology Language that us based on Description Logics, F-logic has its foundation in logic programming languages. More specifically, F-logic extends horn-logic language with constructs of frame languages supporting the straightforward representation of class-based knowledge representation. The OntoBroker inference engine translates these constructs back into horn logic and uses standard logic programming techniques for answering queries. The use of horn logic has some implications for the expressive power of F-logic as compared to OWL that we will briefly summarize in the following.

Correspondences with OWL

Focusing on a frame-based representation of knowledge, F-logic has a number of commonalities with OWL, in particular with OWL Lite. We summarize these common features in the following.

- *Classes.* F-logic can be used to express class membership and subclassing. Assigning an instance I to a class C is denoted as `I:C`, which corresponds to the OWL expression `Instance(I type(C))`. Further, a class C can be declared to be a subclass of another class D using the axiom `C::D`. This corresponds to the OWL expression `SubClassOf(C D)`.

- *Range Restrictions.* F-Logic can express a special type of property restriction. In particular, we can restrict the types of values that are allowed to be in the range of an attribute A that is assigned to a particular class C to some other class D. The corresponding F-Logic expression `C[A =>> D]` has the same effect as the OWL statement `SubClassOf(C restriction(A allValuesFrom(D)))`.

- *Facts.* Finally, we can express information about actual instances of an ontology in a frame-like fashion. For stating that an object O is of type C and shows a value V in the attribute A we write `O:C[A->V]`. In OWL we would express the same information using the following statement: `Instance(O type(C) value(A V))`.

We see that the direct overlap between F-Logic and OWL is a fragment of OWL that allows us to state simple schema information. In particular, the fragment always exactly corresponds to the OWL part of RDF Schema. We will see, however, that F-logic offers other means for defining the meaning of information mainly in terms of its rule language. In contrast to the original proposal , the variant on F-Logic implemented in Ontobroker is based on a semantics that borrows from logic programming rather than the standard semantics of first order logic. In fact, the DLP fragment discussed briefly in Chap. 3 also corresponds to the largest segment on which the different semantics of OWL and F-Logic intersect, adding further interest to this fragment.

Differences from OWL

Being based on logic programming rather than description logics, F-Logic offers some features that go beyond the expressive power of OWL. These additional features can be used to capture some of the build in modelling primitives of OWL using special axioms.

- *General relations.* An often criticized limitation of OWL is the restriction to binary relations between objects. F-logic does not have this restriction and is able of representing predicates of arbitrary arity for capturing complex relations between multiple objects.
- *Parameterized attributes.* A special case of the use of general relations in F-Logic is the ability to parameterize the attributes of a class. We denote that V is the value of an attribute A of object O with respect to a certain parameter P (e.g. the length in inches) as `O[A@(P) ->> V]`. This feature is useful for describing different scales and measures.
- *Rules and queries.* The main difference between OWL and F-Logic is the axiom and rule language. F-Logic offers the possibility to state general implication axioms that act as rules and queries. The general form of a rule is `FORALL V, H <- B`, where V is a list of goal variables, H is the head and B the body of the rule. The body of a rule consists of an arbitrary F-Logic formula containing the operators `AND`, `OR`, `NOT`, `<-`, `->` or `<->` and quantifiers `FORALL` and `EXISTS`. Queries are rules with an empty head.

F-Logic rules can be used to model OWL features like the disjointness of classes, transitivity and inverses of relations and others. Beyond that, rules provide a powerful mechanism for encoding other features such as relational algebra and domain-specific knowledge about relations. In the following we will see how this can be used to mediate between different information sources in our example problem.

9.1.2 Ontologies, sources and queries

The OntoBroker strategy of using F-logic as a uniform language for information items and ontological background knowledge leads to a very flexible way of managing knowledge and information sources in the system. In particular, arbitrary F-logic files can be loaded into the OntoBroker system regardless of whether they contain information, ontological information or both. The corresponding interface of the standard client is shown in Fig. 9.2a. Here the user can also choose to compile out the rule base in order to increase run-time performance. The specifications in the different files loaded to the system are treated as one big knowledge base that can be used to answer queries about information and background knowledge. In particular, all schema information is considered as representing one ontology common to all information sources. Fig. 9.2b shows the ontology interface of the OntoBroker client that allows

(a) Source management

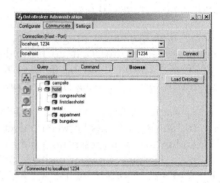

(b) Ontology browser

Fig. 9.2. The OntoBroker client

the user to browse the ontological knowledge of the system.

Applying OntoBroker to our example problem first of all requires us to wrap the different information sources into a common F-logic representation and load the corresponding knowledge to the system. Each row in Table 9.1 is translated into an object with certain values for the relevant attributes corresponding to the columns of the table. The F-logic representations of the three example entries in the table are the following:

```
radisson:congresshotel[location->denmark; price->580].
mercure:four-star[location->germany; price->210].
ritz:first-class[location->england; price->130].
```

The first heterogeneity problem mentioned in the problem statement is the use of different categories of hotels. This problem can be addressed by a common ontology that relates the different types mentioned in the data to the more general concept hotel that can be used to query objects belonging to the different special types of hotels. The corresponding part of the F-logic definition is the following:

```
congresshotel::hotel
four-star::hotel
first-class::hotel
```

Using this ontology, we can query the system for all hotels that have a price of less than 200 using the following query:

```
FORALL Y,X <- Y:hotel[price->X] AND lessorequal(X,200).
```

The system returns the `ritz` as the answers to the query, because it can be shown to belong to the class of hotels and to have a price of less that 200. Fig. 9.3 summarizes the situation.

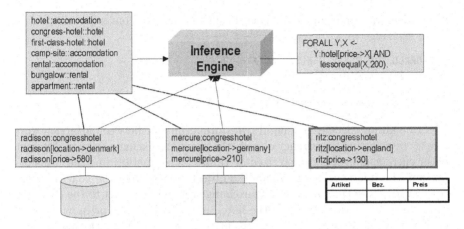

Fig. 9.3. Example of ontology-based retrieval

Using the rule language allows us to retrieve objects and their values based on complex criteria and background knowledge. In that OntoBroker behaves like a knowledge-based system capable of deriving new facts from given ones.

9.1.3 Context transformation

The use of an ontology of different types of hotels helps us to cope with the different hotel categories mentioned in the information sources. It cannot, however, solve the problem of differences in units and scales used in the description of attribute values. In our example, the prices for a room are given in different local currencies, which are Euros, UK Pounds and Danish Crowns. In order to make these prices comparable to each other and to the criteria given in the query, we have to normalize them to a common currency, say US Dollars. This problem corresponds to the notion of context transformation used before. In order to be able to transform from one context (in this case currency) to another, we first have to make the context of a piece of information explicit. Parameterized attributes are an elegant and flexible way of doing this. We therefore extend the description of information items by a currency parameter for the price attribute:

```
radisson:congresshotel[price@(dkcrowns)->580].
mercure:four-star[price@(euro)->210].
ritz:first-class[price@(ukpounds)->130].
```

The actual transformation between different contexts can be specified using complex F-logic rules that specify the value of an attribute in one context in terms of its value in other contexts. The translation can either be point-wise, from one specific context to another, or general. In the case of different currencies, we can formulate a general rule for currency conversion that refers to an exchange rate.

```
FORALL X,Y,Z,A,B,C X[price@(A)->Y] <-
    X[price@(B)->Z] AND
    (Y is (Z*C)/100) AND
    A[exchangerate@(B)->C].
```

The rule above specifies a general transformation rule between arbitrary currencies by referring to currency objects that have the exchange rate to different other currencies as a parameterized attribute. When performing the transformation, the inference engine binds the object representing the goal currency to the variable in the rule, reads its exchange rate with respect to the currency mentioned in the description of the hotel and calculates the price in the goal currency, which is returned as the result. For the case of US Dollars, we use the following definitions of the currency object usdollar.

```
usdollar[exchangerate@(euro)->90].
usdollar[exchangerate@(ukpounds)->173].
usdollar[exchangerate@(dkcrowns)->27].
```

The currency transformation is now triggered by explicitly mentioning a goal currency in the query. In our case, we now look for hotels that have a price of less than 200 US Dollars:

```
FORALL Y,X <- Y:hotel[price@(usdollar)->X] AND lessorequal(X,200).
```

As summarized in Fig. 9.4, the result is no longer the ritz, but the two other hotels, because the price of 130 UK pounds corresponds a a much higher price in US Dollar while the prices denoted in Euro and Danish Crowns are actually lower than 200 if measured in Dollars.

The application of this kind of context transformation is of course not limited to measures and scales. We can also formulate rules that establish between different classes of hotels (for example first class and four star hotels). These rules, however, will always depend on the specific domain. We will turn our attention to systems that offer generic solutions for translating between different classifications in the following section.

9.2 OBSERVER

The OntoBroker approach described above can be seen as a good example of the core functionality an ontology-based information-integration system provides. In practice, however, some of the design decisions made for OntoBroker turn out to be unrealistic. The first is the restriction to a single ontology that covers all sources of data. As mentioned before, the restriction to a single ontology leads to significant maintenance problems when new

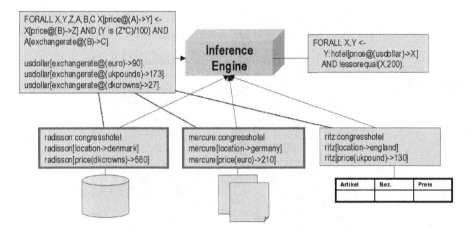

Fig. 9.4. Example context transformation

information sources are added. The other problematic aspect is the need to create and maintain a logical representation of information items as instances of the ontology. In the presence of large information sources the logical representation becomes the bottleneck of the system. In this section we will discuss the OBSERVER system, which provides solutions for the two problems mentioned above: the system allows the existence of multiple ontologies, including the use of different ontologies to represent different views on the same domain, and provides and uses the semantic information to generate plans of how to query the different sources rather than including individual information items into the reasoning process.

In the following, we describe how OBSERVER addresses the example integration problem focusing on these two aspects.

9.2.1 Query Processing in OBSERVER

The OBSERVER system implements a special query-processing strategy for dealing with multiple information sources that are based on different ontologies. This strategy consists of three basic steps shown in Fig. 9.5. The strategy is incremental in the sense that the system first tries to answer a query only using data that is linked to the user's ontology and establishes connection to other information sources one by one in case the user is not satisfied with the result so far. In the following, we briefly discuss the different steps shown in Fig. 9.5.

- *Query Formulation.* in the first step the user selects one of the existing ontologies in the system as source for the query vocabulary. In the following,

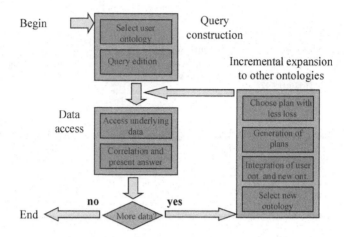

Fig. 9.5. Incremental query extension in OBSERVER

we call this ontology the user ontology. After having decided on a particular ontology, a query to the system can be formulated using the terms of the ontology that can be combined using operators of the CLASSIC description logic [Borgida et al., 1989].

- *Data access.* in OBSERVER an ontology is associated with a number of information sources. In this step, the system retrieves answers to the user query from the data sources associated with the ontology chosen in the first step. The user query is processed by expanding the query into an extended relational algebra expression. This expression is evaluated on the information source using special wrappers and the results are passed to the user as a partial answer to the query.
- *Query expansion.* if the user is not satisfied with the answer given by the system, the user query is incrementally expanded to other information sources. As these sources use different ontologies, the user query has to be re-written into the terminology used by the additional source (target ontology). For this purpose, OBSERVER uses semantic relations between the different ontologies in the system. These semantic relations include synonym, hypernym and hyponym relations as well as overlap, disjointness and coverage. These relations that are stored in a central repository can be interpreted as equivalence and subsumption in the description logic used to represent knowledge in the system. When re-formulating the query, OBSERVER distinguishes two cases:
  - In some cases, all terms in the query can be replaced by synonym terms in the target ontology. In this case, the re-formulated query is equivalent to the original one and there is no loss of information resulting from the translation (referred to as full translation).

– Often, not all the terms in a user query have synonym terms in the target ontology. In this case, OBSERVER performs a partial translation of these terms using a similar approach to the one described in Sect. 6.2. In particular, the terms are replaced by unions of hyponym or intersections of hyperym terms and the corresponding query is used to retrieve data accepting a certain loss of information. This case is referred to as partial translation.

In the case of a partial translation, there are different possibilities of combining replacements of terms in the query. For each of these possible translations, OBSERVER estimates the loss of information and selects the approach that can be assumed to have the smallest loss.

As shown in Fig. 9.5 steps two and three are repeated iteratively incorporating more and more information sources until the user is satisfied with the result. After the first iteration, the second step also includes a re-formulation of the retrieved information into the user ontology.

9.2.2 Vocabulary integration

We consider an extension of our example integration problem, where the information shown in Table 9.1 is taken from two different sources of information. Each of these information sources uses a different ontology that provides the terms used to describe the category of the accommodation. We assume that the information sources use the ontologies shown in Fig. 9.6. The hierarchy on the left-hand side is the user ontology that is used to formulate the query.

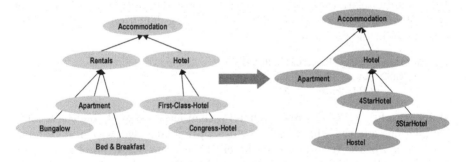

Fig. 9.6. The ontology integration problem

Using this ontology the user states the query for hotels with a price of less than 200. In the following, we focus our attention on the type information contained in the query. The restriction on the price and the necessary currency conversion are assumed to be handled by information-source wrappers.

Looking at the information in Table 9.1, we see that consulting the information source associated with the user ontology will only produce the first item in the table as a result. The other two information items are classified according to the ontology on the right-hand side of Fig. 9.6. In order to decide whether this information is an answer to the query for hotels, the user ontology has to be integrated with this ontology using information about semantic relations between terms in the two models. We use the set of semantic relations shown in Table 9.2 to combine the two ontologies.

Table 9.2. Data from the example problem

IAO.APARTMENT	is a synonym of SAO.apartment
IAO.HOTEL	is a hyponym of SAO.hotel
IAO.HOTEL	is a hypernym of SAO.4StarHotel
IAO.HOTEL	is a hypernym of SAO.5StarsHotel
<IAO.HOTEL,80% > overlaps	<SAO.Hotel,50%>
IAO.PRICE	is a synonym of SAO.price

The semantic relations in Table 9.2 indicate that the terms apartment, hotel and price used in both models are synonyms. Further, we find the information that 4StarHotel and 5StarHotel are hyponyms of hotel and that the term hotel in the user ontology refers to a more specific concept than the term accommodation in the ontology of the additional information. In addition to the semantic relations, the system uses semantic descriptions of the different concepts in the ontologies. Consider the following definition of the term first class hotel in the user ontology:

```
(define-concept FirstClassHotel
    (AND Hotel
        (ALL Stars (> 3)))
```

It defines a first-class hotel to be a hotel with at least 4 stars. Using the semantic relations and the semantics of the description language, we can determine the relation of the term first class hotel to the terms 4 star hotel and 5 star hotel from the target ontology that have the following definition:

```
(define-concept 4StarHotel
    (AND Hotel
        (ALL Stars (= 4))))
```

```
(define-concept 5StarHotel
```

```
(AND Hotel
     (ALL Stars (= 5))))
```

Using a description-logic reasoner we can compute semantic relations between
all the terms in the user and the target ontology. The resulting integrated
model (Fig. 9.7) provides the basis for re-formulating user queries that do not
have a full translation.

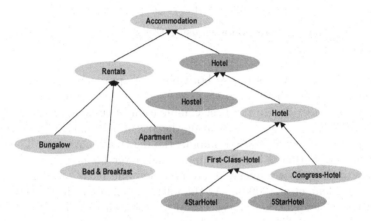

Fig. 9.7. Combined view on the ontologies

9.2.3 Query plan generation and selection

The integrated ontology now provides a basis for re-formulating queries across
the different ontologies present in the system. While terms that have a direct
synonym in the target ontology are just replaced by this synonym, terms
without a direct correspondence have to be approximated by a combination
of similar terms. This can be done in different ways, leading to a situation
where one query can be translated in different ways. We will illustrate this
using our example problem.

In order to answer our example query we will state a query in terms of a
concept expression describing hotels with a price of less than 200. Using the
logic provided in OBSERVER, this concept expression is the following:

```
(AND Hotel (ALL price (<200)))
```

Here, the terms *Hotel* and *price* are both taken from the user ontology. As we
can see from the semantic relations, the term price has a corresponding term
in the target ontology and can therefore be directly replaced. Although there is
also a term "hotel" in the target ontology, it is not a synonym. We therefore

have to consider different approximation of this term. The approximation approach taken in OBSERVER is similar to the one described in Sect. 6.2. In particular, each term that does not have a synonym is either replaced by the conjunction of its parents or the union of its children in the integrated concept hierarchy. In our example this results in two possible translations of the query:

1. `(AND Hotel (ALL price (<200))`
2. `(AND (OR 4StarHotel 5StarHotel) (ALL price (<200)))`

The first alternative corresponds to using the upper, the second to using the lower approximation.

As OBSERVER allows us to use both kinds of approximations and even to mix them in cases where more than one term has to be approximated, we need a criterion to choose the best combination of these approximations. In OBSERVER this is done by estimating the loss of information for each possible translation based on statistics about the information sources. The notion of loss of information is based on upper and lower bounds on the expected precision and recall of a query, where precision and recall are defined in the usual way [Mena et al., 2000b]. As the following example shows, the estimation of loss of information is also useful in cases where we only replace one term as in the example above, as it helps us to choose between the upper and the lower approximations. Using the measures defined in [Mena et al., 2000b] we get the following figures:

Replacement	Hotel	(OR 4StarHotel 5StarHotel)
Precision	(23%, 30%)	(100%, 100%)
Recall	(100%, 100%)	(22%, 50%)
Loss	(53%, 62%)	(33%, 63%)

As the figures show, in contrast to our expectation, replacing the term hotel from the user ontology by the term hotel from the target ontology is not the best choice in our case. While it has about the same maximal possible loss of information, replacing the term by its lower approximation leads to a better lower bound in the loss (one-third as opposed to one-half of the information). In our example, OBSERVER will therefore decide to use the lower approximation for the term hotel and return all four and five star hotels from the information sources classified by the target ontology.

9.3 The BUSTER system

While the OBSERVER approach to information integration is quite similar to the techniques described in this part of the book (in particular Chap.

6), the need to create and maintain sematic relations between multiple ontologies in the system is a drawback. In order to cope with this problem OBSERVER is able to deduce new semantic relations from combinations of existing ones using canonical terms. This can be seen as a step in the direction of the hybrid integration approach mentioned in Chap. 2. The BUSTER system [Visser and Schuster, 2002], developed at the University of Bremen, is an example of a system that more explicitly uses the hybrid approach, implementing the methods described in this book. In the following we will briefly describe the BUSTER system focusing on those features distinguishing it from systems like OBSERVER, in particular the extensive use of a shared base vocabulary and methods for retrieval based on spatial criteria.

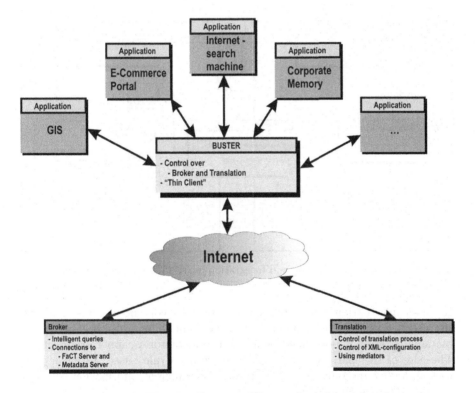

Fig. 9.8. BUSTER – Intelligent middleware for information sharing

BUSTER is meant to provide an intelligent middleware for information sharing. We envision that the BUSTER system is used by many different applications like search engines, e-commerce platforms or corporate memories in order to access heterogeneous and distributed information resources. For this purpose, the BUSTER system provides two subsystems, one for information filtering and one for information integration. These subsystems are mainly independent of each other and can be accessed by clients over the World Wide Web (compare Fig. 9.8).

Fig. 9.9 shows the interaction of the two subsystems in a typical integration scenario. In a first step, relevant information sources are selected based on the user's information need. This is done by a broker component were information sources register and provide access information. The decision whether a source is relevant is based on source metadata provided by a metadata server. A user request is matched against the metadata of an information source that, same as the user query, is based on a shared vocabulary. The actual decision step uses an external OWL reasoner for deductive matching.

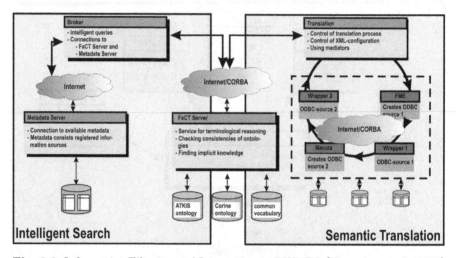

Fig. 9.9. Information Filtering and Integration in BUSTER [Neumann et al., 2001]

After an information source has been chosen, its content is translated into the user's format by the integration component. This structural and syntactic integration is performed by a classical mediator–wrapper architecture. The core of this part is the MECOTA system, a rule based mediator that uses abductive reasoning to translate between different information contexts [Wache, 1999, Wache, 2003].

9.3.1 The use of shared vocabularies

In principle, the query processing in BUSTER works quite similarly to the OBSERVER system: user queries are translated into the vocabulary provided by the ontologies assigned to different sources. The main difference lies in the fact that the user does not commit to a user ontology representing his personal view of the domain but rather to a basic vocabulary that is used to define concepts in all the source ontologies (compare Sect. 2.4.2).

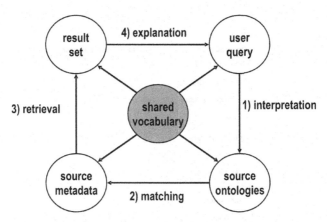

Fig. 9.10. The role of shared vocabularies in BUSTER

By formulating the user query in terms of this basic vocabulary we ensure that the query can interpreted with respect to all source ontologies in the system. In particular, we can determine these concepts in a source ontology that are most similar to the concept we asked for. Here, being similar means the direct parents and children of the query concept after we have classified it into the source ontology. After translating the query into the terminology provided by a source ontology – this is done as described in Sect. 6.2, we can match the query against metadata provided for the information source. The metadata for an information source is comparable to the descriptions used in the OntoBroker system. In particular, information items contained in the source and their properties are described using terms from the shared vocabulary. This again guarantees that we can determine those items that are an answer to the translated query by logical deduction. Finally, the descriptions of matching information items are returned to the user and a short explanation is given why the item has been matched – currently this explanation points to the concept in the source ontology that has been used for matching. Fig. 9.10 provides an overview of the process.

9.3.2 Retrieving accommodation information

For our example problem we use a shared vocabulary containing basic relations and terms from the accommodation domain that can be used to specify different types of accommodations as well as to describe actual accommodations. In the initial interaction with the system the user will be asked to select a domain and the corresponding vocabulary (see Fig. 9.11).

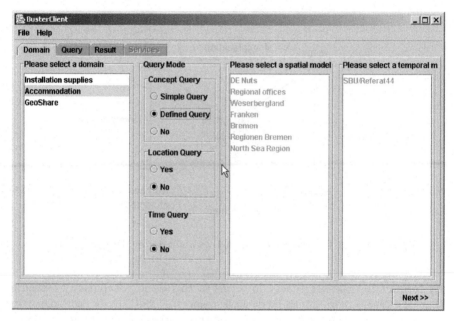

Fig. 9.11. Selection of shared models

After having selected a query the user is asked to formulate a query using the shared vocabulary. The query formulation is supported by a query-construction interface which is dynamically generated from the chosen vocabulary. As shown in Fig. 9.12 the vocabulary for the accommodation domain specifies five properties for the concept accommodation that can be further specified:

- *Meals.* Information about available meals for example used to distinguish full-pension, half-pension and bed and breakfast.
- *Facilities.* Information about available facilities including fixed installation such as TV-sets as well as services offered.
- *Stars.* Number of stars assigned to the accommodation. This can also be used describe other kinds of distinctions received by the accommodation.
- *Building.* Information about the type of building, e.g. apartments vs. one single complex.

Units: the size of the accommodation in terms of number of units.

For each of these properties, the vocabulary also defines a set or even a hierarchy of possible values. In Fig. 9.12 we see parts of the fillers for the facility property.

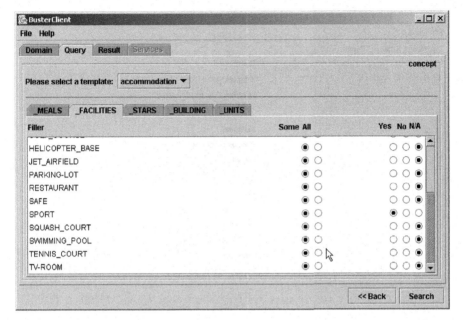

Fig. 9.12. Query construction based on shared terminology

Based on the query formulated by the user the system now searches the different information sources and returns relevant results. Fig. 9.13 shows a situation where the user is looking for a sports hotel. The results are shown as a list on the left-hand side of the screen. The right-hand side contains an explanation for the currently selected result. The explanation consists of the actual query being asked by the user, the matching concept from the source ontology – in this case "golf hotel" – and the metadata describing the result.

9.3.3 Spatial and temporal information

The systems we have discussed so far – and this observation also holds for information integration systems in general – are mainly focusing on the integration of conceptual information. We have seen how the systems deal with different classifications of information items and differences in underlying measures and scales. If we look at our example problem, however, it is quite obvious that there is not only a conceptual side to the integration problem. When looking for a certain accommodation, we also have to take care of spatial and temporal aspects of the information:

- Is the accommodation close enough to the place we really want to go to, e.g. the location of a conference?
- Is the accommodation available at the respective time we need to be at the place, e.g. the duration of the conference?

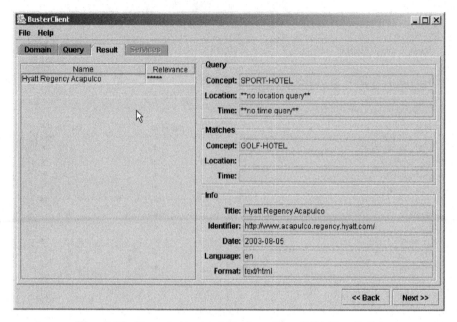

Fig. 9.13. Presentation and Explanation of the Result Set

Currently, these aspects are not well supported by many systems, because they require different kinds of reasoning mechanisms. While many systems rely on reasoning about class hierarchies, in particular about the subclass relation, reasoning about spatial relevance of a piece of information needs inferences over part-of hierarchies and neighborhood graphs. The BUSTER system tries to close this gap by distinguishing between conceptual, spatial and temporal aspects of an information request. Each of these components is evaluated separately and only information meeting all of the criteria is returned. In the following, we briefly describe the processing of spatial queries in the BUSTER system.

The idea behind processing spatial queries in BUSTER is the use of names of spatial locations. These names can include the names of cities and countries, but also less well-defined locations such as regions or landscapes. A problem that arises with the use of place names is the fact that different information sources will often use different place names. This might be due to the fact that the same place has different names (e.g. Chemnitz vs. Karl-Marx Stadt), to differences in the granularity of the information (countries vs. federal states) or the use of special names that do not have a counterpart in other terminologies (sales regions of a certain company). Fig. 9.14 shows the query interface of the system that allows the user to specify spatial criteria.

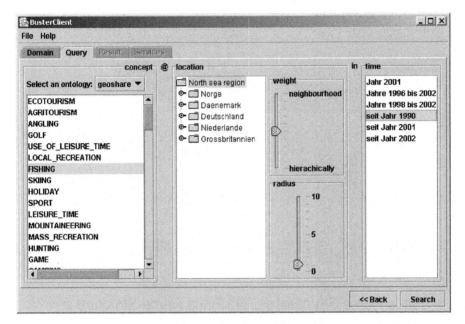

Fig. 9.14. Query interface for conceptual, spatial and temporal criteria

Once such a name appears in a user query, the system has to determine which part of the information that satisfies the conceptual part of the query is also relevant with respect to the place name in the query. In order to deal with this problem, the BUSTER system uses so called place-name structures [Voegele et al., 2003]. Place-name structures consist of a combination of a partonomy of spatial regions each connected with a name. In our example, this partonomy would for example contain the path: Europe, Scandinavia, Denmark. Depending on the spatial region chosen by the user, different answers will be returned. If the user selects the name Europe, all three hotels will be returned as they are all located in cities that are part of Europe. If the user narrows down the requested region to Scandinavia, only the Radisson in Copenhagen will be returned, because the other cities are not considered to belong to Scandinavia. The upper-left part of Fig. 9.15 shows a similar partonomy related to federal states in Germany.

Besides clearly defined regions such as countries, a place-name structure may also contain names of less well-defined regions such as mountain ranges or seas. The upper right part of Fig. 9.15 shows an example of a mountain range (square box in the hierarchy) inserted into the partonomy by relating its spatial extension to federal states. In the case of our example, the user might ask for a hotel on the Baltic Sea. Clearly none of the hotels are part of the Baltic Sea, making clear that a partonomy alone is not enough to process spatial queries. For this purpose, BUSTER combines the partonomy with a

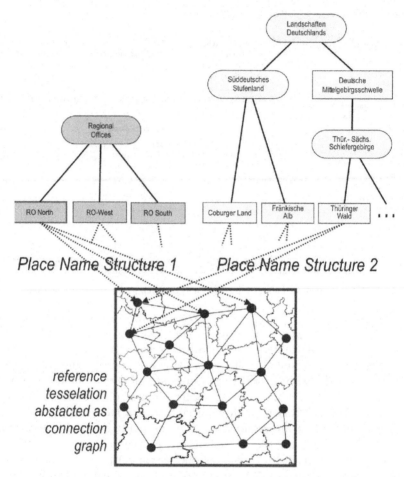

Fig. 9.15. Representation of spatial knowledge (from [Voegele et al., 2003])

connection graph for an underlying tessellation of spatial regions with well defined boundaries (compare the lower part of Fig. 9.15). In our example this connection graph provides the knowledge that Denmark as well as Germany are connected to the Baltic Sea and are therefore more relevant than the UK. Therefore, the Radisson in Copenhagen and the Mercure in Hamburg are returned as results.

Another function of the tessellations underlying the place-name structures is the integration of spatial information during query answering. It allows different information sources to use different partonomies of place names.

As long as they are based on the same underlying tessellation, the spatial relevance can still be determined based on this shared model.

9.4 Conclusions

The systems discussed in this chapter address various aspects of identifying and integrating heterogeneous and distributed information sources of related topics. The integration problem is addressed on different levels including syntax, structure and semantic integration. The systems have successfully been applied in different domains such as database integration, experience management in large companies and geographic information processing. These applications show that the models and methods described in this book are not only of theoretical interest, but that they contribute to a practical solution for information-sharing problems. Especially, we conclude that the general framework described in this book can be put to work using existing Web technologies: shared ontologies can be encoded in RDF Schema, OWL can be used to build source ontologies. Information sources in terms of collections of HTML documents can be linked to these ontologies using specialized wrappers and annotation tools. Finally, mapping and filtering methods can be implemented on top of existing subsumption reasoners that can be accessed over the Web. This tight coupling with existing technologies makes us optimistic about the potential contribution of the framework to a more intelligent Semantic Web. We also have to notice, however, that currently successful applications are only reported in rather restricted application domains rather than an open Semantic Web environment. Issues such as scalability and automatic generation of mappings still need investigation before systems are ready to move out to the Web.

Further reading

The OntoBroker system is presented in [Decker et al., 1999] in more detail. Frame-logic, the logical formalism used in OntoBroker is introduced in [Kifer et al., 1995]. The most complete description of the OBSERVER system is in [Mena and Illarramendi, 2001]. The methods for query planning based on approximate re-writing is discussed in [Mena et al., 2000b]. A description of the BUSTER system can be found in [Visser and Schuster, 2002]. The methods for determining spatial relevance in the BUSTER system are described in [Schlieder et al., 2001] and [Voegele et al., 2003].

Part IV

Distributed ontologies

10

Modularization

Summary. In Chap. 3 we introduced the Web Ontology Language as a suitable way of describing information on the Semantic Web. We described the use of the language for integrating different information sources. In this context, we always considered ontologies as monolithic entities. In particular, we assumed that reasoning is performed on the complete set of consistent definitions from all relevant ontologies. On the Web it is much more likely, however, that the ontologies themselves are distributed and describe the same domain in different, potentially mutually inconsistent ways. In this chapter, we propose an extension of OWL that deals with distributed ontologies and show its benefits compared to direct use of OWL.

Throughout this book we have considered distributed information sources and semantic descriptions of the information contained therein. One of the principles of our approach is the use of source ontologies that formalize the conceptualization of a single information source. Being based on the representations found in the particular source, these ontologies will be distributed and will often describe the same domain of interest in different ways. Most existing tools, however, treat ontologies as monolithic entities and provide little support for specifying, storing and accessing ontologies in a modular manner. Existing proposals trying to fill this gap lack a formal underpinning. Examples can be found with respect to ontology editors [Noy et al., 2000, Bechhofer et al., 2001], reasoning systems [Haarslev and Moeller, 2001, Horrocks, 1998] and more recently storage and query systems (e.g. [Broekstra et al., 2002]). We think that the distributed nature of ontologies used for information sharing on the Semantic Web requires an adequate treatment of distributed ontologies. In particular, there is a need for a formal foundation and an appropriate infrastructure for representing and managing distributed ontologies. In this chapter, we propose a formal foundation for distributed ontology modules that are connected by specialized mappings. We show that the expressiveness of our model goes beyond the import mechanism provided by OWL and analyze the model with respect to formal properties and supported inferences.

In this chapter, we first motivate and explain our approach for defining and reasoning with modular ontologies. After a brief review of related work on modular representation, we propose and architecture and semantics for modular ontologies. The definition of our model is followed by a comparison with OWL and its possibility to modularize and to link representations. Aferwards, the problem of reasoning with and about modular ontologies is discussed.

10.1 Motivation

Beyond the use of ontologies as local descriptions of information sources there are many reasons for thinking about ontology modularization. Our work is mainly driven by three arguments. These also bias the solution we propose, as it is aimed at improving the current situation with respect to the following aspects.

- *Distributed systems.* In distributed environments like the Semantic Web, the question for modularization arises naturally. Ontologies in different places are built independent of each other and can be assumed to be highly heterogeneous. Unrestricted referencing to concepts in a remote ontology can therefore lead to serious semantic problems as the domain of interpretation may differ even if concepts appear to be the same on a conceptual level. The introduction of modules with local semantics and clearly specified interfaces can help to overcome this problem.
- *Large ontologies.* Modularization is not only desirable in distributed environments, it also helps to manage very large ontologies we find for example in medicine or biology. These ontologies that sometimes contain more than a hundred thousand concepts are hard to maintain as changes are not contained locally but can affect large parts of the model. Another argument for modularization in the presence of large ontologies is reuse as, in most cases, we are not interested in the complete ontology when building a new system, but only in a specific part. Experiences from software engineering show that modules provide a good level of abstraction to support maintenance and re-use.
- *Efficient reasoning.* A specific problem that occurs in the case of distributed ontologies as well as very large models is the problem of efficient reasoning. While the pure size of the ontologies causes problems in the latter case, in a distributed setting hidden dependencies and cyclic references can cause serious problems. The introduction of modules with local semantics and clear interfaces will help us to analyze distributed systems and provides a basis for the development of methods for localizing inference.

10.1.1 Requirements

There are a couple of requirements a modular ontology architecture has to fulfill in order to improve ontology maintenance and reasoning in the way suggested above. The requirements will be the main guidelines for the design of our solution proposed in this work.

- *Loose coupling.* In general, we cannot assume that two ontology modules have anything in common. This refers to the conceptualization as well as the specific logical language used for the interpretation of objects, classes or relations. Our architecture has to reflect this by providing an extremely loose coupling of modules. Especially, we have to prevent unwanted interactions between modules. For this purpose, mappings between modules have to be distinguished from local definitions on the semantic as well as the conceptual level.
- *Self-containment.* In order to facilitate the re-use of individual modules from a larger, possibly interconnected system, we have to make sure that modules are self-contained. In especially, the result of certain reasoning tasks such as subsumption or query answering within a single module has to be possible without having to access other modules. This is also important if we want to provide efficient reasoning. Further, we have to ensure correctness and, whenever possible, completeness of local reasoning for obvious reasons.

10.1.2 Our approach

In the following, we describe our approach to ontology modularization on an abstract level. We emphasize the main design decisions and motivate them on the basis of the requirements defined above. The technical details of the approach will be given in the following sections.

- *View-based mappings.* The first design decision made concerns the way different ontology modules are connected. In our work, we adopt the approach of view-based information integration. Ontology modules are connected by conjunctive queries. Especially, the extension of a concept in one module can be claimed to be equivalent to the (intentional) answer set of a conjunctive query over the vocabulary of another module. This way of connecting modules is more expressive than simple one-to-one mappings between concept names. Further, the same technique can be used to define relations of any arity based on other modules. Compared to the use of arbitrary axioms, our approach is less expressive. We decide to sacrifice a higher expressiveness for the sake of conceptual simplicity and desirable semantic properties such as directedness of the mapping. Especially, the definition of a query mapping does not influence the interpretation of the queried ontology.

- *Interface compilation.* The use of conjunctive queries guarantees a loose coupling on a conceptual and semantic level. However, it does not provide self-containment, because reasoning in an ontology module depends on the answer sets of the queries used to connect it to other modules. These answer sets have to be determined by actually querying the other ontology module. In order to make local reasoning independent from other modules, we use a knowledge-compilation approach. The idea is to compute the result of each mapping query off-line and add the result as an axiom to the ontology module using the result. During reasoning, these axioms replace the query thus enabling local reasoning. As the results of queries are considered to be defined intentionally rather than extensionally, the result of the compilation of a query is not a set of instances retrieved from other modules, but a concept expression that contains all the information necessary to perform local reasoning. In our case this expression is the conjunction of all concepts of the other ontology module that subsume the query expression.

10.1.3 Related work

Our work relates to two main areas of research on representing and reasoning about ontological knowledge. The first area is concerned with distributed and modular knowledge representation where we use ideas from theorem proving and knowledge engineering. The second area of related work is concerned with managing knowledge models. Here previous work exists in knowledge engineering as well as in databases and information systems.

While the principle of modularity has widely been adopted in software engineering it has got less attention in the area of knowledge representation and reasoning. Some fundamental work on the modularization of representations can be found in the area of theorem proving. Farmer and colleagues promote the use of combinations of "little theories", representations of a specific mathematical structure in order to reason about complex problems [Farmer et al., 1992]. They show the advantages of this modular approach in terms of reusability and reduced modelling effort.

The idea of reusing and combining chunks of knowledge rather than building knowledge bases from scratch has later been adopted by the knowledge engineering community for building real-world knowledge bases (see e.g. [Clark et al., 2001]). McIlraith and Amir argue that a modularization of knowledge bases also has advantages for reasoning, even if the modularization is done a posteriori. They present algorithms for breaking down existing representations into a set of modules with minimal interaction and define reasoning procedures for propositional [Amir and McIlraith, 2000] and first-order logic [McIlraith and Amir, 2001]. The work reported is motivated by well-established techniques from uncertain reasoning, where an a posteriori modularization of large theories is a common way to reduce run time complexity (see e.g. [Lauritzen and Spiegelhalter, 1988]).

As we are interested in representations of ontological knowledge, approaches from the area of logics for representing terminologies, so-called description logics, are of special interest for our work. In this area, we find the same arguments for a modularized representation as in the area of theorem proving. Rector proposes a strategy for modular implementation of ontologies using description logics [Rector, 2003]. The approach is based on a set of orthogonal taxonomies that provide a basis for defining more complex concepts. Rector argues for the benefits of this strategy in terms of easier creation and reuse of ontological knowledge. Buchheit and others propose a similar structuring on the language level by dividing the terminological part of a knowledge base into a schema part that corresponds to the basic taxonomies and a view part [Buchheit et al., 1994]. They show that this distinction can be used to achieve better run-time behavior for complex view languages. While these approaches still assume the overall model to be a single ontology providing a coherent conceptualization of the World, Giunchiglia and others propose a more radical approach to distributed representations. They propose the local model semantics as an extension of the standard semantics of first-order logics [Ghidini and Giunchiglia, 2001]. This semantics allows different modules to represent different views of the same part of the World and the definition of directed partial mappings between different modules. Recently, Borgida and Serafini defined a distributed version of description logics based on local model semantics that has all advantages of the contextual representations [Borgida and Serafini, 2002].

The problem of combining and reasoning with ontological modules is has become of central importance in research on knowledge representation and reasoning on the so-called Semantic Web. Current proposals for languages to encode ontological knowledge on the World Wide Web, i.e. the RDF Schema [Brickley and Guha, 2004] and the Web Ontology Language OWL [McGuinness and van Harmelen, 2003], provide some basic mechanisms for combining modular representations. The abilities for combining different models are restricted to the import of complete models and to the use of elements from a different model in definitions by direct reference. It is assumed that references to external statements are only made for statements from imported models; however, this is strictly speaking not required. In first case the complete semantics of the external ontology is adopted. In the latter case, the external elements are treated as atomic elements with no further definition. As a consequence, mappings rather implicitly exist in terms of mutual use of statements across models. Volz and colleagues discuss different interpretations of the import statement that range from purely syntactic to schema-aware interpretations of the imported knowledge [Volz et al., 2002a]. An alternative way of relating different RDF models to each others that is much closer to our ideas is discussed by Oberle [Volz et al., 2003], who defines a view language for RDF and defines some consistency constraints for the resulting model.

10.2 Modular ontologies

In order to put a higher-level modularization infrastructure for ontologies into place, extensions of existing technologies are necessary at different levels. On the syntactic level, we have to extend existing language standards like OWL with a language for defining module interfaces and mappings between different modules. On the semantic level, we have to define the interpretation of mappings as well as the relation between definitions in different modules in such a way that we achieve independence between modules. In this section we will present a framework for representing modular ontologies. In Sect. 10.2.1 we define a syntax for representing modular ontologies and provide an intuitive description of its meaning. Section 10.2.2 underpins the syntax with a model-theoretic semantics for modular ontologies that uses the notion of a distributed interpretation across different abstract domains to define an novel notion of logical consequence that better fits the intuition of distributed models than the standard notion used by languages like OWL.

10.2.1 Syntax and architecture

What makes up a modular ontology is the possibility to use ontology-based queries in order to define concepts in one module in terms of a query over another module. For this purpose, we divide the set of concepts in a module into internally defined concepts $\mathcal{C}_I$ and externally defined concepts $\mathcal{C}_E$, resulting in the following definition of $\mathcal{C}$:

$$\mathcal{C} = \mathcal{C}_I \cup \mathcal{C}_E, \; \mathcal{C}_I \cap \mathcal{C}_E = \emptyset \qquad (10.1)$$

Internally defined concepts are specified by using concept expressions in the spirit of description logics [Baader et al., 2002]. We do not require a particular logic to be used.

Definition 10.1 (internal concept definition). *An internal concept definition is an axiom of one of the following forms $C \sqsubseteq D, C \equiv D$, where $C \in \mathcal{CN}$ and D is a concept expression of the form $f(t_1, ..., t_n)$, where the terms t_i are either concept names or concept expressions and f is an n-ary concept-building operator.*

Besides this standard way of defining concepts, we consider externally defined concepts that are assumed to be equivalent to the result of a query posed to another module in the modular ontology. This way of connecting modules is very much in the spirit of view-based information integration, which is a standard technique in the area of database systems [Halevy, 2001]. The choice of conjunctive queries for connecting different modules is motivated by the trade-off between expressiveness of the mapping and conceptual as well as computational simplicity. Our approach is more expressive than simple one-to-one mappings; having more complex mappings would contradict the principle of loose coupling of different modules. We now use the notion of an ontology-based query in order to define concepts using queries over a different ontology (module) that have exactly one free variable.

Definition 10.2 (external concept definition). *An external concept definition is an axiom of the form: $C \equiv M : Q$, where M is a module and Q is an ontology-based query over the signature of M with exactly one free variable.*

Further, we allow relations to be defined in terms of query expressions with two free variables. By convention, we call these variables x and y where x always denotes the variable in the first and y the variable in the second place of the binary relation. Analogously to external concept definitions, we get the following definition for externally defined relations $R_{\mathcal{E}}$.

Definition 10.3 (External Relation Definition). *An external relation definition is an axiom of the form: $R \equiv M : Q$ Where M is a module and Q is an ontology-based query over the signature of M with exactly two free variable. We denote the set of all external relations $R_{\mathcal{E}}$.*

A modular ontology is now simply defined as a set of modules that are connected by external concept and relation definitions. In particular we require that all external definitions are contained in the modular system.

Definition 10.4 (modular ontology). *A modular ontology $\mathcal{M} = \{M_1, ..., M_m\}$ is a set of modules such that, for each externally defined concept $C \equiv M_i : Q$ and each external relation definition $R \equiv M_i : Q$, M_i is also a member of $\mathcal{M}$.*

We will use this notion of a modular ontology in the following to investigate the problem of integrity of logical reasoning across modules.

10.2.2 Semantics and logical consequence

After having defined a representation syntax for modular ontologies, we now have to define how a modular ontology should be interpreted. Such a semantic underpinning in necessary to define the notion of logical consequence which serves as a basis for any kind of reasoning. Further, having a formal semantics makes it easier to compare our model to existing proposals for ontologies on the Web as well as to investigate the formal properties of the kind of mapping relations chosen.

When defining the semantics of our model, we have to find a trade-off between backward compatibility with existing standards and new ways of defining logical semantics that better fit the distributed nature of a modular ontology. In order to meet both requirements, we define a local semantics that applies to individual modules and a distributed semantics that defines how the relations between elements in different modules are interpreted. The local semantics directly corresponds to the Tarskian-style semantics of description logics and is therefore very close to the semantics of OWL-DL, which can be seen as a special kind of description logics. The distributed semantics borrows from the notion of distributed first-order logics and more specifically distributed description logics defining the interaction between different local models referring to the local semantics.

Local semantics

We can define semantics and logical consequence of a terminological knowledge base using an interpretation mapping $(.)^{\Im}$ into an abstract domain Δ such that:

- $c^{\Im} \subseteq \Delta$ for all class definitions c in the way defined above,
- $r^{\Im} \subseteq \Delta \times \Delta$ for all relation definitions r,
- $o^{\Im} \in \Delta$ for all object definitions o.

This type of denotational semantics is inspired by description logics [Donini et al., 1996]; however, we are not specific about operators that can be used to build class definitions which are of central interest of these logics. Using the interpretation mapping, we can define the notion of a model in the following way:

Definition 10.5 (Model of a terminological knowledge base). *An interpretation $\Im$ is a model for the knowledge base $\mathcal{T}$ if $\Im \models A$ for every axiom $A \in (\mathcal{C} \cup \mathcal{R} \cup \mathcal{O})$, where $\models$ is defined as follows.*

- $\Im \models c \equiv (o_1, ..., o_n)$, *iff* $c^{\Im} = \{o_1^{\Im}, ..., o_n^{\Im}\}$
- $\Im \models c_1 \sqsubseteq c_2$, *iff* $c_1^{\Im} \subseteq c_2^{\Im}$
- $\Im \models r \sqsubseteq (c_1, c_2)$, *iff* $r^{\Im} \subseteq c_1^{\Im} \times c_2^{\Im}$
- $\Im \models r_1 \sqsubseteq r_2$, *iff* $r_1^{\Im} \subseteq r_2^{\Im}$
- $\Im \models o : c$, *iff* $o^{\Im} \in c^{\Im}$
- $\Im \models (o_1, o_2) : r$, *iff* $(o_1^{\Im}, o_2^{\Im}) \in r^{\Im}$

These definitions enable us to perform reasoning using the notion of logical consequence:

Definition 10.6 (logical consequence). *An axiom A logically follows from a set of axioms $\mathcal{S}$ if $\Im \models \mathcal{S}$ implies $\Im \models A$ for every model $\Im$. We denote this fact by $\mathcal{S} \models A$.*

Global semantics

We define a model-based semantics for modular ontologies using the notion of a distributed interpretation proposed in [Borgida and Serafini, 2002] in the context of distributed description logics:

Definition 10.7 (distributed interpretation). *A distributed interpretation* $\Im = \langle \{\Im_i\}_{i \in Index}, r \rangle$ *of a modular ontology* $\mathcal{M}$ *consists of interpretations* $\Im_i$ *for the individual module* M_i *over domains* Δ_i, *such that:*

- $C_i^{\Im} \subseteq \Delta_i$ *for all concept definitions* $C \in \mathcal{C}_i$,
- $R_i^{\Im} \subseteq \Delta_i \times \Delta_i$ *for all relation definition* $R \in \mathcal{R}_i$,
- $O_i^{\Im} \in \Delta_i$ *for all object definitions* $O \in \mathcal{O}_i$

and functions b^k *associating to each pair of indices* i, j *binary relations* $b_{ij}^k \subseteq \Delta_i^k \times \Delta_j^k$. $b_{ij}^k(d)$ *denotes the set* $\{d' \in \Delta_j^k \mid (d, d') \in b_{ij}^k\}$; *for every* $D \subseteq \Delta_i^k$ $b_{ij}^k(D)$ *denotes* $\bigcup_{d \in D} b_{ij}^k(d)$.

The assumption of disjoint interpretation domains again reflects the principle of loose coupling underlying our approach. Based on the notion of a distributed interpretation we can define a model of a modular ontology as an interpretation that satisfies the constraints imposed by internal and external concept definitions. In contrast to [Borgida and Serafini, 2002] , we do not introduce special operators for defining the relations between different domains, we rather interpret external concept definitions as constraints on the relation between the domains:

Definition 10.8 (Logical consequence). *A distributed interpretation* $\Im$ *is a model for a modular ontology* $\mathcal{M}$ *if for every module* M_i *we have* $\Im \models X$ *for every concept or relation definition* X *in* M_i, *where* $\models$ *is defined using Definition 10.5 for internal definitions and the following equations:*

- $\Im \models C \equiv M_j : Q$, *iff* $C^{\Im_i} = b_{ji}^1(Q^{\Im_j})$,
- $\Im \models R \equiv M_j : Q$, *iff* $R^{\Im_i} = b_{ji}^2(Q^{\Im_j})$.

Here $Q^{\Im_j}$ *denotes the interpretation of the set of answers to query* Q. *An axiom* A *logically follows from a set of axioms* $\mathcal{S}$ *if* $\Im \models \mathcal{S}$ *implies* $\Im \models A$ *for every model* $\Im$. *We denote this fact by* $\mathcal{S} \models A$.

The actual definitions of concepts impose further constraints on the interpretation of a modular ontology. For the case of internally defined concepts, these constraints are provided by the definition of concept-building operators of description logics. For the case of externally defined concepts, the situation is more complicated and will be discussed in more detail in the next section.

10.3 Comparison with OWL

Different from the mainstream work on distributed ontology definitions, our approach uses a mapping language that is different from the logical language used to specify the local ontologies themselves. In particular, we use conjunctive queries over concepts and binary relations. At first glance this seems to be a serious restriction of the expressiveness of our language as mappings contain no negation, disjunction or other terminological operators. A careful investigation of the semantics of our model, however, reveals that the use of conjunctive queries actually leads to a higher expressiveness as opposed to the standard approach of linking ontologies by directly referring to elements of remote models in a local specification (compare [Dean et al., 2002]). In this section we show that the direct reference scheme used in languages like OWL can be simulated using a trivial mapping scheme; further, we argue that our model is more expressive than the direct use of elements, because it allows us to specify relations in terms of complex expressions. Finally, we sketch how our model can be extended in a straightforward way to also capture relations of arbitrary arity.

10.3.1 Simulating OWL import

Aiming at the Semantic Web, the language we have to compare ourselves to is the Web Ontology Language OWL. In the current proposals for OWL, the notion of mapping is not explicitly contained in the language. The abilities for combining different models are restricted to the import of complete models and to the use of elements from a different model in definitions by direct reference. It is assumed that references to external statements are only made for statements from imported models; however, this is strictly speaking not required. As a consequence, mappings rather implicitly exist in terms of mutual use of statements across models. While being quite simple, this way of connecting ontologies is quite flexible and allows for complex arrangements of elements from different models into one expression. In this section, we show that this ability can easily be encoded in our model using examples from the OWL language guide. The basic idea is the following: we create a local copy C of each external concept E involved using a trivial mapping of the form $C(X) \equiv M : E(X)$ and then combine these local copies in a complex definition using OWL class building operators.

Simple references

The most basic kind of reference to other ontologies mentioned in the OWL documentation is to state the equivalence of two classes using the `owl:equivalentClass` statement. The following example is taken from the OWL language guide:

```
Class(Wine)
Equivalent(Wine wine:Wine)
```

Assuming that the external ontology, described by the prefix `wine` is imported by the local ontology, this statements claims that the extensions of the two concepts are actually the same. We can model this constraint on the interpretation of the local ontology using the following trivial definition of the external concept Wine:

$$Wine(X) \equiv M_{vin} : Wine(X)$$

In this case, we could directly encode the OWL reference mechanism in terms of our model. Having restricted the definitions of external concepts to equivalence statements, however, we cannot directly encode the weaker `subclassOf` relation to external concepts like the one in the example below:

```
Class(WineGrape)
SubClassOf(WineGrape food:Grape)
```

At this point, we have to apply the modelling trick mentioned above: We create a local copy of the concept "Grape" using the same trivial mapping as above and declare the local concept "WineGrape" to be a subclass of this local copy:

$$C \equiv M_{food} : Grape(X)$$
$$WineGrape(X) \sqsubseteq C \qquad\qquad (10.2)$$

Combining internal and external definitions

The simple strategy of creating local copies of external concepts allows us to easily combine external and local definitions into more complex concepts. Again, we use an example from the OWL language guide, where Wine is defined as a subclass of the intersection of potable liquids and things made from grapes. Here, potable liquids are defined elsewhere, whereas the restricted relation "madeFromGrape" is contained in the local ontology:

```
Class(Wine)
SubClassOf(Wine intersectionOf(
    food:PotableLiquid
    restriction(madeFromGrape
        minCardinality(1))))
```

Using the same strategy as before, we create a copy of the externally defined concept "potableLiquid". Using this copy, we simply define the concept Wine locally using the description-logic counterparts of the OWL operations used in the example:

$$C(X) \equiv M_{food} : PotableLiquid(X)$$
$$Wine \sqsubseteq C \sqcap (\leq 1 \ madeFromGrape) \qquad (10.3)$$

Complex external references

The ability to make complex assertions about local copies from (maybe different) models also helps us to overcome the restricted expressiveness of our mapping language. Having restricted external definitions to conjunctive queries, we cannot directly express conjunction or negation in the definitions. However, we can use disjunction, negation and other OWL operators locally in order to define complex concepts on the basis of local copies of concepts from other ontologies. In order to illustrate this possibility, we use the following concept definition that uses concepts from three different external models:

```
Class(LiquidPoison)
SubClassOf(LiquidPoison intersectionOf(
    physics:LiquidSubstance
    unionOf(
        medicine:Drug
        food:PotableLiquid)))
```

In order to directly capture this definition in terms of an external concept definition, the mapping language would have to contain disjunction (for expressing `owl:unionOf`) and negation (for expressing `owl:complementOf`). Instead, we can encode the above concept expression in the following way that leads us to an internal concept expression with the same meaning as the example above.

$$C_1(X) \equiv M_{physics} : LiquidSubstance(X)$$
$$C_2(X) \equiv M_{medicine} : Drug(X)$$
$$C_3(X) \equiv M_{food} : PotableLiquid(X)$$
$$LiquidPoison \sqsubseteq C_1 \sqcap (C_2 \sqcup \neg C_3) \qquad (10.4)$$

Relation definitions

Concerning the definition of relations, the abilities of OWL are quite limited. Most of the assertions that can be made about relations do not depend on other elements of the ontologies but solely address the mathematical properties of a relation (such as transitivity or functionality). Assertions than can be made about a relation and its dependence on elements from other ontologies are `subPropertyOf`, `inverseOf` as well as domain and range restrictions. A slightly modified example from the OWL documentation is the following:

```
ObjectProperty(madeFromGrape
    InverseOf(wine:usedFor)
    domain(wine:Wine)
```

```
range(wine:WineGrape)
super(physical:madeOf))
```

In order to capture this definition in our mapping framework, we can combine the direct use of our mapping language and the use of local copies. Defining a relation to be the inverse of an external one can directly be done using a mapping query and inverting the order of the return variables:

$$madeFromGrapes(X, Y) \equiv M_{wine} : usedFor(Y, X)$$

For the domain and range restrictions, we create local copies and define the relation to range over these local copies (compare the section on axioms for defining ontological knowledge). As both kinds of restrictions, the mapping on the inverse of an external relation and the local restriction of the domain and range apply to the definition of the "madeFromGrape" relation, the semantics of its definition is the same as for the example definition.

$$C_1(X) \equiv M_{wine} : Wine(X)$$
$$C_2(X) \equiv M_{wine} : WineGrape(X)$$
$$madeFromGrapes \sqsubseteq (C_1 \times C_2) \tag{10.5}$$

The representation of subproperty relationship can be done analogously to the subclass relation described above. We introduce a new relation R, define it to be equivalent to the "madeOf" relation and add an axiom stating that "madeFromGrape" is a subproperty of R.

$$R(X, Y) \equiv M_{physical} : madeOf(X, Y)$$
$$madeFromGrape(X, Y) \sqsubseteq R(X, Y) \tag{10.6}$$

10.3.2 Beyond OWL

The examples given above raise the question of the advantages of a mapping language based on conjunctive queries. In this section, we argue that our mapping language extends the expressiveness of existing ontology languages that are solely based on description logics, and in particular OWL, by adding more possibilities for defining properties. In contrast to existing approaches for combining description logics with rule languages such as [Levy and Rousset, 1996] or [Donini et al., 1998], our approach only allows us to use rules in a very specific way, namely to define relations between disjoint interpretation domains, and therefore does not suffer from the technical problems of many other approaches. As a consequence, we can allow for complex terminological definitions such as the ones described above. In addition, we can define local relations by complex expressions over predicates in another model. Examples of such definitions that go beyond the expressiveness of OWL are given below.

Combining relations

The major advance of our approach over the abilities of OWL is the possibility to intentionally define relations using concepts, relations and also instances of a remote model. Based on these definitions, our model allows to derive subsumption relations between externally defined relations, while OWL only allows us to explicitly state subsumption relations between relations and use them to derive subsumption between relations. The example below describes the relation between employees and the companies they were employed by in a particular year:

$$employedIn2003(X,Y) \equiv M : employmentContract(Z) \wedge employee(Z,X)$$
$$\wedge year(Z,2003) \wedge employer(Z,Y) \qquad (10.7)$$

We now consider the more general relation of legal partners defined by the more general concepts of contract and beneficiary without reference to a particular year. Assuming that the model M provides the corresponding background knowledge $employmentContract \sqsubseteq contract$, $employee \sqsubseteq beneficiary$ and $employer \sqsubseteq beneficiary$ we can, based on the notion of logical consequence, derive that the following relation subsumes the one described above:

$$legalpartner(X,Y) \equiv M : contract(Z) \wedge beneficiary(Z,X) \wedge beneficiary(Z,Y)$$
$$(10.8)$$

n-ary Relations

A more ambitious extension to OWL expressiveness, that is supported by our model (though it is not worked out in this chapter) is the ability to express relations of an arbitrary arity. This is supported by the mapping language as well as the formal semantics of our approach. In our model, an n-ary relation can be defined using a query expression with n free variables. An example for a tertiary relation that connects an employee with his or her employer depending on a certain year is given below:

$$employed(X,P,Y) \equiv M : employmentContract(Z) \wedge beneficiary(Z,X)$$
$$\wedge year(Z,P) \wedge employer(Z,Y) \qquad (10.9)$$

On the semantic level, relations of higher arity are supported by the use of the relations b_{ij}^k that connect the different interpretation domains. Up to now we are only using these relations with the arity parameter k set to 1 for concepts and 2 for relations. The semantics of the tertiary relation above can be defined using the relation b_{ij}^3. Reasoning about these relations is equivalent to the problem of query containment under constraints, which is known to be decidable for many interesting cases [Calvanese et al., 1998a].

10.4 Reasoning in modular ontologies

Using the notion of logical consequence defined above, we now turn our attention to the issue of reasoning in modular ontologies. For the sake of simplicity, we only consider the interaction between two modules in order to clarify the basic principles. Further, we assume that only one of the two modules contains externally defined concepts in terms of queries to the other module. As mentioned in the introduction, we are interested in the possibility of performing local reasoning. For the case of ontological reasoning, we focus on the task of deriving implied subsumption relations between concepts within a single module. For the case of internally defined concepts this can be done using well-established reasoning methods [Donini et al., 1996]. Externally defined concepts, however, cause problems: being defined in terms of a query to the other module, a local reasoning procedure will often fail to recognize an implied subsumption relation between these concepts. Consequently, subsumption between externally defined concepts requires reasoning in the external module as the following theorem shows. We define the notion of implied subsumption starting with subsumption between atomic concepts before extending the results to arbitrarily complex concept expressions

10.4.1 Atomic concepts and relations

The most simple case of implied subsumption is the case where we want to decide whether two externally defined concepts subsume each other. Assuming that these concepts are solely defined in terms of their mapping to another ontology, we can define when these concepts subsume each other on the basis of query subsumption in the external ontology:

Theorem 10.9 (implied subsumption). *Let E_1 and E_2 be two concepts (or relations) in module M_i that are externally defined in module M_j by queries Q_1 and Q_2; then $\Im \models E_1 \sqsubseteq E_2$ if $\Im_j \models Q_1 \sqsubseteq Q_2$.*

The result presented above implies the necessity to decide subsumption between conjunctive queries in order to identify implied subsumption relations between externally defined concepts. In order to decide subsumption between queries, we translate them into internally defined concepts in the module they refer to. A corresponding sound and complete translation is described in [Horrocks and Tessaris, 2000]. Using the resulting concept definition, to which we refer as *query concepts*, we can decide subsumption between externally defined concepts by local reasoning in the external ontology.

10.4.2 Preservation of Boolean operators

Things become a bit more complicated when we consider the case where externally defined concepts are further used to define complex concepts. What is needed is a general result on the preservation of subsumption relationships between concept expressions in different modules that are defined in the same way. In the following we will call these expressions isomorphic.

Definition 10.10 (isomorphic concepts). *Let $M_i : C$ and $M_j : D$ be two concepts defined in modules M_i and M_j, respectively, then $M_i : C$ and $M_j : D$ are said to be isomorphic if*

- $M_i : C(x) \equiv M_j : D(x)$ *or*
- $M_i : C \equiv f(E_1, ..., E_n)$, $M_j : D \equiv f(F_1, ..., F_n)$, E_i *and* F_i *are isomorphic.*

We can use the notion of isomorphic concepts we presented above in order to extend Theorem 10.9. While the theorem only makes assertions about concepts that are directly defined by external mappings, we saw above that under certain assumptions there is also a semantic connection between concepts that are not directly connected but built from other connected concepts (see Equation A.2). The table below summarizes these results:

b^1_{ji}	Atomic Concepts	Disjunction	Conjunction	Negation
Relation	X			
Function	X	X		
Injective function	X	X	X	
Bijective function	X	X	X	X

We see that there is a semantic relation between isomorphic concepts defined using only disjunction is provided if the semantic mapping is functional. If conjunction is used as well, the semantic mapping has to be an injective function in order to guarantee that a semantic relation exists between isomorphic concepts. If negation is used to define concepts, only a semantic mapping, which is a bijective function implies Equation A.2. Based on this observation, we formulate the following extension of Theorem 10.9.

Theorem 10.11 (Implied Subsumption (extended)). *Let E_1 and E_2 be two concepts in module M_i and $\Im_i \not\models E_1 \sqsubseteq E_2$. Let further be F_1 and F_2 be concepts in module M_j with $\Im_j \models F_1 \sqsubseteq F_2$. We have $\Im \models E_1 \sqsubseteq E_2$ if:*

- *Theorem 10.9 applies.*
- *E_1, F_1 and E_2, F_2 are isomorphic, b^1_{ji} is a function and only disjunction is used to define concepts.*
- *E_1, F_1 and E_2, F_2 are isomorphic, b^1_{ji} is an injective function and only disjunction and conjunction are used to define concepts.*
- *E_1, F_1 and E_2, F_2 are isomorphic, b^1_{ji} is a bijective function and only disjunction, conjunction and negation are used to define concepts.*

The crucial question connected to these technical results is about the suitability of the assumptions we make about the semantic relation. In order to get an idea about these assumptions, we will take a look at the formal properties of the semantic relation and discuss the intuition connected with these properties.

In the most general case, b_{ji} is just a general relation with no further restrictions. As a result it provides a high flexibility with respect to the links that exist between modules. This general relation allows us for example to connect models with different levels of granularity as one element in the domain of one module may correspond to several elements in the domain of the other module. This flexibility leads to a very loose coupling of different modules as no operators are preserved. In principle, we only know connections between modules that are explicitly stated. This changes when we assume that the semantic relation is functional. In this case every element in the domain of M_i corresponds to exactly one element in M_j. This means that the goal module is at least as fine grained (or exact) as the target. Still, it can be the case that the target is an abstraction, because more than one element of the goal domain corresponds to one element in the target domain. Choosing an injective b_{ji} that establishes a one-to-one mapping between elements of different domains means that we only allow domains of the same level of abstraction. While being at the same level of detail, an injective semantic relation does not restrict the coverage of the two domains. They may overlap because we neither require b_{ji} to be non-partial nor do we assume that it covers all of the target domain. The latter is required if we want to preserve negation. In a logic where negation is defined by set difference with respect to the complete domain it is clear that negation will only have the same effect if the domains are comparable, which is only given in case of a bijective b_{ji}.

From a practical point of view, some of the assumptions are more likely to hold for modular ontologies than others. While we can often assume that different modules are at the same level of abstraction, their coverage may vary as sometimes one module will just be a different view of exactly the same set of objects and sometimes they will cover completely different aspects of a domain, being only related by a few concepts. Therefore, we think that defining the semantic relation to be an injective function is a good compromise between flexibility of coupling and preservation of operator semantics.

10.4.3 Compilation and integrity

The bottom line of the investigations above is that in order to completely determine the subsumption relations in an ontology module that contains externally defined concepts, we might also have to perform subsumption reasoning in the modules the external concepts are mapped to. This fact contradicts the requirement of local reasoning stated in the motivation as subsumption reasoning in the external module may in turn require reasoning in modules this one is linked to, and so on. In order to reach the goal of local reasoning, we therefore have to find a way to avoid the need to look beyond the border of a module at run time.

We can avoid the need to perform reasoning in external modules each time we perform reasoning in a local module using the idea of knowledge compilation [Cadoli and Donini, 1997]. The idea of compilation is to perform the external reasoning once and add the derived subsumption relations as axioms to the local module. These new axioms can then be used for reasoning instead of the external definitions of concepts. This set of additional axioms can be computed using Algorithm 2.

Algorithm 2 Compile

Require: the module $M = \langle C_I \cup C_E, R, O \rangle$
Require: the external module $M_j = \langle C_j, R_j, O_j \rangle$
    for all $E \equiv M_j : Q \in C_E$ **do**
      $C'_E := C'_E \cup \{E \sqsubseteq C | C \in C_j, \Im_j \models E \sqsubseteq Q\}$
    end for
    return C'_E

If we want to use the compiled axioms instead of external definitions, we have to make sure that this will not invalidate the correctness of reasoning results. We call this situation, where the compiled results are correct, integrity. We formally define integrity as follows:

Definition 10.12 (Integrity). *We consider integrity of two ontology modules M, M_j to be present if $M, M_j \models M^c$ where M^c is the result of replacing the set of external concept definitions in M by $compile(M, M_j)$.*

At the time of applying the compilation this is guaranteed by Theorem 10.9; however, integrity cannot be guaranteed over the complete life-cycle of the modular ontology. The problem is that changes to the external ontology module can invalidate the compiled subsumption relationships. In this case, we have to perform an update of the compiled knowledge. This problem is discussed in more detail in the next section.

10.5 Conclusions

In this chapter, we discussed an infrastructure for representation and reasoning with modular ontologies. The intent was to enhance the existing Semantic Web infrastructure with notions of modularization that have been proven useful in other areas of computer science, in particular in software engineering. We defined a set of requirements for modular ontologies that arise from expected benefits such as enhanced reuse and more efficient reasoning. Taking the requirements of loose coupling, self-containment and integrity as a starting point, we defined a framework for modular ontologies providing the following contributions to the state of the art in ontology representation for the Semantic Web:

1. We presented a formal model for describing dependencies between different ontologies. We proposed conjunctive queries for defining concepts using elements from another ontology and presented a model-based semantics in the spirit of distributed description logics that provides us with a notion of logical consequence across different ontologies.

2. We compared our model with existing standards, in particular the Web Ontology Language OWL, and showed that the OWL import facilities can easily be captured as a special case in our model. We further showed that our model provides additional expressiveness in particular with respect to modelling relations. In order to get a better idea of the improvements of our model over OWL, we investigated the formal properties of inter-module mappings, their impact on reasoning and their intuition.

In summary, this chapter covered the representation of modular ontologies on a syntactic and semantic level as well as the notion of logical consequence as a basis for inferencing. The notions defined here can be exploited by knowledge engineers to design newly created ontologies in a modular fashion. What is still missing in order to support a wide adoption of this infrastructure are methods that support the process of migrating existing ontologies to this new infrastructure. As the way of defining concepts we propose is equivalent to OWL, the missing part is a set of methods that analyze ontologies and split them up into modules according to the principles of maximal internal cohesion and maximal external independence. A number of such methods are known from the area of object-oriented databases, where so-called fragmentation methods are used to determine an optimal distribution of object definitions over different object bases. Further, in the area of parallel processing algorithms for partitioning graphs into a set of subgraphs have been developed that could be applied to ontologies when regarding the RDF encoding of the ontology as a graph that has to be split up. Such methods for identifying modules are not only interesting for splitting up existing ontologies; they can also be used as a design tool to help knowledge engineers to come up with a useful set of modules.

Further reading

Early work on a modular representation of logical theories and their benefits is [Farmer et al., 1992]. Halevy gives a survey of the use of view-based mappings in the area of database systems [Halevy, 2001]. The use of knowledge compilation techniques for improving the efficiency of logical reasoning is surveyed in

[Cadoli and Donini, 1997]. Borgida and Serafini introduce the notion of distributed interpretation that is also used to define the semantics of modular ontologies in this chapter [Borgida and Serafini, 2002]. In [Bouquet et al., 2003] we introduce an extension of OWL for representing ontologies in a distributed and modular way.

11

Evolution management

Summary. In the last chapter we introduced modular ontologies as a natural way of representing terminological information on the Semantic Web. We proposed to use compilation techniques for improving the efficiency of reasoning. In this section we address the problem of maintaining modular ontologies. In particular, we present an update strategy that guarantees the integrity of compiled knowledge in a modular ontology.

The advantages of having self-contained ontology modules as described in the last chapter have their price in terms of potential inconsistencies that arise from changes in other ontology modules. While being independent from accessing other modules at reasoning time, the correctness of reasoning within a self-contained module may still depend on knowledge in other ontologies. If this knowledge changes, reasoning results in a self-contained module may become incorrect with respect to the overall system, and we will not even notice it. We have to provide mechanisms for checking whether relevant knowledge in other systems has changed and for adapting the reasoning process if needed to ensure correctness. Our approach of compiling mappings and adding the result to the ontology models is very sensitive against changes in ontology modules. Once a query has been compiled, the correctness of reasoning can only be guaranteed as long as the class hierarchy of the queried ontology module does not change. On the other hand, not every change in the hierarchy really influences the compiled result. Problems only arise if concepts used in the query change or if the set of classes subsuming the query is changed. In the second case, we will have to compile the interface again. In the first case we might even have to consider a re-definition of the query. In order to decide whether the compiled axiom is still valid, we propose a change-detection mechanism that is based on a taxonomy of ontological changes and their impact of the class hierarchy in combination with the position of the affected class in that hierarchy.

We further exploit an explicit representation of the dependencies between ontology modules in order to propagate changes in the system when necessary.

In this chapter, we first discuss the possibility of detecting and analyzing changes in an ontology module with respect to the integrity of s modular ontology as defined in the last chapter. For this purpose the notion of a harmless change is defined and methods for classifying changes as harmless or harmful are preseted. After discussing the application of these methods in a small case study, we define an update procedure for modular ontologies that ensures integrity in the presence of changes.

11.1 Change detection and classification

In principle, testing integrity might be very costly as it requires reasoning within the external ontology. In order to avoid this, we propose a heuristic change-detection procedure that analyzes changes with respect to their impact on compiled subsumption relations. Work on determining the impact of changes on a whole ontology is reported in [Heflin and Hendler, 2000]. As our goal is to determine whether changes in the external ontology invalidate compiled knowledge, we have to analyze the actual impact of changes on individual concept definitions. We want to classify these changes as either *harmless* or *harmful* with respect to compiled knowledge.

11.1.1 Determining harmless changes

As compiled knowledge reflects subsumption relations between query concepts, a harmless change is a set of modifications to an ontology that does not change these subsumption relations. Finding harmless changes is therefore a matter of deciding whether the modifications affect the subsumption relation between query concepts. We first look at the effect of a set of modifications on individual concepts:

Assuming that C represents the concept under consideration before and C' the concept after the change, there are four ways in which the old version C may relate to the new version C':

1. the meaning of a concept is not changed: $C \equiv C'$ (e.g. because the change was in another part of the ontology, or because it was only syntactical);
2. the meaning of a concept is changed in such a way that concept becomes more general: $C \sqsubseteq C'$;
3. the meaning of a concept is changed in such a way that concept becomes more specific: $C' \sqsubseteq C$;
4. the meaning of a concept is changed in such a way that there is no subsumption relationship between C and C'.

The same observations can be made for relations before and after a change, denoted as R and R', respectively. The next question is how these different types of changes influence the interpretation of query concepts. We take advantage of the fact that there is a very tight relation between changes in concepts of the external ontology and implied changes to the query concepts using these concepts:

Lemma 11.1 (monotonicity of effect). *Let $c(Q)$ be the set of all concept names and $r(Q)$ the set of all relation names occurring in query Q; let further $C \in c(Q)$ and $R \in r(Q)$. Then changing C has the same impact on the interpretation of Q as it has on the interpretation of C; in particular, we have $C \sqsubseteq C' \Longrightarrow Q \sqsubseteq Q'$ and $C' \sqsubseteq C \Longrightarrow Q' \sqsubseteq Q$, where Q' is the query as being interpreted after changing C. Analogously, a change of R has the same effect on the complete query.*

We can exploit this relation between the interpretation of concepts and queries in order to identify the effect of changes in the external ontology on the subsumption relations between different query concepts. First of all, the above result directly generalizes to multiple changes with the same effect, i.e. a query Q becomes more general (specific) or stays the same if none of the elements in $c(Q) \cup r(Q)$ become more specific(general). Further, the subsumption relation between two query concepts does not change if the more general (specific) query becomes even more general (specific) or stays the same. Combining these two observations, we derive the following characterization of harmless change.

Theorem 11.2 (harmless change). *A change is harmless with respect to compiled knowledge (i.e. $Q_1 \sqsubseteq Q_2 \Longrightarrow Q'_1 \sqsubseteq Q'_2$) if for all compiled subsumption relations $C_1 \sqsubseteq C_2$, where C_i is defined by query Q_i, we have:*

- $X' \sqsubseteq X$ *for all* $X \in c(Q_1) \cup r(Q_1)$,
- $X \sqsubseteq X'$ *for all* $X \in c(Q_2) \cup r(Q_2)$.

The theorem provides us with a correct but incomplete method for deciding whether a change is harmless. This basic method can be refined by analyzing the overlap of $c(Q_1)$ and $c(Q_2)$ in combination with the relations they restrict. This more accurate method is not topic of this chapter, but it relies on the same idea as the theorem given above.

11.1.2 Characterizing changes

Now that we are able to determine the consequence of changes in the concept hierarchy on the integrity of the mapping, we still need to know what the effect of specific modifications on the interpretation of a concept is (i.e. whether it becomes more general or more specific). As our goal is to determine the integrity of mappings without having to do classification, we describe what theoretically could happen to a concept as result of a modification in the ontology. To to so, we have listed all possible change operations to an ontology according to the OWL Lite[1] knowledge model in the same style as done in [Banerjee et al., 1987]. The list of operations is extendable to other knowledge models; we have chosen the OWL Lite model because of its simplicity and its expected important role on the Semantic Web. Apart from *atomic change operations* to an ontology – like *add range restriction* or *delete subclass relation* – the list also contains some *complex change operations*, which consist of multiple atomic operations and/or incorporate some additional knowledge. The complex changes are often more useful to specify effects than the basic changes. For example, for operations like *concept moved up*, or *domain enlarged*, we can specify the effect more accurately than for the atomic operations *subclass relation changed* and *domain modified*[2]. Atomic changes can be detected without using the knowledge in the ontology itself, only using the knowledge of the knowledge model, i.e. the language. These changes are detected at a structural level. To identify complex changes, we also need to use the content of the ontology itself. We are currently working on rules and heuristics to distill complex changes from sets of atomic changes. Table 11.1 contains some examples of operations and their effect on the classification of concepts. The table only shows a few examples, although our full ontology of change operations contains around 120 operations. This number is still growing as new complex changes are defined. A snapshot of the change ontology can be found online[3].

Table 11.1. Some modifications to an ontology and their effects on the classification of concepts in the hierarchy.

Operation	Effect
Attach a relation to concept C	C: Specialized
Complex: change the superclass of concept C to a concept lower in the hierarchy	C: Specialized
Complex: restrict the range of a relation R *(effect on all C that have a restriction on R)*	R: Specialized, C: Specialized
Remove a superclass relation of a concept C	C: Generalized
Change the concept definition of C from primitive to defined	C: Generalized
Add a concept definition A	C: Unknown
Complex: add a (not further specified) subclass A of C	C: No effect
Define a relation R as functional	R: Specialized

The specification of effects is not complete, in the sense that it describes "worst-case" scenarios, and that for some operations the effect is "unknown"

---

[1] See http://www.w3.org/TR/owl-features/

[2] For a complete list, see http://wonderweb.man.ac.uk/deliverables/D20.shtml

[3] http://ontoview.org/changes/1/3/

(i.e. unpredictable). In contrast to [Franconi et al., 2000] who provide complete semantics of changes, we prefer to use heuristics in order to avoid expensive reasoning about the impact of changes.

11.1.3 Update management

With the elements that we described in this section, we now have a complete procedure to determine whether compiled knowledge in other modules is still valid when the external ontology is changed. The complete procedure is as follows:

1. create a list of concepts and relations that are part of the "subsuming" query of any compiled axiom;
2. create another list of concepts and relations that are part of the "subsumed" query of any compiled axiom;
3. achieve the modifications that are performed in the external ontology;
4. use the modifications to determine the effect on the interpretation of the concepts and relations;
5. check whether there are concepts or relations in the first, "subsuming", list that became more specific, or concepts or relations in the second, "subsumed", list that became more general, or concepts or relations in either of the lists with an unknown effect; if not, the integrity of the mapping is preserved.

In cases where we cannot guarantee that integrity is preserved, we recompute and re-compile the implied subsumption statements. We thus restore integrity and make correct local reasoning possible.

Algorithm 3 Update

Require: Ontology Module M
Require: Ontology Module M_j
  for all compiled axioms $C_1 \sqsubseteq C_2$ in M^c **do**
    for all $X \in c(Q_1) \cup r(Q_1)$ **do**
      if effect on C is 'generalized' or 'unknown' **then**
        $M^c := Compile(M, M_j)$
      end if
    end for
    for all $X \in c(Q_2) \cup r(Q_2)$ **do**
      if effect on X is 'specialized' or 'unknown' **then**
        $M^c := Compile(M, M_j)$
      end if
    end for
  end for

We describe the procedure in a more structured way in Algorithm 3. The algorithm triggers a (re-)compilation step only if it is required in order to resume integrity. Otherwise no action is taken, because the previously compiled knowledge is still valid. All the steps can be automated. A tool that helps to automate steps 3 and 4 is described in [Klein et al., 2002]. This tool will compare two versions of an ontology and derive the list of change operations that is necessary to transform the one into the other. It will also be able to detect some of the *complex* operations. The tool will also annotate the definitions in an ontology with the effect that the change has on its place in the hierarchy.

11.2 Application in a case study

In order to support the claims made about the advantage of modular ontologies, we applied our model in a case study that has been carried out in the course of the WonderWeb project. Our main intention was to show that the update-management procedure presented in the last section can be used to avoid the computation of subsumption relations in many cases. For this purpose, we defined a small example ontology using mappings to a Human Resource ontology that was developed stepwise in the case study. We used the changes that occurred in the human resource ontology during the different steps of the case study and determined the impact on our example ontology. Besides this, the case study provides us with examples of implied subsumption some of which are non-trivial but likely to occur in real-life situations.

11.2.1 The WonderWeb case study

The WonderWeb case study assumes that an existing database schema is used as the basis for an ontology that should function on the Semantic Web. A database in the human resource (HR) domain is used as an example. The first version of the ontology is created by a tool that automatically converts a schema into an ontology [Volz et al., 2002b]. In the next phase, the quality of the ontology is improved by relating this ontology to the foundational ontology DOLCE [Gangemi et al., 2002]. First, the HR ontology is aligned with the DOLCE ontology, and in several successive steps the resulting ontology is further refined. During this process, the ontology changes continuously, which causes problems when other ontologies refer to definitions in the evolving ontology. Therefore, in our case study, evolution management is important during the entire life-cycle of the ontology-development process. Besides this DOLCE+HR ontology, we assume that we have another ontology (we call it the *local ontology*) that uses terms and definitions from the evolving DOLCE+HR ontology (the *external ontology*). As an example, we define a very simple ontology about employees (see Fig. 11.1). Our example ontology introduces the concept *FulltimeEmployee* and defines a superclass *Employee* and two subclasses *DepartmentMember* and *HeadOfDepartment* using terms from the DOLCE+HR ontology.

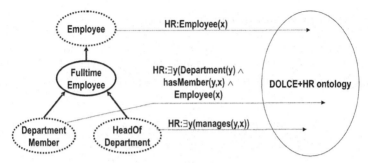

Fig. 11.1. A simple ontology (left) with some concepts (dashed ovals) that are defined using terms from the DOLCE+HR ontology (schematically represented by a large oval).

The specific problem in our case is that the changes in the DOLCE+HR ontology could affect the reasoning in the local ontology. We want to be able to predict whether or not the reasoning in the local ontology is still valid for specific changes in the external ontology.

The evolution of the DOLCE+HR ontology consisted of several steps. Each of these steps involves some typical changes. We will briefly summarize them and show some changes that are typical for a specific step.

- In the first step, the extracted HR ontology is aligned with the DOLCE foundational ontology, i.e. the concepts and properties in the HR ontology are connected to concepts and properties in the DOLCE ontology via subsumption relations. For example, the concept *Departments* from the HR ontology is made a subclass of *Social-Unit* in DOLCE.
- The refinement step involves a lot of changes. Some property restrictions are added, and some additional concepts and properties are created to define the HR concepts more precisely. For example, the concept *Administrative-Unit* is introduced as a new subclass of *Social-Unit*, and the concept *Departments* is made a subclass of it. Also, the range of the property *email* is restricted from *Abstract-Region* to its new subclass *Email*.
- In the next step, a number of concepts and properties are renamed to names that better reflect their meaning. For example, *Departments* is renamed to *Department* (singular), and the two different variants of the relation *manager-id* are renamed to *employee-manager* and *department-manager*.
- In the final step, the tidying step, all properties and concepts that are not necessary any more are removed and transformed into property restrictions. For example, the property *employee-email* is deleted and replaced by an existential restriction in the class *Employee* on the property *abstract-location* to the class *Email*.

11.2.2 Modularization in the case study

If we now consider the problem statement from the case study, we have a local ontology with a concept hierarchy that is built up by the following explicitly stated subsumption relations (see Fig. 11.1 again):

$$FulltimeEmployee \sqsubseteq Employee$$
$$DepartmentMember \sqsubseteq FulltimeEmployee$$
$$HeadOfDepartment \sqsubseteq FulltimeEmployee$$

This ontology introduces *FulltimeEmployee* as a new concept, not present in the case study ontology. Consequently, this concept is only defined in terms of its relation to other concepts in the local ontology.

All other concepts are externally defined in terms of ontology based queries over the case study ontology. The first external definition concerns the concept *Employee* that is equivalent to the "Employee" concept in the case study ontology. This can be defined by the following trivial view:

$$Employee \equiv HR : Employee(x)$$

Another concept that is externally defined is the "head of department" concept. We define it to be the set of all instances that are in the range of the "department manager" relation. The definition of this view given below shows that our approach is flexible enough to define concepts in terms of relations.

$$HeadOfDepartment \equiv HR : \exists y[departmentManager(y, x)]$$

An example of a more complex external concept definition is the concept *DepartmentMember*, which is defined using a query that consists of three conjuncts, claiming that a department member is an employee that is in the has-member relation with a department.

$$
\begin{aligned}
DepartmentMember \equiv HR : \exists y \, [Department(y) \, \wedge \\
hasmember(y, x) \, \wedge \\
Employee(x)]
\end{aligned}
\tag{11.1}
$$

Implied subsumption relations

If we now consider logical reasoning about these external definitions, we immediately see that the definition of employee subsumes the definition of *DepartmentMember*, as the former occurs as part of the definition of the latter.

$$\models DepartmentMember \sqsubseteq Employee \tag{11.2}$$

At a first glance, there is no relation between the definition of a head of department and the other two statements as it does not use any of the concept or relation names. However, when we use the background knowledge provided by the case study ontology we can derive some implied subsumption relations. The reasoning is as follows. Because the range of "department manager" is set to "department" and the domain to "employee", the definition of "HeadofDepartment" is equivalent to:

$$\exists y[Department(y) \land departmentManager(y, x) \land Employee(x)]$$

As we further know that manager is a subclass of employee and "departmentManager" is a subrelation of "has-member", we can derive the following subsumption relation between the externally defined concepts:

$$\models HeadOfDepartment \sqsubseteq Employee \tag{11.3}$$
$$\models HeadOfDepartment \sqsubseteq DepartmentMember \tag{11.4}$$

When the relations 11.2–11.4 are added to the local ontology, it possible to do subsumption reasoning without having to access the DOLCE+HR ontology any more.

11.2.3 Updating the models

We will now illustrate that the conclusions of the procedure are correct by studying the impact of changes mentioned in the problem statement.

Example 1: the employee concept

The first change we observed is the removal of properties from the employee concept. Our rules tell us that this change makes the new version more general compared to its old version:

$$Employee \sqsubseteq Employee'$$

According to our procedure, this should not be a problem because employee is in the "subsuming list".

When we analyze this change, we see that it has an impact on the definition of the concept "DepartmentMember" as it enlarges the set of objects allowed to take the first place in the has-member relation. This leads to a new definition of $DepartmentMember'$ with $DepartmentMember \sqsubseteq DepartmentMember'$. As "DepartmentMember" was already more general than "HeadOfDepartment" and the employee concept is not used in the definition of the latter the, implied subsumption relation indeed still holds.

Example 2: the department-manager relation

The second example, we have to deal with a change affecting a relation that is used in en external definition. The relation department-manager is specialized by restricting its range to the concept "manager" (which is a subclass of employee) making it a subrelation of its previous version:

$$department - manager \sqsupseteq department - manager'$$

Again, this is harmless according to our procedure, as department_manager is in the "subsumed list".

The analysis show that this change has an impact on the definition of the concept "HeadOfDepartment" as it restricts the allowed objects to the more specific Class "Manager". The new definition $HeadOfDepartment'$ is more specific that the old one: $HeadOfDepartment' \sqsubseteq HeadOfDepartment$. As the old version was already more specific than the definition of "DepartmentMember" and the "department-manager" relation is not used in the definition of the latter the implied subsumption is indeed still valid.

The situation is different if the range of the "department-manager" relation is changed to the concept "person" which is more general than "employee". In this case the definition of the concept "department-manager" also becomes more general. This means that we cannot guarantee that it is still subsumed by "DepartmentMember". In this case we have to recompute and compile the implied subsumption relations in order to guarantee integrity.

Example 4: the department concept

The different changes of the definition of the "department" concept left us with no clear idea of the relation between the old and the new versions. In this specific case, however, we can still make assertions about the impact on implied subsumption relations. The reason is that the concept occurs in both definitions. Moreover, it plays the same role, namely restricting the domain of the relation that connects an organizational unit with the set of objects that make up the externally defined concept. As a consequence, the changes have the same impact on both definitions, thus not invalidating the implied subsumption relation.

11.3 Conclusions

We described a method for detecting changes in an ontology and for assessing their impact. The main feature of this method is the derivation of conceptual changes from purely syntactic criteria. These conceptual changes in turn provide input for a semantic analysis of the effect on dependent ontologies, in particular, on the validity of implied subsumption relations. We applied heuristics to determine the impact of changes without logical reasoning. However, many relevant questions occurring in practical information management are not captured by the model. In particular, these questions relate to the impact of changes of concrete information that is connected to the ontologies that are subject to the impact of the changes. Some key questions are the following:

- *What parts of the information are affected?* The fact that the content of an information source has changed may or may not have influence on a task like answering a query for objects with certain properties. Deciding whether the result of such a task is affected by a change in the background knowledge depends on the set of objects and the specific properties that are affected by the change.
- *What is the effect on that information?* Often, it is important to know about the nature of the effect on certain objects in the information source. Are new properties derivable for an object, or have some disappeared? Has the classification of the object changed to a more general or a more specific class? Answers to question like these are valuable for evolution management as we obtain the possibility to react to these changed more specifically.
- *What part of the ontology caused it?* In order to be able to repair harmful or include beneficial changes to background knowledge, we have to be able to identify which portion of the background knowledge actually caused a specific change of the information content in a particular source. The ability to locate the cause of changes also helps to more precisely define relevant background knowledge and isolate it from the portion that is not relevant for a given set of information.

Preliminary work on the diagnosis of ontologies exists [Schlobach and Cornet, 2003] but the problem is far from being solved. We consider the development of a comprehensive framework for managing ontological changes in the context of information management as a major challenge for future research on information sharing on the Semantic Web.

Further reading

The idea of describing model evolution in terms of change operations is described in [Banerjee et al., 1987]. The use of this idea for detecting, analyzing and modelling ontology evolution is discussed in [Klein, 2004] and [Heflin and Hendler, 2000]. A formal characterization of schema evolution using description logics is described in [Franconi et al., 2000]. A detailed description of the Wonderweb case study can be found in [Bechofer et al., 2003].

Part V

Conclusions

12

Conclusions

After extensive work on information sharing on the Semantic Web, most of which is reported in this book, we can draw some general conclusions about successful ways of using Semantic Web technology. These conclusions consider the choice of representations as well as methodologies for creating semantic descriptions and methods for using them. In the following, we present our main conclusions and discuss the state of the art of the Semantic Web technology with respect to these conclusions.

12.1 Lessons learned

The first condition for a successful application of ontologies to information sharing is the existence of a representational infrastructure. This infrastructure has to ensure that the potential benefits of ontologies can be exploited.

Semantics and reasoning

On a logical level, the representational infrastructure has to have a clear logical semantics that supports reasoning about contextual information. Having reasoning support is important, because the possibility to reason about the meaning of information is one of the major benefits of using ontologies in systems and not only for communication between people. Semantics and reasoning can be used at ontology-development time for consistency checking or at run time for classifying individuals or performing semantic mappings. In our approach, the Web Ontology Language OWL is used to represent and reason about ontologies.

Shared and Contextual Meaning

On the content level, the benefits of ontologies can be that they define a common understanding of specific terms. Thus, the reference to a term in such a shared ontology makes it possible to communicate between systems on a semantic level. On the other hand, ontologies can be used to explicate background knowledge by defining what a certain term means in the context of the corresponding source. In order to make use of both of these benefits of ontologies the representational infrastructure has to consist of a mixture of shared and non-shared representations. In our framework non-shared representations define the meanings of classes in a specific information source using only terms from a shared ontology. This ensures that we can capture the contextual information of every information source but still have a basic understanding of terms that are shared between systems.

Content Metadata

In order to be useful, definitions of contextual interpretations have to be directly connected with concrete information, because we use ontologies as a tool for information sharing. The connection has to be tight enough to make the transfer of reasoning results from the logical level to the information. On the other hand, the connection must be flexible enough to be applicable to weakly structured information without having to build these structures from scratch. In our framework, we use an assignment of complete Web pages to ontological classes with RDF Schema metadata. This assignment is easy to establish by means of machine-learning techniques and it supports many useful methods like validation, querying and content-based browsing of Web resources.

Another important point is that it is not sufficient to define an infrastructure for information sharing. Providing methodologies and tools for supporting the development of this infrastructure is at least equally important since knowledge acquisition is well known to be one of the main bottlenecks in the application of knowledge-based technology.

Ontology construction

The success of ontology-based information sharing heavily depends on the quality of the ontologies used. Building them in an ad hoc way leads to serious shortcomings. In an early case study on semantic matching we encountered huge problems that were mostly caused by sloppy ontology development. It clearly displayed the need for modelling guidance. Existing ontology-engineering approaches are often very general; they state general principles but only provide limited support for a more concrete modelling task. We found out that for the case of building source ontologies and shared vocabularies, a bottom-up approach is suitable that takes the actual integration problem as a starting point and consults general models like top-level ontologies and linguistic resources only if necessary. The resulting vocabularies are general enough to cover at least a certain class of integration problems. We think that this is more valuable than a general top-down approach because it solves real-world problems without losing the connection to basic ontological principles.

Metadata generation

Metadata plays an important role especially in weakly structured environments. At the same time, the creation of such metadata is harder the less structure is present to refer to. Despite these problems we think that successful approaches to applying ontologies in these environments will have to live with the existing structures, in our case HTML documents, because the freedom from the need to encode sophisticated data structures is one of the secrets behind the success of the World Wide Web. We therefore proposed an approach for mostly automatically generating metadata that links information to ontologies. We claim that the assignment of individual Web pages to classes in an ontology provides a good trade-off between the strength of the connection and the effort of establishing it. We show that Web-page classification can be done using classification rules that refer to the structure of HTML documents. The resulting classification can be used for content-based navigation and search. We also demonstrated that structural classification rules can be generated in a mostly automatic way using techniques from machine learning.

The final important condition for the successful application of ontologies for information sharing is that the approach chosen scales up to real-life problems. This claim raises new questions with respect to compatibility with existing technology and with tolerance for imperfect data and knowledge.

Compatibility

Solutions developed in science often fail to make their way into real applications due to a lack of compatibility with industrial standards. Considering the World Wide Web as a target application area, the World Wide Web Consortium provides a platform where science and industry make an effort for the development of joint standards. We therefore think that any approach to ontology-based information sharing on the World Wide Web should be compatible with W3C standards. The general framework described in this book can be put to work using existing Web technologies: shared ontologies can be encoded in RDF Schema, OWL can be used to build source ontologies. Information sources in terms of collections of HTML documents can be classified using the WebMaster system. Finally, mapping and filtering methods can be implemented on top of existing subsumption reasoners that can be accessed over the Web.

Robust methods

Unlike conventional approaches to knowledge representation and reasoning, the application of ontologies in weakly structured and heterogeneous environments can in principle make no assumption about the quality of the information that has to be handled. As argued above, we can provide methodological guidance for the development of ontologies and the generation of metadata, but we still may have to face inconsistencies or incompleteness when trying to perform reasoning across different systems. We claim that there is a need for developing new reasoning techniques that are more flexible and fault tolerant than classical deduction systems in order to cope with the nature of the application environment. The approximate mapping approach proposed in Chap. 7 is an example of such a more flexible method. We can answer Boolean queries over concept names by replacing unknown concept names by their lower bound in the corresponding source ontology. The resulting query can be processed in the context of the remote information source delivering a query result that can be proven to be a correct approximation of the intended result.

Evolution and maintenance

In a distributed environment without a central authority, changes in the information to be shared as well as in the representations of information semantics are a big problem. Successful approaches for information sharing have to be able to deal with changes. This requires sophisticated methods for detecting changes, analyzing their impact and reacting to the changes. In order to support these mechanisms, the underlying languages and storage structures should provide support for evolution and maintenance. Change logs and representations of histories are as important as stable interfaces.

12.2 Assumptions and Limitations

In the previous section we discussed the lessons learned from developing and testing a framework for information sharing on the Semantic Web. We in particular, we discussed the role and the benefits of the different methods and design decisions. Most of these decisions that were made to make information sharing possible, however, also introduce some assumptions and limitations that have to be taken into account when designing information sharing solutions. In the following, we discuss assumptions and limitations of the three main aspects of our framework: the use of shared vocabularies as a basis for specifying information semantics and the process of semantic translation as introduced in this book.

12.2.1 Shared Vocabularies

The main aspect that distinguishes our approach from related work in the area of information integration is the use of a shared vocabulary as a basis for the integration of information, while other approaches either rely on a completely shared ontology or on mappings between different ontologies.

The use of such a shared model requires a certain degree of agreement amongst the sources on both the representations used and the conceptualization of the domain of interest. The development of the shared vocabulary can only be done if all sources are known and the conceptualization of each source is accessible. Consequently, the approach is not really feasible in a completely open environment, but is suitable for a particular domain (e.g. tourism) where relevant sources can be determined. A typical example of such a setting are online marketplaces. In this case the market place provides the organizational instance needed to establish and maintain the agreement encoded in the shared vocabulary.

Another limitation of the approach is the fact that establishing the representational infrastructure needed to support information sharing requires an somewhat high initial investment. The effort of creating shared vocabularies and source ontologies is only justified in terms of benefits achieved from being able to share information over a longer period to amortize the initial investment. This is normally connected with a commercial interest. We therefore cannot assume that the methods for information sharing described in this book are adopted on the same scale as other Web technologies with low start-up costs such as HTML.

As with every ontology-based approach, the performance heavily relies on the quality of the ontologies used. We provided some guidelines for the creating of ontologies that are suited for the purpose of our approach, but we cannot guarantee that the definitions in the source ontologies actually reflect the intended meaning of the information. From our point of view this is a fundamental problem and the quality of models can only be determined for a concrete task to be solved.

12.2.2 On demand translation

The second choice we made is to integrate the ontologies of different information sources at run time by approximating concepts in a joint concept hierarchy. This choice was made in order to better respond to the dynamic nature of the World Wide Web, as sources can be integrated only if needed.

The choice of an on-demand translation of information between different sources has the disadvantage of a high computational complexity compared to approaches, where the alignment of different conceptualizations is done off-line. In particular, our approach relies on terminological reasoning over OWL representations. While modern reasoners perform quite efficiently on most reasoning problems that do not involve large instance sets, it is well known that there are cases where even small ontologies cannot be reasoned about efficiently. The approach also does not really allow to restrict the use of OWL to a subset of constructs with better computational complexity because the approach relies on an accurate description of local semantics that requires a high expressiveness. As a consequence, we were forced to reduce for example the expressiveness of queries for retrieving information and to abandon the idea of a tight integration of terminological and spatial reasoning.

the use of approximation techniques allows us to compare different ontologies, it also introduces a certain error in the translation. As shown in Chap. 6, we can give certain guarantees concerning the logical properties of the approximation (e.g. correctness), but we cannot quantify the degree of error induced by the approximation. This is a serious drawback, because the ability to provide users with feedback on the rationales and the quality of the approximation and a ranking of results are important techniques to improve the retrieval performance. A particular problem is associated with the techniques of query relaxation, because it is often hard to decide what kinds of relaxations are acceptable and which not. This highly depends on the preferences and restrictions of the user and often remain implicit during query processing. What is needed is a mechanism that enables the user to indicate which parts of a query can be relaxed without leading to unacceptable results thereby reducing the precision of the query.

12.2.3 Modular Ontologies

The other of our main contributions in this work is a proposal for the representation of distributed ontologies based on a non-standard semantics that allows us to represent and reason about complex mappings between different models. We argued for the benefits of this alternative representation in terms of expressive power and maintainability. Not surprisingly, these advantages obtained by the use of distributed description logics only comes with a number of limitations. As a result of the non-standard semantics we actually use the a number of inferences that could have been drawn in a more traditional setting. As shown in Chap. 10, certain logical operators such as conjunction and disjunction are only preserved if we make additional assumptions. In particular, the straightforward use of distributed description logics does not preserve negation. As a consequence, we lose the ability to verify our local ontology by referring to a standard definition. A typical scenario would be the alignment of a domain ontology with an upper level ontology that defines some basic distinctions of a domain, e.g. that entities and processes are disjoint concepts. Ideally, if we link all classes that describe entities to the entity class all process-related concepts to the process concept in the upper level ontology, we would like our ontology to become inconsistent in cases where we mixed up entities and processes in the domain ontology. As negation is not preserved this is not possible. Even though it can be argued that on the Semantic Web, we often prefer this kind of behavior there are still cases, where the weak semantics is a limitation.

The second major limitation of the current framework is that it is limited to the terminological knowledge and to the basic reasoning service connected to terminological knowledge which is subsumption. When talking about information sharing, however, we are mostly interested in the actual information represented as instances of the ontologies. Therefore future work on evolution management will have to focus on extending the framework towards assessing the impact of changes on the information that is to be shared.

12.3 Where are we now?

The final question we want to address now is whether the current state of the art in Semantic Web technology addresses the points raised in the general conclusions above.

Our first point was concerned with a representational infrastructure for ontologies and metadata. Looking at the developments on the Semantic Web, we see that this point has been addressed from the beginning, resulting in language standards like RDF and OWL that have been proven useful not only in our work. These languages provide us with the expressive power and the semantics needed to represent and reason about the meaning of information. An increasing set of software tools is available to support the use of these languages. From this point of view we are doing fine. A problem that still exists, however, is the strong focus on shared conceptualizations we can observe especially with respect to the Web Ontology Language. In [Bouquet et al., 2003], we argue for an extension of the Web Ontology Language by mechanisms for also representing contextual information. The proposed language C-OWL is currently under development and will provide a flexible framework for representing ontologies as well as contextual information in the spirit of modular ontologies described in Chap. 10. More specifically, C-OWL is based on the same semantic model (distributed description logics), but has a more flexible language architecture. In particular C-OWL treats mappings as first-class citizen that are specified in a separate model. This makes it possible to have multiple different mappings between the same ontologies. Further, in C-OWL mappings can be defined between arbitrary concept expressions rather than just between atomic concept names and expressions corresponding to conjunctive queries.

Concerning the existence of support for building up a representational infrastructure, an increasing number of software tools is available supporting the complete life cycle of RDF models. Editors and converters are available for the generation of RDF Schema representations from scratch or for extracting such descriptions from database schemas or software design documents. Storage and retrieval systems have been developed that can deal with RDF models containing millions of statements, and provide query engines for a number of RDF query languages. Annotation tools support the user in the task of attaching RDF descriptions to Web pages and other information sources either manually or semi-automatically using techniques from natural language processing. Finally, special purpose tools support the maintenance of RDF models in terms of change detection and validation of models. A problem that still remains is the interoperability of these tools. Despite the standardization of RDF, the different tools often use different conventions for representing knowledge and data that makes it hard to exchange models between them. Recently, this problem is being addressed by standardizing interfaces for particular types of tools (a first standard interface exists for OWL reasoners) and by the development of middleware components that mediate between different tools.

Concerning the use of Semantic Web infrastructure for information sharing, we see more and more researchers trying to apply or relate their technology to Semantic Web languages in order to be compatible with the emerging standards. This is a first step towards successful information sharing as a large set of useful techniques and tools become available. As already mentioned above, compatibility of the different tools and representations is still a problem. In particular, different strategies in the use of name spaces and the influence of legacy data models cause problems. Concerning the methods themselves, we often miss the robustness and flexibility needed to deal with real life data. Especially, tools for dealing with ontologies are in most cases based on classical logic and fail to produce any reasonable result in the case of inconsistency or incompleteness of information. Some work on robust methods exists in the area of query processing, but we think that there is a large potential for the development of robust methods that could significantly improve the quality of information sharing on the Semantic Web.

12.4 Is that all there is?

Have we, at the end of this book, really dealt with all the questions regarding *information sharing* that we identified in the introductory chapter? By no means. At the end of this book we briefly list a number of issues which are still very much under investigation in the research community.

Degree of automation

The main thesis of this book is that the problem of information sharing can only be solved by attaching semantic meta-data to information items, and by relating these metadata to each other through background knowledge in the form of ontologies. We have shown in Chap. 5 how some of the meta-data can be generated automatically, by exploiting machine-learning techniques. In contrast, Chap. 4, which discussed the creation of the ontologies, relied entirely on manual construction of the ontology. Not only was ontology construction a manual process, but it also requires considerable skill in knowledge modelling. *Will it be possible to provide more automated support for the process of ontology modelling?* Given that an ontology is supposed to encode the *shared* interpretation of concepts and relations between different parties, and given that such sharing is by definition a social process, is it even possible in principle to entirely automate this process? And even if human involvement in the loop remains necessary, to which extent can machines be exploited to support the human effort? Current research on concept extraction, using either statistical or natural-language analysis techniques, is aiming to do exactly this.

Degree of centralization

Contrary to its original motivation, the current Web has an almost client–server architecture: the number of information-providing servers is an order of magnitude smaller than the number of information-consuming clients and, even among the servers, the information streams are dominated by a very small number of very large servers. Also, in this book, most if not all of the example systems we discussed were centralized information servers, and many of our techniques relied on this.

The advantages of more distributed systems such as peer-to-peer architectures are by now widely recognized, both in research and in industry. *To what extent can the techniques discussed in this book also be applied to such peer-to-peer architectures?*

The Semantic Web community is already working on these questions, for example, the SWAP research project [Ehrig et al., 2003], the FOAF initiative[1], and the Edutella project [Nejdl et al., 2002].

Semantic weight of the metadata

The term "ontology" is applied to a very wide variety of structures, with very different semantic weight. A structures such as the Open Directory topic hierarchy[2] is only a very loosely organized hierarchy of terms, without any clear semantic definitions. A hierarchy such as `Computers -- Artificial Intelligence -- People` has a very unclear semantics (it is certainly not a subclass-hierarchy). Yet, even with such lightweight content, the hierarchy has turned out to be very useful for many different purposes, including structuring of results from Google.

---

[1] `http://www.foaf-project.org/`
[2] `http://dmoz.org`

On the other end of the spectrum we have such heavyweight semantic structures as Cyc[3], with hundreds of thousands of carefully engineered logical axioms.

Will the main benefit of ontologies come from a small number of heavily axiomatized ontologies, or instead from a large number of semantically lightweight ontologies?

This dichotomy between lightweight and heavyweight ontologies is also visible in the design of the Semantic Web languages: while RDF Schema is sufficient to capture the Open Directory hierarchy, even OWL Full is not powerful enough (by far) to capture the richness of Cyc.

And, if the future is with large numbers of lightweight ontologies (as many of us believe), then the problem of ontology mapping which was so extensively discussed in this book, becomes even more urgent. Unfortunately, most of these mapping techniques work best on heavily axiomatized ontologies, so many problems remain to be solved in this area.

We have hardly touched on many of these questions in this book. All of these questions are still very much under investigation in the research community, and other books remain to be written regarding their answers.

---

[3] http://cyc.com

A

Proofs of theorems

A.1 Theorem 6.6

The approximation from Definition 6.5 is correct in the sense that:

- If $M'(x, c_1) = 1$ then $x^{\Im} \in d_1(c_1)^{\Im}$
- If $M'(x, c_1) = 0$ then $x^{\Im} \notin d_1(c_1)^{\Im}$

Proof. (1) If the classification returns $M'(x, c_1) = 1$ then $x :$ ($\bigvee_{c \in glb_{IS_2}(c_1)} d_2(c)$). Using Definition 6.4 we get that for all c we have $d_2(c) \sqsubseteq d_1(c_1)$ and therefore also ($\bigvee_{c \in glb_{IS_2}(c_1)} d_2(c)) \sqsubseteq d_1(c_1)$ (by set theory). Using the definition of subsumption we can conclude that $x^{\Im, \mathcal{A}} \in d_1(c_1)^{\Im, \mathcal{A}}$.

(2) Using Definition 6.3 we deduce that for all c we have $d_1(c_1) \sqsubseteq d_2(c)$ and therefore $d_1(c_1) \sqsubseteq \bigwedge_{c \in lub_{IS_2}(c_1)} d_2(c)$. This means that $x^{\Im, \mathcal{A}} \in d_1(c_1)^{\Im, \mathcal{A}}$ only if $x^{\Im, \mathcal{A}} \in (\bigwedge_{c \in lub_{IS_2}(c_1)} d_2(c))^{\Im, \mathcal{A}}$. However, if the classification returns $M'(x, c_1) = 0$ then $x : \neg(\bigwedge_{c \in lub_{IS_2}(c_1)} d_2(c))$, which is equivalent to $x^{\Im, \mathcal{A}} \notin (\bigwedge_{c \in lub_{IS_2}(c_1)} d_2(c))^{\Im, \mathcal{A}}$. Therefore, we also have $x^{\Im, \mathcal{A}} \notin d_1(c_1)^{\Im, \mathcal{A}}$.

A.2 Theorem 6.11

An information item x is in the result of a query Q if

$$M_2(x, C) \wedge d(C) \sqsubseteq Q$$

Proof. By definition we have $x^{\Im, \mathcal{A}} \in d(C)^{\Im, \mathcal{A}}$. From Theorem 6.11 we get that $x^{\Im, \mathcal{A}} \in Q^{\mathcal{I}}$, because $d(C) \sqsubseteq Q$ and therefore $d(M(x))^{\Im, \mathcal{A}} \subseteq Q^{\mathcal{I}}$.

A.3 Theorem 6.14

The notion of query re-writing defined above is correct in the sense that:

$$x : Q' \implies x^{\Im} \in Q^{\mathcal{I}}$$

Proof. From Theorem 6.6 we get that $x : (\bigwedge_{c' \in lub_{IS_2}(c)} c')$ implies $x^{\Im,\mathcal{A}} \in c^{\Im,\mathcal{A}}$
and that $x : \neg(\bigvee_{c' \in glb_{IS_2}(c)} c')$ implies $x^{\Im,\mathcal{A}} \notin c^{\Im,\mathcal{A}}$. This establishes the
correctness of re-writing for atomic queries, i.e. non-negated and negated concept names. Assuming queries in negation normal form, it remains to be shown that the correctness is preserved for conjunctions and disjunctions of negated and non-negated concept names.

We prove the overall correctness by induction over the definition of legal query expressions. By the induction hypothesis (established above) we have $x \in e'_1 I \implies x\Im, \mathcal{A} \in e^{\mathcal{I}}_1$ and $x : e'_2 \implies x^{\Im,\mathcal{A}} \in e^{\mathcal{I}}_2$. For the induction step we have to distinguish the following cases:

(case 1: $q = e_1 \wedge e_2$) as $x\Im, \mathcal{A}$ is in $e^{\mathcal{I}}_1$ and $e^{\mathcal{I}}_2$ by the induction hypothesis it is also in $e^{\mathcal{I}}_1 \cap e^{\mathcal{I}}_2$ and therefore in $q^{\mathcal{I}}$.

(case 2: $q = e_1 \vee e_2$) as $x\Im, \mathcal{A}$ is in $e^{\mathcal{I}}_1$ or in $e^{\mathcal{I}}_2$ by induction hypothesis it is also in $e^{\mathcal{I}}_1 \cup e^{\mathcal{I}}_2$ and therefore in $q^{\mathcal{I}}$.

A.4 Theorem 10.9

Let E_1 and E_2 be two concepts (or relations) in module M_i that are externally defined in module M_j by queries Q_1 and Q_2; then $\Im \models E_1 \sqsubseteq E_2$ if $\Im_j \models Q_1 \sqsubseteq Q_2$.

Proof. For $a \in \{1, 2\}$ we have:

$$\Im_j \models Q_1 \sqsubseteq Q_2 \Rightarrow Q_1^{\Im_j} \subseteq Q_1^{\Im_j}$$
$$\Rightarrow b^a_{ji}(Q_1^{\Im_j}) \subseteq b^a_{ji}(Q_1^{\Im_j})$$
$$\Rightarrow E_1^{\Im_i} \subseteq E_1^{\Im_i}$$
$$\Rightarrow \Im \models E_1 \sqsubseteq E_2 \tag{A.1}$$

A.5 Theorem 10.11

Let E_1 and E_2 be two concepts in module M_i and $\Im_i \not\models E_1 \sqsubseteq E_2$. Let further be F_1 and F_2 be concepts in module M_j with $\Im_j \models F_1 \sqsubseteq F_2$. We have $\Im \models E_1 \sqsubseteq E_2$ if:

- Theorem 10.9 applies.
- E_1, F_1 and E_2, F_2 are isomorphic, b_{ji}^1 is a function and only disjunction is used to define concepts.
- E_1, F_1 and E_2, F_2 are isomorphic, b_{ji}^1 is an injective function and only disjunction and conjunction are used to define concepts.
- E_1, F_1 and E_2, F_2 are isomorphic, b_{ji}^1 is a bijective function and only disjunction, conjunction and negation are used to define concepts.

Proof. We formulate the following hypothesis about isomorphic concepts: For every pair of isomorphic concepts C and D we have

$$C^{\Im_i} = b_{ji}^1(D_i^{\Im}) \tag{A.2}$$

We try to prove the hypothesis by induction over the definition of isomorphic concepts. The induction hypothesis is directly established by Definition 10.8. We therefore consider case 2 in Definition 10.10. From the induction hypothesis, we know that $E_i^{\Im_i} = b_{ji}^1(F_j^{\Im_j})$. As

$$C^{\Im_i} = b_{ji}^1(D_i^{\Im}) \Leftarrow C^{\Im_i} = b_{ji}^1(f(F_1, ..., F_n)^{\Im_j})$$

in order to prove the lemma we have to show that b_{ji}^1 distributes over f; in particular, that

$$b_{ji}^1(f(F_1, ..., F_n)^{\Im_j}) = f(b_{ji}^1(F_1^{\Im_j}), ..., b_{ji}^1(F_n^{\Im_j}))^{\Im_i}$$

because in this case, we can use the induction hypothesis to replace the arguments of f resulting in $C^{\Im_i} = f(E_i^{\Im_j}, ..., E_n^{\Im_j})^{\Im_i}$, which directly follows from the definition.

We investigate the above statement with respect to the Boolean operators over class names. For the sake of readability, we use b instead of b_{ji}^1 to denote the semantic relation between M_j and M_i.

Disjunction

Disjunction is defined in terms of the union of the extensions of concepts. We have to show that: $b(C^{\Im_j} \cup D^{\Im_j}) = b(C^{\Im_j}) \cup b(D^{\Im_j})$.

($\subseteq$) For each element $x \in b(C^{\Im} \cup D^{\Im})$ there is an element $y \in (C^{\Im} \cup D^{\Im})$ with $b(y, x)$. For this y we know that either $y \in C^{\Im}$ or $y \in C^{\Im}$. As b is defined for y, we also have an object x' with $b(y, x')$ and either $x' \in b(C^{\Im_j})$ or $x' = b(D^{\Im_j})$ and therefore $x' \in b(C^{\Im} \cup D^{\Im})$. What is left to be shown is that $x' = x$. This actually is only given if b is a function, which we have to take as a premise.

($\supseteq$) For each element $x \in b(C^{\Im}) \cup b(C^{\Im})$ we know that $x \in b(C^{\Im})$ or $x \in b(D^{\Im})$. Therefore, there is an element y with $b(y, x)$ and either $y \in C^{\Im}$

or $y \in D^{\Im}$. We conclude that $y \in (C^{\Im} \cup D^{\Im})$. As b is defined for y there is an element x' with $b(y, x')$ and $x' \in b(C^{\Im} \cup D^{\Im})$. As above, what is left to be shown is $x = x'$, which is the case if b is a function.

Conjunction

Conjunction is defined in terms of the intersection of the extensions of concepts. We have to show that: $b(C^{\Im_j} \cap D^{\Im_j}) = b(C^{\Im_j}) \cap b(D^{\Im_j})$.

($\subseteq$) For each element $x \in b(C^{\Im} \cap D^{\Im})$ there is an element $y \in (C^{\Im} \cap D^{\Im})$ with $b(y, x)$. For this y we know that $y \in C^{\Im}$ and $y \in D^{\Im}$. We conclude (as b is defined for y) that there is an x' with $b(y, x')$ and $x' \in b(C^{\Im}) \cap b(C^{\Im})$. What is left to be shown is that $x' = x$. This actually is only given if b is a function, which we have to take as a premise.

($\supseteq$) For each element $x \in b(C^{\Im}) \cap b(C^{\Im})$ we know that $x \in b(C^{\Im})$ and $x \in b(D^{\Im})$. Therefore, there are elements y_1, y_2 with $y_1 \in C^{\Im}, b(y, x)$ and $y_2 \in D^{\Im}, b(y', x)$. What we are looking for is an element y with $y \in (C^{\Im} \cap D^{\Im}), b(y, x)$. In this case we could use the same argument as above to show that the subset equation holds if b is a function. Actually, we have such an element y if we could show that $y_1 = y_2$. This is actually the case if b is an injective function which is another premise.

Negation

OWL uses negation in terms of the `owl:complementOf` operator. Its semantics is defined in terms of set complement with respect to the domain of interpretation, i.e. $(\neg C)^{\Im_i} = \Delta_i - C^{\Im_i}$. We have to show that $b(\Delta_j - C^{\Im}) = \Delta_i - b(C^{\Im})$.

($\subseteq$) For every $x \in b(\Delta_j - C^{\Im})$ we know that there is an element y with $b(y, x)$ and $y \notin C^{\Im}$. As we know that b is defined for y, there is an x' with $b(y, x')$. Two things need to shown for this x'. That it is not in $b(C^{\Im})$ and that $x = x'$. The latter is given if b is a function. The former can be guaranteed if b is injective since for each element $x'' \in b(C^{\Im})$ there is an element $y' \in C^{\Im}$. From the injectivity of b it would follow that $y' = y$, which results in a conflict as we know that $y \notin C^{\Im}$.

($\supseteq$) Let $x \in \Delta_i - b(C^{\Im})$. We assume that there is an element y with $b(y, x)$ and $y \notin C^{\Im}$. We assume that $y \in C^{\Im}$. Therefore there exists an element x' with $x' \in b(C^{\Im})$. For the case that b is a function, we can derive a conflict, because in this case $x = x'$ and $x \notin b(C^{\Im})$. If follows that $y \in \Delta_j - C^{\Im}$. As b is defined for y there is an element x'' with $b(y, x'')$ such that $x'' \in b(\Delta_j - C^{\Im})$. Again, if b is a function, we have $x = x''$, which establishes the result under the assumption that we can find a suitable y. This, however, can only be guaranteed if b is also surjective, as otherwise it might be the case that x is not in the image of b. Summarizing, we can say that the set inclusion only holds if b is a bijective function.

A.6 Lemma 11.1

Let $c(Q)$ be the set of all concept names and $r(Q)$ the set of all relation names occurring in query Q; let further $C \in c(Q)$ and $R \in r(Q)$. Then changing C has the same impact on the interpretation of Q as it has on the interpretation of C; in particular, we have $C \sqsubseteq C' \implies Q \sqsubseteq Q'$ and $C' \sqsubseteq C \implies Q' \sqsubseteq Q$, where Q' is the query as being interpreted after changing C. Analogously, a change of R has the same effect on the complete query.

Proof (sketch). The idea of the proof is the following: queries contain conjuncts of the form $C(x)$ or $R(x, y)$. Conjuncts of the first form are interpreted as $\{x | x \in C^{\Im}\}$. It directly follows that changing the interpretation of the concept C referred to in a conjunct of this type leads to the same change in the interpretation of the conjunct and, because conjunction is interpreted as set intersection, the whole query. Conjuncts of the second type are interpreted as $\{x | \exists y : (x, y) \in R^{\Im}\}$. The variable y can be further constrained by a conjunct of the first type. Again changes in the interpretation of the concept that further restrict y have the same effect on possible interpretations of y and therefore also on the interpretation of conjuncts of the second type. Using the same argument, we see that making R more general/specific (allowing more/fewer tuples in the relation) makes conjuncts of the second form more general/specific. Using these basic conclusions, we can prove the lemma by induction over the lengths of the path in the dependency graph of the query, where nodes represent conjuncts and arcs co-occurrence of variables.

The theorem is proven in the same way as Theorem 10.9 where the third step of the derivation is justified by Equation (A.2), which has been shown in the last section.

A.7 Theorem 11.2

A change is harmless with respect to compiled knowledge (i.e. $Q_1 \sqsubseteq Q_2 \implies Q_1' \sqsubseteq Q_2'$) if for all compiled subsumption relations $C_1 \sqsubseteq C_2$, where C_i is defined by query Q_i, we have:

- $X' \sqsubseteq X$ for all $X \in c(Q_1) \cup r(Q_1)$,
- $X \sqsubseteq X'$ for all $X \in c(Q_2) \cup r(Q_2)$.

Proof. We assume that $X' \sqsubseteq X$ for all $X \in c(Q_1) \cup r(Q_1)$. Applying Lemma 11.1 with respect to all $X \in c(Q_1) \cup r(Q_1)$ we derive $Q_1' \sqsubseteq Q_1$. We further assume that $X \sqsubseteq X'$ for all $X \in c(Q_2) \cup r(Q_2)$. Using lemma 1 we get that $Q_2 \sqsubseteq Q_2'$. This leads us to $Q_1' \sqsubseteq Q_1 \sqsubseteq Q_2 \sqsubseteq Q_2'$. Theorem 11.2 is established by transitivity of the subsumption relation.

References

[Aben, 1993] Aben, M. (1993). Formally specifying re-usable knowledge model components. *Knowledge Acquisition Journal*, 5:119–141.

[AdV, 1998] AdV (1998). Amtliches Topographisch Kartographisches Informationssystem ATKIS. Technical report, Landesvermessungsamt NRW, Bonn.

[Amir and McIlraith, 2000] Amir, E. and McIlraith, S. (2000). Partition-based logical reasoning. In *7th International Conference on Principles of Knowledge Representation and Reasoning (KR'2000)*.

[Antoniou and van Harmelen, 2003] Antoniou, G. and van Harmelen, F. (2003). Web ontology language: Owl. In Staab, S. and Studer, R., editors, *Handbook on Ontologies in Information Systems*, Berlin. Springer.

[Antoniou and van Harmelen, 2004] Antoniou, G. and van Harmelen, F. (2004). *The Semantic Web: A Primer*. MIT Press, Cambridge, MA.

[Arens et al., 1993] Arens, Y., Chee, C. Y., Hsu, C.-N., and Knoblock, C. A. (1993). Retrieving and integrating data from multiple information sources. *International Journal of Intelligent and Cooperative Information Systems*, 2(2):127–158.

[Arens et al., 1996] Arens, Y., Hsu, C.-N., and Knoblock, C. A. (1996). Query processing in the sims information mediator. In *Advanced Planning Technology*. AAAI Press, Menlo Park, CA.

[Baader et al., 2002] Baader, F., Calvanese, D., McGuinness, D., Nardi, D., and Patel-Schneider, P., editors (2002). *The Description Logic Handbook: Theory, Implementation and Applications*. Cambridge University Press.

[Banerjee et al., 1987] Banerjee, J., Kim, W., Kim, H.-J., and Korth, H. F. (1987). Semantics and Implementation of Schema Evolution in Object-Oriented Databases. *SIGMOD Record*, 16(3):311–322.

[Basili et al., 2001] Basili, R., Moschitti, A., and Pazienza, M. T. (2001). NLP-driven IR: Evaluating performances over a text classification task. In Nebel, B., editor, *Proceedings of the 13th International Joint Conference on Artificial Intelligence (IJCAI-01)*, pages 1286–1294.

[Bechhofer et al., 2001] Bechhofer, S., Horrocks, I., Goble, C., and Stevens, R. (2001). OilEd: A reason-able ontology editor for the semantic web. In Baader, F., Brewka, G., and Eiter, T., editors, *KI 2001: Advances in Artificial Intelligence*, pages 396–408. Springer.

[Bechofer et al., 2003] Bechofer, S., Gangemi, A., Guarino, N., van Harmelen, F., Horrocks, I., Klein, M., Masolo, C., Oberle, D., Staab, S., Stuckenschmidt, H., and

Volz, R. (2003). Tackling the ontology acquisition bottleneck: An experiment in ontology re-engineering. Technical Report, Computer Science Department, University of Manchester.

[Bechofer et al., 1999] Bechofer, S., Horrocks, I., Patel-Schneider, P. F., and Tessaris, S. (1999). A proposal for a description logic interface. In *Proceedings of the Description Logic Workshop DL'99*, pages 33–36.

[Beeri et al., 1997] Beeri, C., Levy, A., and Rousset, M.-C. (1997). Rewriting queries using views in description logics. In *Proceedings of the 16th ACM SIGACT SIGMOD SIGART Symposium on Principles of Database Systems (PODS-97)*, pages 99–108.

[Belkin and Croft, 1992] Belkin, N. and Croft, B. (1992). Information filtering and information retrieval: two sides of the same coin? *Communications of the ACM*, 35(12):29–38.

[Benjamins and Fensel, 1998] Benjamins, V. and Fensel, D. (1998). The ontological engineering initiative (KA)^2. In Guarino, N., editor, *Proceedings of the International Conference on Formal Ontologies in Information Systems (FOIS-98)*, pages 287–301. IOS Press, Trento, Italy.

[Biron and Malhotra, 2001] Biron, P. V. and Malhotra, A. (2001). Xml schema part 2: Datatypes. Recommendation, W3C. http://www.w3.org/TR/2001/REC-xmlschema-2-20010502/.

[Boley et al., 1999] Boley, D., Gini, M., Gross, R., Han, E.-H. S., Hastings, K., Karypis, G., Kumar, V., Mobasher, B., and Moor, J. (1999). Document categorization and query generation on the world wide web using webace. *AI Review*, 13(5–6):365–391.

[Borgida et al., 1989] Borgida, A., Brachman, R. J., McGuinness, D. L., and Resnick, L. A. (1989). CLASSIC: a structural data model for objects. In *Proceedings of the ACM SIGMOD International Conference on Management of Data*, pages 58–67, Portland OR.

[Borgida and Serafini, 2002] Borgida, A. and Serafini, L. (2002). Distributed description logics: Directed domain correspondences in federated information sources. In Meersman, R. and Tari, Z., editors, *On The Move to Meaningful Internet Systems 2002: CoopIS, Doa, and ODBase*, volume 2519 of *Lecture Notes in Computer Science*, pages 36–53, Berlin. Springer.

[Bouquet et al., 2003] Bouquet, P., Giunchiglia, F., van Harmelen, F., Serafini, L., and Stuckenschmidt, H. (2003). C-OWL: Contextualizing ontologies. In Sekara, K. and Mylopoulis, J., editors, *Proceedings of the Second International Semantic Web Conference*, volume 2870 of *Lecture Notes in Computer Science*, pages 164–179, Berlin. Springer.

[Brachman, 1977] Brachman, R. (1977). What's in a concept: Structural foundations for semantic nets. *International Journal of Man–Machine Studies*, 9(2):127–152.

[Brickley and Guha, 2004] Brickley, D. and Guha, R. (2004). Rdf vocabulary description language 1.0: Rdf schema. Recommendation, W3C. http://www.w3.org/TR/2004/REC-rdf-schema-20040210/.

[Broekstra et al., 2002] Broekstra, J., Kampman, A., and van Harmelen, F. (2002). Sesame: A generic architecture for storing and querying rdf and rdf schema. In *The Semantic Web – ISWC 2002*, volume 2342 of *Lecture Notes in Computer Science*, pages 54–68. Springer.

[Buchheit et al., 1994] Buchheit, M., Nutt, F. D. W., and Schaerf, A. (1994). Terminological systems revisited: Terminology = schema + views. In *Proceedings of the 12th National Conference on Artificial Intelligence (AAAI-94)*.

[Cadoli and Donini, 1997] Cadoli, M. and Donini, F. (1997). A survey on knowledge compilation. *AI Communications*, 10(3–4):137–150.

[Calvanese et al., 1998a] Calvanese, D., Giacomo, G. D., and Lenzerini, M. (1998a). On the decidability of query containment under constraints. In *Proc. 17th ACM Symposium on Principles of Database Systems (PODS-98)*, pages 149–158.

[Calvanese et al., 1998b] Calvanese, D., Giacomo, G. D., Lenzerini, M., Nardi, D., and Rosati, R. (1998b). Description logic framework for information integration. In *Proceedings of the International Conference on Principles of Knowledge Representation and Reasoning, KR-98*, pages 2–13.

[Catarci et al., 1998] Catarci, T., D'Angiolini, G., and Lenzerini, M. (1998). Concept description language for statistical data modelling. In *Proceedings of the VLDB Conference*.

[Champin, 2000] Champin, P.-A. (2000). RDF tutorial. Available at http://www710.univ-lyon1.fr/ champin/rdf-tutorial/.

[Chang and Garcia-Molina, 2001] Chang, K.-C. and Garcia-Molina, H. (2001). Approximate query mapping: Accounting for translation closeness. *The VLDB Journal*, 10:155–181.

[Chen, 1976] Chen, P.-S. (1976). The entity relationship model - towards a unified view of data. *ACM Transactions on Database Systems*, 1(1):9–36.

[Clark and DeRose, 1999] Clark, J. and DeRose, S. (1999). Xml path language (xpath) version 1.0. Recommendation, W3C. http://www.w3.org/TR/1999/REC-xpath-19991116.

[Clark et al., 2001] Clark, P., Thompson, J., Barker, K., Porter, B., Chaudhri, V., Rodriguez, A., Thomere, J., Mishra, S., Gil, Y., Hayes, P., and Reichherzer, T. (2001). Knowledge entry as the graphical assembly of components. In *Proceedings of the 1st International Conference on Knowledge Capture (K-Cap'01)*.

[Clementini et al., 1997] Clementini, E., Felice, P. D., and Hernandez, D. (1997). Qualitative representation of positional information. *Artificial Intelligence*, 95:317–356.

[Cohn, 1997] Cohn, A. (1997). Qualitative spatial representation and reasoning techniques. In Brewka, G., editor, *KI-97 Advances in Artificial Intelligence*, pages 1–30, Berlin. Springer.

[Collet et al., 1991] Collet, C., Huhns, M. N., and Shen, W.-M. (1991). Resource integration using a large knowledge base in carnot. *IEEE Computer*, 24(12):55–62.

[Craven et al., 2000] Craven, M., DiPasquo, D., Freitag, D., McCallum, A., Mitchell, T., Nigam, K., and Slattery, S. (2000). Learning to construct knowledge bases from the world wide web. *Artificial Intelligence*, 118(1–2):69–113.

[de Berg et al., 2000] de Berg, M., van Kreveld, M., Overmars, M., and Schwarzkopf, O. (2000). *Computational Geometry: Algorithms and Applications*. Springer, Berlin.

[De Giacomo and Naggar, 1996] De Giacomo, G. and Naggar, P. (1996). Conceptual data model with structured objects for statistical databases. In *Proceedings of the 8th International Conference on Scientific and Statistical Data Base Management*, pages 168–175, Stockholm, Sweden.

[De Rougemont and Schlieder, 1997] De Rougemont, M. and Schlieder, C. (1997). Spatial navigation with uncertain deviations. In *Proceedings of the 14th National Conference on Artificial Intelligence (AAAI'97)*, pages 649–654.

[Dean et al., 2002] Dean, M., Connolly, D., van Harmelen, F., Hendler, J., Horrocks, I., McGuinness, D., Patel-Schneider, P., and Stein, L. (2002). Web ontology language (owl) reference version 1.0. Working draft, W3C. http://www.w3.org/TR/owl-ref/.

[Decker et al., 1999] Decker, S., Erdmann, M., Fensel, D., and Studer, R. (1999). Ontobroker: Ontology based access to distributed and semi-structured information. In R. Meersman et al., editor, *Semantic Issues in Multimedia Systems. Proceedings of DS-8*, pages 351–369. Kluwer, Boston, MA.

[Decker et al., 2000] Decker, S., Melnik, S., van Harmelen, F., Fensel, D., Klein, M., Broekstra, J., Erdmann, M., and Horrocks, I. (2000). The semantic web: The roles of XML and RDF. *IEEE Expert*, 15(3):63–74.

[Deerwester et al., 1990] Deerwester, S. C., Dumais, S. T., Landauer, T. K., Furnas, G. W., and Harshman, R. A. (1990). Indexing by latent semantic analysis. *Journal of the American Society of Information Science*, 41(6):391–407.

[Denk and Froeschl, 2000] Denk, M. and Froeschl, K. (2000). The idaresa data mediation architecture for statistical aggregates. *Research in Official Statistics*, 3(1):7–38.

[Donini et al., 1996] Donini, F. M., Lenzerini, M., Nardi, D., and Schaerf, A. (1996). Reasoning in description logics. In Brewka, G., editor, *Principles of Knowledge Representation*, pages 191–236. CSLI Publications, Stanford, California.

[Donini et al., 1998] Donini, F. M., Lenzerini, M., Nardi, D., and Schaerf, A. (1998). AL-log: Integrating datalog and description logics. *Journal of Intelligent Information Systems*, 10(3):227–252.

[Duineveld et al., 1999] Duineveld, A., Stoter, R., Weiden, M., Kenepa, B., and Benjamins, V. (1999). Wondertools? A comparative study of ontological engineering tools. In [Gaines et al., 1999].

[Egenhofer, 1991] Egenhofer, M. J. (1991). Reasoning about binary topological relations. In Günther, O. and Schek, H.-J., editors, *Advances in Spatial Databases, Second International Symposium, (SSD'91)*, volume 525 of *Lecture Notes in Computer Science*, pages 143–160, Zürich, Switzerland. Springer.

[Ehrig et al., 2003] Ehrig, M., Tempich, C., Broekstra, J., van Harmelen, F., Sabou, M., Siebes, R., Staab, S., and Stuckenschmidt, H. (2003). A metadata model for semantics-based peer-to-peer systems. In *Proceedings of the Second Konferenz Professionelles Wissensmanagement*, Lucern.

[European Environmental Agency, 1999a] European Environmental Agency (1999a). Corine land cover, technical guide. Technical report, European Environmental Agency. ETC/LC, European Topic Centre on Land Cover.

[European Environmental Agency, 1999b] European Environmental Agency (1999b). GEMET – general multilingual environmental thesaurus. Technical report, European Topic Centre on Catalogue of Data Sources (ETC/CDS). European Environmental Agency. Version 2.0.

[Fallside, 2001] Fallside, D. (2001). Xml schema part 0: Primer. Recommendation, W3C. http://www.w3.org/TR/2001/REC-xmlschema-0-20010502/.

[Farmer et al., 1992] Farmer, W., Guttman, J., and Thayer, F. (1992). Little theories. In Kapur, D., editor, *Proceedings of the Eleventh International Conference on Automated Deduction*, volume 607 of *Lecture Notes in Computer Science*, pages 567–581, Berlin. Springer.

[Farquhar and Gruninger, 1997] Farquhar, A. and Gruninger, M. (1997). Proceedings of the AAAI spring symposium on ontological engineering. Technical report, AAAI, Stanford, CA.

[Fellbaum, 1998] Fellbaum, C., editor (1998). *WordNet: An Electronic Lexical Database*. Language, Speech, and Communication Series. MIT Press, Cambridge, MA.

[Fensel, 1999] Fensel, D., editor (1999). *Proceedings of the IJCAI-99 Workshop on Intelligent Information Integration*, volume 23 of *CEUR Workshop Proceedings*. CEUR Publications and AIFB Karlsruhe.

[Fensel and Brodie, 2003] Fensel, D. and Brodie, M. (2003). *Ontologies: A Silver Bullet for Knowledge Management and Electronic Commerce*. Springer-Verlag, Berlin, 2nd edition.

[Fensel et al., 1998] Fensel, D., Decker, S., Erdmann, M., and Studer, R. (1998). Ontobroker: The very high idea. In *11th International Flairs Conference (FLAIRS-98)*, pages 131–135, Sanibal Island, USA.

[Fensel et al., 1997] Fensel, D., Erdmann, M., and Studer, R. (1997). Ontology groups: Semantically enriched subnets of the WWW. In *Proceedings of the International Workshop on Intelligent Information Integration during the 21st German Annual Conference on Artificial Intelligence*, Freiburg, Germany.

[Fensel et al., 2001] Fensel, D., Horrocks, I., van Harmelen, F., McGuinness, D. L., and Patel-Schneider, P. F. (2001). OIL: An ontology infrastructure for the semantic web. *IEEE Intelligent Systems*, 16(2):38–44.

[Fluit et al., 2003] Fluit, C., Sabou, M., and van Harmelen, F. (2003). Ontology-based information visualisation. In Geroimenko, V. and Chen, C., editors, *Visualizing the Semantic Web*, Berline. Springer.

[Fox and Grninger, 1998] Fox, M. S. and Grninger, M. (1998). Enterprise modelling. *AI Magazine*, 19(3):109–121.

[Frakes and Baeza-Yates, 1992] Frakes, W. B. and Baeza-Yates, R. (1992). *Information Retrieval: Data Structures and Algorithms*. Prentice-HALL, North Virginia.

[Franconi et al., 2000] Franconi, E., Grandi, F., and Mandreoli, F. (2000). A semantic approach to schema evolution and versioning in object-oriented databases. In *Proceesing of CL 2000*, volume 1861 of *Lecture Notes in Artificial Intelligence*, pages 1048–1062. Springer Verlag.

[Frank, 1992] Frank, A. (1992). Qualitative spatial reasoning about distances and directions in geographic space. *Journal of Visual Languages and Computing*, 3:343–371.

[Freitag and Kushmerick, 2000] Freitag, D. and Kushmerick, N. (2000). Boosted wrapper induction. In *Proceedings of AAAI-00*, pages 577–583, Austin, TX.

[Gaines et al., 1999] Gaines, B., Kremer, R., and Musen, M. (1999). Proceedings of the 12th Banff knowledge acquisition for knowledge-based systems workshop. Technical report, University of Calgary/Stanford University.

[Gaizauskas and Humphreys, 1997] Gaizauskas, R. and Humphreys, K. (1997). Using a semantic network for information extraction. *Journal of Natural Language Engineering*, 3(2–3):147–169.

[Gangemi et al., 2002] Gangemi, A., Guarino, N., Masolo, C., Oltramari, A., and Schneider, L. (2002). Sweetening ontologies with DOLCE. In *13th International Conference on Knowledge Engineering and Knowledge Management (EKAW02)*, volume 2473 of *Lecture Notes in Computer Science*, page 166 ff, Sigüenza, Spain. Springer.

[Ganter and Wille, 1999] Ganter, B. and Wille, R. (1999). *Formal Concept Analysis - Mathematical Foundations*. Springer.

[Garcia-Molina et al., 1995] Garcia-Molina, H., Papakonstantinou, Y., Quass, D., Rajaraman, A., Sagiv, Y., Ullman, J., and Widom, J. (1995). The TSIMMIS approach to mediation: Data models and languages. In *Next Generation Information Technologies and Systems (NGITS-95)*, Naharia, Israel. Extended Abstract.

[Genesereth and Fikes, 1992] Genesereth, M. and Fikes, R. (1992). Knowledge interchange format version 3.0 reference manual. Report of the Knowledge Systems Laboratory KSL 91-1, Stanford University.

[Ghidini and Giunchiglia, 2001] Ghidini, C. and Giunchiglia, F. (2001). Local models semantics, or contextual reasoning = locality + compatibility. *Artificial Intelligence*, 127(2):221–259.

[Giunchiglia and Shvaiko, 2003] Giunchiglia, F. and Shvaiko, P. (2003). Semantic matching. In *Proceedings of the IJCAI-03 Workshop on Ontologies and Distributed Systems*, volume 71 of *CEUR Workshop Proceedings*.

[Glasgow et al., 1995] Glasgow, J., Narayanan, H., and Chandrasekaran, B. (1995). *Diagrammatic Reasoning: Cognitive and Computational Perspectives*. MIT Press, Cambridge, MA.

[Goasdoue et al., 2000] Goasdoue, F., Lattes, V., and Rousset, M.-C. (2000). The use of CARIN language and algorithms for information integration: The PICSEL system. *International Journal of Cooperative Information Systems*, 9(4):383–401.

[Goasdoue and Reynaud, 1999] Goasdoue, F. and Reynaud, C. (1999). Modeling information sources for information integration. In Fensel, D. and Studer, R., editors, *Knowledge Acquisition, Modeling and Management*, volume 1621 of *Lecture Notes in Artificial Intelligence*, pages 121–138, Berlin. Springer.

[Goh, 1997] Goh, C. H. (1997). *Representing and Reasoning about Semantic Conflicts in Heterogeneous Information Sources*. Phd thesis, MIT.

[Gomez-Perez, 2002] Gomez-Perez, A. (2002). A survey on ontology tools. Deliverable 1.3 of the OntoWeb Thematic Network. Available at http://www.ontoweb.org.

[Gomez-Perez and Corcho, 2002] Gomez-Perez, A. and Corcho, O. (2002). Ontology languages for the semantic web. *IEEE Intelligent Systems*, January/February:54–60.

[Gomez-Perez et al., 1996] Gomez-Perez, A., Fernandez, M., and de Vicente, A. (1996). Towards a method to conceptualize domain ontologies. In *Workshop on Ontological Engineering, ECAI '96*, pages 41–52, Budapest, Hungary.

[Gomez-Perez and Juristo, 1997] Gomez-Perez, M. F. A. and Juristo, N. (1997). Methontology: From ontological arts towards ontological engineering. In [Farquhar and Gruninger, 1997], pages 33–40.

[Grosof et al., 2003] Grosof, B., Horrocks, I., Volz, R., and Decker, S. (2003). Description logic programs: combining logic programs with description logic. In *Proceedings of the twelfth international World Wide Web Conference*, pages 48 – 57, Budapest, Hungary.

[Grossmann, 2002] Grossmann, W. (2002). Structures for metadata. In Kent, J.-P., editor, *Work Package 1: Methodology and Tools*. MetaNet Project.

[Gruber, 1991] Gruber, T. (1991). Ontolingua: A mechanism to support portable ontologies. KSL Report KSL-91-66, Stanford University.

[Gruber, 1993] Gruber, T. (1993). A translation approach to portable ontology specifications. *Knowledge Acquisition*, 5(2):199–220.

[Gruber, 1995] Gruber, T. (1995). Toward principles for the design of ontologies used for knowledge sharing. *International Journal of Human–Computer Studies*, 43:907–928.

[Guarino and Giaretta, 1995] Guarino, N. and Giaretta, P. (1995). Ontologies and knowledge bases: Towards a terminological clarification. In Mars, N., editor, *Towards Very Large Knowledge Bases: Knowledge Building and Knowledge Sharing*, pages 25–32, Amsterdam. IOS Press.

[Guarino et al., 1999] Guarino, N., Masolo, C., and Vetere, G. (1999). Ontoseek: Content-based access to the web. *IEEE Intelligent Systems*, 14(3):70–80.

[Haarslev et al., 1998] Haarslev, V., Lutz, C., and Moeller, R. (1998). Foundations of spatioterminological reasoning with description logics. In *Principles of Knowledge Representation and Reasoning*, pages 112–123.

[Haarslev and Moeller, 1997] Haarslev, V. and Moeller, R. (1997). Spatioterminological reasoning: Subsumption based on geometrical inferences. In *Proceedings of the International Workshop on Description Logics*.

[Haarslev and Moeller, 2001] Haarslev, V. and Moeller, R. (2001). Description of the RACER system and its applications. In *Proceedings of the Description Logics Workshop DL-2001*, pages 132–142, Stanford, CA.

[Haarslev et al., 1994] Haarslev, V., Moeller, R., and Schroeder, C. (1994). Combining spatial and terminological reasoning. In Nebel, B. and Dreschler-Fischer, L., editors, *KI-94: Advances in Artificial Intelligence – Proceedings of the 18th German Annual Conference on Artificial Intelligence*, volume 861 of *Lecture Notes in Artificial Intelligence*, pages 142–153, Berlin. Springer Verlag.

[Halevy, 2001] Halevy, A. (2001). Answering queries using views – a survey. *The VLDB Journal*, 10(4):270–294.

[Hartmann, 2002] Hartmann, J. (2002). Lernen struktureller Regeln zur Klassifikation von Web Dokumenten. Master's thesis, University of Bremen.

[Hartmann and Stuckenschmidt, 2002] Hartmann, J. and Stuckenschmidt, H. (2002). Automatic metadata analysis for environmental information systems. In *Proceedings of the International Symposium on Environmental Informatics*.

[Heflin and Hendler, 2000] Heflin, J. and Hendler, J. (2000). Dynamic ontologies on the web. In *Proceedings of American Association for Artificial Intelligence Conference (AAAI-2000)*, Menlo Park, CA. AAAI Press.

[Heflin et al., 1999] Heflin, J., Hendler, J., and Luke, S. (1999). SHOE: A knowledge representation language for internet applications. Technical Report CS-TR-4078, Institute for Advanced Computer Studies, University of Maryland.

[Hirst and St-Onge, 1998] Hirst, G. and St-Onge, D. (1998). Lexical chains as representations of context for the detection and correction of malapropisms. In [Fellbaum, 1998], pages 305–332.

[Horrocks, 1998] Horrocks, I. (1998). The FaCT system. In de Swart, H., editor, *Automated Reasoning with Analytic Tableaux and Related Methods: International Conference Tableaux'98*, volume 1397 of *Lecture Notes in Artificial Intelligence*, pages 307–312. Springer-Verlag, Berlin.

[Horrocks and Tessaris, 2000] Horrocks, I. and Tessaris, S. (2000). A conjunctive query language for description logic aboxes. In *Proceedings of the National Conference on Artificial Intelligence AAAI/IAAI 2000*.

[Hwang, 1999] Hwang, C. H. (1999). Incompletely and imprecisely speaking: Using dynamic ontologies for representing and retrieving information. In Franconi, E. and Kifer, M., editors, *Proceedings of the 6th International Workshop on Knowledge Representation meets Databases (KRDB'99)*, pages 14–20.

[ISO-8879, 1986] ISO-8879 (1986). Information processing – text and office systems – standard generalized markup language (SGML). Standard by the International Organization for Standardization.

[Jasper and Uschold, 1999] Jasper, R. and Uschold, M. (1999). A framework for understanding and classifying ontology applications. In [Gaines et al., 1999].

[Jones et al., 1998] Jones, D. M., Bench-Capon, T., and Visser, P. (1998). Methodologies for ontology development. In Cuena, J., editor, *Proceedings of the IT&KNOWS Conference of the 15th IFIP World Computer Congress*, Budapest. Chapman-Hall.

[Jonker and Verwaart, 2003] Jonker, C. and Verwaart, D. (2003). Intelligent support for solving classification differences in statistical information integration. In *Procedings of IEA/AEI 2003*.

[Kapur and Mundy, 1988] Kapur, D. and Mundy, J. (1988). Geometric reasoning and artificial intelligence. *Artificial Intelligence*, 37(1-3):1–11.

[Karp et al., 2002] Karp, P., Chaudri, V., and Thomere, J. (2002). An XML-based ontology exchange language. Available at http://www.ai.sri.com/ pkarp/xol.

[Karp, 1993] Karp, P. D. (1993). The design space of frame knowledge representation systems. Technical Note 520, AI Center SRI International, Menlo Park, CA.

[Kashyap and Sheth, 1996] Kashyap, V. and Sheth, A. (1996). Schematic and semantic similarities between database objects: A context-based approach. *The International Journal on Very Large Data Bases*, 5(4):276–304.

[Kashyap and Sheth, 1997] Kashyap, V. and Sheth, A. (1997). Semantic heterogeneity in global information systems: The role of metadata, context and ontologies. In Papazoglou, M. P. and Schlageter, G., editors, *Cooperative Information Systems*, pages 139–178. Academic Press, San Diego.

[Kent, 2002] Kent, R. (2002). Conceptual knowledge modelling language. Available at http://www.ontologos.org/CKML/.

[Kifer et al., 1995] Kifer, M., Lausen, G., and Wu, J. (1995). Logical foundations of object-oriented and frame-based systems. *Journal of the ACM*, 42:741–84.

[Kim and Seo, 1991] Kim, W. and Seo, J. (1991). Classifying schematic and data heterogeneity in multidatabase systems. *IEEE Computer*, 24(12):12–18.

[Klein, 2004] Klein, M. (2004). *Change Management for Distributed Ontologies*. PhD thesis, Vrije Universiteit Amsterdam.

[Klein et al., 2002] Klein, M., Fensel, D., Kiryakov, A., and Ognyanov, D. (2002). Ontology versioning and change detection on the web. In *13th International Conference on Knowledge Engineering and Knowledge Management (EKAW02)*, volume 2473 of *Lecture Notes in Computer Science*, page 197 ff, Sigüenza, Spain. Springer.

[Klinkert et al., 2000] Klinkert, M., Treur, J., and Verwaart, D. (2000). Knowledge-intensive gathering and integration of statistical information on European fisheries. In Loganantharaj, R., Palm, G., and Ali, M., editors, *Proceedings IEA/AIE 2000*, volume 1821 of *Lecture Notes in Artificial Intelligence*. Springer.

[Kottmann, 1999] Kottmann, C. (1999). Semantics and information communities. OGC Abstract Specification Topic 14, The Open GIS Consortium.

[Kutz et al., 2002] Kutz, O., Wolter, F., and Zakharyaschev, M. (2002). Connecting abstract description systems. In Fensel, D., Giunchiglia, F., McGuinness, D., and Williams, M., editors, *Proceedings of the 8th International Conference of Knowledge Representation and Reasoning (KR-2002)*, pages 215–227, San Mateo, CA. Morgan Kaufmann.

[Lauritzen and Spiegelhalter, 1988] Lauritzen, S. and Spiegelhalter, D. (1988). Local computations with probabilities on graphical structures and their application to expert systems. *Journal of the Royal Statistical Society*, 50:157–224.

[Leacock and Chodorow, 1998] Leacock, C. and Chodorow, M. (1998). Combining local context and wordnet similarity for word sense identification. In [Fellbaum, 1998].

[Lenat, 1998] Lenat, D. (1998). The dimensions of context space. Available on the Web site of the Cycorp Corporation. (http://www.cyc.com/publications).

[Lenat, 1995] Lenat, D. B. (1995). Cyc: A large-scale investment in knowledge infrastructure. *Communications of the ACM*, 38(11):33–38.

[Levy et al., 1996] Levy, A., Rajaraman, A., and Ordille, J. J. (1996). Querying heterogeneous information sources using source descriptions. In *Proceedings of the 22nd International Conference on Very Large Databases, VLDB-96*, pages 251–262, Bombay, India.

[Levy and Rousset, 1996] Levy, A. and Rousset, M.-C. (1996). Carin: A representation language combining horn rules and description logics. In *Proceedings of the 12th European Conference on Artificial Intelligence (ECAI-96)*, pages 323–327.

[Lewis, 1996] Lewis, D. D. (1996). Natural language processing for information retrieval. *Communcations of the ACM*, 39(1):92–101.

[Luke and Hefflin, 2002] Luke, S. and Hefflin, J. (2002). SHOE 1.01 proposal specification. Available at http://www.cs.umd.edu/projects/plus/SHOE.

[Manola and Miller, 2003] Manola, F. and Miller, E. (2003). RDF primer. Proposed recommendation, W3C.

[Manola and Miller, 2004] Manola, F. and Miller, E. (2004). Rdf primer. Recommendation, W3C. http://www.w3.org/TR/2004/REC-rdf-primer-20040210/.

[Marriott and Stuckey, 1998] Marriott, K. and Stuckey, P. (1998). *Programming with Constraints*. MIT Press, Cambridge, MA.

[Maynard and Ananiadou, 1998] Maynard, D. and Ananiadou, S. (1998). Term sense disambiguation using a domain-specific thesaurus. In *Proceedings of 1st International Conference on Language Resources and Evaluation (LREC)*, Granada, Spain.

[McGuinness, 2002] McGuinness, D. (2002). Ontologies come of age. In Fensel, D., Hendler, J., Lieberman, H., and Wahlster, W., editors, *Spinning the Semantic Web: Bringing the World Wide Web to Its Full Potential*, page 171ff. MIT Press, Cambridge, MA.

[McGuinness and van Harmelen, 2003] McGuinness, D. and van Harmelen, F. (2003). Owl web ontology language overview. Proposed recommendation, W3C. http://www.w3.org/TR/owl-features/.

[McIlraith and Amir, 2001] McIlraith, S. and Amir, E. (2001). Theorem proving with structured theories. In Nebel, B., editor, *Proceedings of IJCAI'01*, pages 624–634, San Mateo. Morgan Kaufmann.

[Mena and Illarramendi, 2001] Mena, E. and Illarramendi, A. (2001). *Ontology-Based Query Processing for Global Information Systems*. Kluwer.

[Mena et al., 2000a] Mena, E., Illarramendi, A., Kashyap, V., and Sheth, A. (2000a). OBSERVER: An approach for query processing in global information systems based on interoperation across pre-existing ontologies. *International journal of Distributed And Parallel Databases (DAPD)*, 8(2):223–272.

[Mena et al., 2000b] Mena, E., Kashyap, V., Illarramendi, A., and Sheth, A. (2000b). Imprecise answers in distributed environments: Estimation of information loss for multi-ontology based query processing. *IJCIS*, 9(4):403–425.

[Motik et al., 2004] Motik, B., Stattler, U., and Hustadt, U. (2004). Reducing shiq description logic to disjunctive datalog programs. In *Proceedings of the Ninth In-*

ternational Conference on Principles of Knowledge Representation and Reasoning (KR2004).

[Motik et al., 2003] Motik, B., Volz, R., and Maedche, A. (2003). Optimizing query answering in description logics using disjunctive deductive databases. In *Proceedings of the 10th International Workshop on Knowledge Representation meets Databases (KRDB-2003)*, pages 39–50, Hamburg.

[Motta, 1999] Motta, E. (1999). *Reusable Components for Knowledge Models: Case Studies in Parametric Design Problem Solving*, volume 53 of *Frontiers in Artificial Intelligence and Applications*. IOS Press, Amsterdam.

[Muggleton, 1995] Muggleton, S. (1995). Inverse entailment and Progol. *New Generation Computing, Special Issue on Inductive Logic Programming*, 13(3-4):245–286.

[Muggleton, 1999] Muggleton, S. (1999). Inductive logic programming: issues, results and the LLL challenge. *Artificial Intelligence*, 114(1–2):283–296.

[Muggleton and de Raedt, 1994] Muggleton, S. and de Raedt, L. (1994). Inductive logic programming: Theory and methods. *Journal of Logic Programming*, 19–20:629–679.

[Nejdl et al., 2002] Nejdl, W., Wolf, B., Qu, C., Decker, S., Sintek, M., Naeve, A., Nilsson, M., Palmer, M., and Risch, T. (2002). Edutella: A p2p networking infrastructure based on RDF. In *Proceedings of the Eleventh International World Wide Web Conference*, Honolulu, Hawaii.

[Neumann et al., 2001] Neumann, H., Schuster, G., Stuckenschmidt, H., Visser, U., Voegele, T., and Wache, H. (2001). Intelligent brokering of environmental information with the buster system. In Hilty, L. and Gilgen, P., editors, *Sustainability in the Information Society – 15th International Symposium on Informatics for Environmental Protection*, pages 505–512, Marburg. Metropolis.

[Nodine et al., 1999] Nodine, M., Bohrer, W., and Ngu, A. H. H. (1999). Semantic brokering over dynamic heterogeneous data sources in infosleuth. In *Proceedings of the International Conference on Data Engineering*.

[Noy et al., 2000] Noy, N., Fergerson, R., and Musen, M. (2000). The knowledge model of protege-2000: Combining interoperability and flexibility. In *Proceedings of EKAW 2000*.

[Noy and Musen, 2004] Noy, N. and Musen, M. (2004). The prompt suite: Interactive tools for ontology merging and mapping. *International Journal of Human-Computer Studies*, 59(6):983–1024.

[Pan and Horrocks, 2003] Pan, J. and Horrocks, I. (2003). RDFS(FA) and RDF MT: Two semantics for RDFS. In Fensel, D., Sycara, K., and Mylopoulos, J., editors, *Proceedings of the 2003 International Semantic Web Conference (ISWC 2003)*, volume 2870 of *Lecture Notes in Computer Science*, pages 30–46. Springer.

[Patel-Schneider et al., 2002a] Patel-Schneider, P., Horrocks, I., and van Harmelen, F. (2002a). Reviewing the design of daml+oil: An ontology language for the semantic web. In Dechter, R., Kearns, M., and Sutton, R., editors, *Proceedings of the Eighteenth National Conference on Artificial Intelligence*.

[Patel-Schneider et al., 2002b] Patel-Schneider, P. F., Hayes, P., Horrocks, I., and van Harmelen, F. (2002b). Web ontology language (owl) abstract syntax and semantics. Working draft, W3C.

[Patil et al., 1991] Patil, R., Fikes, R., Patel-Schneider, P., McKay, D., Finin, T., Gruber, T., and Neches, R. (1991). The DARPA knowledge sharing effort: Progress report. In Rich, C., Nebel, B., and Swartout, W., editors, *Principles of Knowledge*

Representation and Reasoning: Proceedings of the Third International Conference, Cambridge, MA.

[Pazzaglia and Embury, 1998] Pazzaglia, J.-C. and Embury, S. (1998). Bottom-up integration of ontologies in a database context. In *KRDB'98 Workshop on Innovative Application Programming and Query Interfaces*, Seattle, WA.

[Pepper and Moore, 2001] Pepper, S. and Moore, G. (2001). XML topic maps (XTM) 1.0. Xtm specification, topicmaps.org. http://www.topicmaps.org/xtm/1.0/.

[Pierre, 2001] Pierre, J. M. (2001). On the automated classification of web sites. *Electronic Transactions on Artificial Intelligence*, 6. http://www.ida.liu.se/ext/etai/ra/seweb/002/.

[Preece et al., 1999] Preece, A., Hui, K.-Y., Gray, W., Marti, P., Bench-Capon, T., Jones, D., and Cui, Z. (1999). KRAFT architecture for knowledge fusion and transformation. In *19th SGES International Conference on Knowledge-based Systems and Applied Artificial Intelligence (ES'99)*, Berlin. Springer.

[Ragget et al., 1999] Ragget, D., Le Hors, A., and Jacobs, I. (1999). HTML 4.01 specification. Recommendation, W3C. http://www.w3.org/TR/1999/REC-html401-19991224.

[Randell et al., 1992] Randell, D., Cui, Z., and Cohn, A. (1992). A spatial logic based on regions and connection. In *Proceedings of the Conference on Knowledge Representation and Reasoning (KR-92)*, pages 165–176.

[Rector, 2003] Rector, A. (2003). Modularisation of domain ontologies implemented in description logics and related formalisms including OWL. In *Proceedings of the 16th International FLAIRS Conference*, Menlo Park, CA. AAAI.

[Resnik, 1995] Resnik, P. (1995). Using information content to evaluate semantic similarity in a taxonomy. In *Proceedings of the 14th International Joint Conference on Artificial Intelligence (IJCAI)*.

[Richter, 1995] Richter, M. (1995). On the notion of similarity in case-based reasoning. In della Riccia, G., Kruse, R., and Viertl, R., editors, *Mathematical and Statistical Methods in Artificial Intelligence*, pages 171–184. Springer, Berlin.

[Rodriguez and Egenhofer, 2003] Rodriguez, A. and Egenhofer, M. (2003). Determining semantic similarity among entity classes from different ontologies. *IEEE Transactions on Knowledge and Data Engineering*, 15(2):442–456.

[Rousset, 1997] Rousset, M.-C. (1997). Verifying the world wide web: a position statement. In van Harmelen, F. and J. van Thienen, editors, *Proceedings of the Fourth European Symposium on the Validation and Verification of Knowledge Based Systems (EUROVAV97)*.

[Rumbaugh et al., 1998] Rumbaugh, J., Jacobson, I., and Booch, G. (1998). *The Unified Modeling Language Reference Manual*. Addison-Wesley.

[Salton, 1986] Salton, G. (1986). Another look at automatic text-retrieval systems. *Communications of the ACM*, 29(7):648–656.

[Salton and McGill, 1983] Salton, G. and McGill, M. (1983). *Introduction to Modern Information Retrieval*. McGraw-Hill, New York, NY.

[Schlieder et al., 2001] Schlieder, C., Voegele, T., and Visser, U. (2001). Qualitative spatial representation for information retreival by gazeteers. In *Proceedings of the International Conference on Spatial Information Theory (COSIT 2001)*.

[Schlobach and Cornet, 2003] Schlobach, S. and Cornet, R. (2003). Non-standard reasoning services for debugging of description logic terminologies. In *Proceedings of the 18th International Conference on Artificial Intelligence (IJCAI 2003)*, Acapulco, Mexico.

[Schreiber et al., 1994] Schreiber, A., Wielinga, B., Akkermans, H., van der Velde, W., and Anjewierden, A. (1994). CML the CommonKADS conceptual modeling language. In Steels, L., Schreiber, G., and van de Velde, W., editors, *A Future of Knowledge Acquisition, Proceedings of the 8th European Knowledge Acquisition Workshop (EKAW 94)*, pages 1–25. Springer, Berlin.

[Schreiber, 2002] Schreiber, G. (2002). The web is not well-formed. *IEEE Intelligent Systems*, 17(2). Contribution to the section Trends and Controversies: Ontologies KISSES in Standardization.

[Selman and Kautz, 1996] Selman, B. and Kautz, H. (1996). Knowledge compilation and theory approximation. *Journal of the ACM*, 43(2):193–224.

[Smith et al., 2003] Smith, M., Welty, C., and McGuinness, D. (2003). Owl web ontology language guide. Proposed recommendation, W3C. http://www.w3.org/TR/owl-guide/.

[Sowa, 1999] Sowa, J. F. (1999). *Knowledge Representation: Logical, Philosophical, and Computational Foundations*. Thomson Learning.

[Staab et al., 2001] Staab, S., Maedche, A., and Handschuh, S. (2001). An annotation framework for the semantic web. In *Proceedings of the First Workshop on Multimedia Annotation*, Tokyo, Japan.

[Stuckenschmidt et al., 2000] Stuckenschmidt, H., Broekstra, J., Fensel, D., van Harmelen, F., Klein, M., and Horrocks, I. (2000). Catalogue integration – a case study in ontology-based semantic translation. FEW Report R-474, Vrije Universiteit Amsterdam.

[Stuckenschmidt and Wache, 2000] Stuckenschmidt, H. and Wache, H. (2000). Context modeling and transformation for semantic interoperability. In *Proceedings of the workshop 'Knowledge Representation Meets Databases' KRDB-2000*, number 29 in CEUR Workshop proceedings, pages 115–126.

[Studer et al., 1998] Studer, R., Benjamins, V. R., and Fensel, D. (1998). Knowledge engineering: Principles and methods. *Data Knowledge Engineering*, 25(1-2):161–197.

[Stumme and Maedche, 2001] Stumme, G. and Maedche, A. (2001). FCA-MERGE: Bottom-up merging of ontologies. In *Proceedings of the 17th International Conference on Artifical Intelligence IJCAI 2001*, pages 225–234, Seattle, WA.

[Sundgren, 1995] Sundgren, B. (1995). Guidelines for the modeling of statstical data and metadata. Technical report, Conference of European Statisticians of the UN Economic Commission for Europe.

[Sure et al., 2002] Sure, Y., Staab, S., and Angele, J. (2002). OntoEdit: Guiding ontology development by methodology and inferencing. In *Proceedings of the International Conference on Ontologies, Databases and Applications of SEmantics ODBASE 2002*, Lecture Notes in Computer Science, University of California, Irvine, CA. Springer.

[Thompson et al., 2001] Thompson, H., Beech, D., Maloney, M., and Mendelsohn, N. (2001). Xml schema part 1: Structures. Recommendation, W3C. http://www.w3.org/TR/2001/REC-xmlschema-1-20010502/.

[Turtle and Croft, 1991] Turtle, H. and Croft, W. (1991). Evaluation of inference network-based retrieval methods. *ACM Transactions on Information Systems*, 9(3):187–222.

[Uschold, 1996] Uschold, M. (1996). Building ontologies: Towards a unified methodology. In *16th Annual Conference of the British Computer Society Specialist Group on Expert Systems*, Cambridge, UK.

[Uschold and Gruninger, 1996] Uschold, M. and Gruninger, M. (1996). Ontologies: Principles, methods and applications. *Knowledge Engineering Review*, 11(2):93–155.

[van Harmelen and Fensel, 1999] van Harmelen, F. and Fensel, D. (1999). Practical knowledge representation for the web. In Fensel, D., editor, *Proceedings of the IJCAI'99 Workshop on Intelligent Information Integration*.

[van Harmelen and van der Meer, 1999] van Harmelen, F. and van der Meer, J. (1999). Webmaster: Knowledge-based verification of web-pages. In Ali, M. and Imam, I., editors, *Proceedings of IEA/AEI99*, Lecture Notes in Artificial Intelligence, pages 147–166, Berlin. Springer.

[van Heijst et al., 1997] van Heijst, G., Schreiber, A., and Wielinga, B. (1997). Using explicit ontologies for KBS development. *International Journal of Human-Computer Studies*, 46(2–3):183–292.

[Visser et al., 1998] Visser, P., Jones, D., Bench-Capon, T., and Shave, M. (1998). Assessing heterogeneity by classifying ontology mismatch. In N. Guarino et al, editor, *Formal Ontology in Information Systems (Proceedings of FOIS'98)*. IOS Press, Trento, Italy.

[Visser et al., 1997] Visser, P. R. S., Jones, D. M., Bench-Capon, T. J. M., and Shave, M. J. R. (1997). An analysis of ontological mismatches: Heterogeneity versus interoperability. In *AAAI 1997 Spring Symposium on Ontological Engineering*, Stanford, CA.

[Visser and Schuster, 2002] Visser, U. and Schuster, G. (2002). Finding and integration of information – a practical solution for the semantic web. In *Proceedings of the ECAI 02, Workshop on Ontologies and Semantic Interoperability*.

[Visser and Stuckenschmidt, 1999] Visser, U. and Stuckenschmidt, H. (1999). Intelligent, location-dependent acquisition and retrieval of environmental information. In Rumor, M., editor, *Information Technology in the Service of Local Government Planning and Management*. The Urban Data Management Society, Venice, Italy.

[Visser et al., 2002] Visser, U., Stuckenschmidt, H., Schuster, G., and Voegele, T. (2002). Ontologies for geographic information processing. *Computers in Geosciences*, 28:103–117.

[Voegele, 2004] Voegele, T. (2004). *Spatial Information Retrieval with Place Names*. PhD thesis, Department of Mathematics and Computer Science, University of Bremen.

[Voegele et al., 2003] Voegele, T., Schlieder, C., and Visser, U. (2003). Intuitive modelling of place name regions for spatial information retrieval. In *Proceedings of the Conference on Spatial Information Theory (COSIT'03)*, Lecture Notes in Computer Science, page Springer.

[Voegele et al., 2000] Voegele, T., Stuckenschmidt, H., and Visser, U. (2000). BUISY - using brokered data objects for environmental information systems. In Tochtermann, K. and Riekert, W.-F., editors, *Hypermedia im Umweltschutz*, pages 68–73, Marburg. Metropolis.

[Volz et al., 2002a] Volz, R., Maedche, A., and Oberle, D. (2002a). Towards a modularized semantic web. In *Proceedings of the ECAI'02 Workshop on Ontologies and Semantic Interoperability*.

[Volz et al., 2002b] Volz, R., Oberle, D., Staab, S., and Studer, R. (2002b). Ontolift prototype. Deliverable D11, EU/IST Project WonderWeb.

[Volz et al., 2003] Volz, R., Oberle, D., and Studer, R. (2003). Views for light-weight web ontologies. In *Proceedings of the ACM Symposium on Applied Computing (SAC 2003)*.

[Wache, 1999] Wache, H. (1999). A rule-based mediator for the integration of heterogeneous sources (extended version). TZI-Berichte, University of Bremen.

[Wache, 2003] Wache, H. (2003). *Semantic Mediation for Heterogeneous Information Sources*. Phd thesis, University of Bremen. In German.

[Wache et al., 1999] Wache, H., Scholz, T., Stieghahn, H., and König-Ries, B. (1999). An integration method for the specification of rule-oriented mediators. In Kambayashi, Y. and Takakura, H., editors, *Proceedings of the International Symposium on Database Applications in Non-Traditional Environments (DANTE'99)*, pages 109–112, Kyoto, Japan.

[Wache et al., 2001] Wache, H., Voegele, T., Visser, U., Stuckenschmidt, H., Schuster, G., and S.Huebner, H. N. (2001). Ontology-based integration of information - a survey of existing approaches. In *Ontologies and Information Sharing*, number 47, pages 108–117, Seattle, WA.

[Weibel, 1999] Weibel, S. (1999). The state of the Dublin Core metadata initiative. *D-Lib Magazine*, 5(4).

[Wiederhold, 1992] Wiederhold, G. (1992). Mediators in the architecture of future information systems. *IEEE Computer*, March:38–49.

[Wiederhold, 1996] Wiederhold, G., editor (1996). *Intelligent Integration of Information*. Kluwer, Boston, MA.

[Yarowsky, 1992] Yarowsky, D. (1992). Word-sense disambiguation using statistical models of Roget's categories trained on large corpora. In *Proceedings of COLING-92*, pages 454–460, Nantes, France.

[Yergeau et al., 2004] Yergeau, F., Bray, T., Paoli, J., Sperberg-McQueen, C., and Maler, E. (2004). Extensible markup language (xml) 1.0. Recommendation, W3C. http://www.w3.org/TR/2004/REC-xml-20040204.

Index